French Polynesia

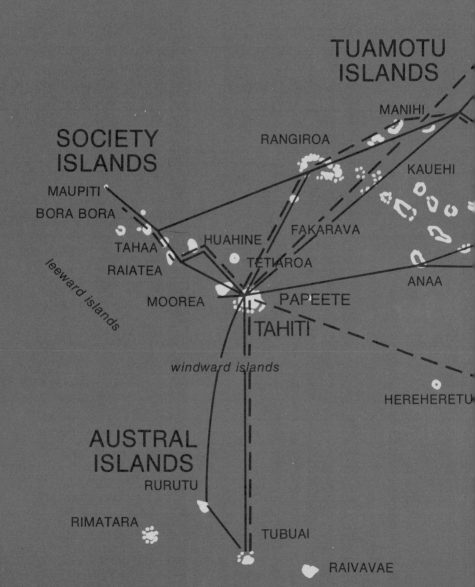

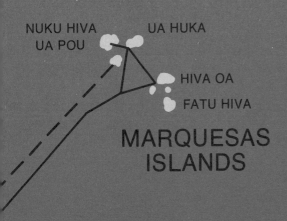

NUKU HIVA   UA HUKA
UA POU

HIVA OA

FATU HIVA

MARQUESAS ISLANDS

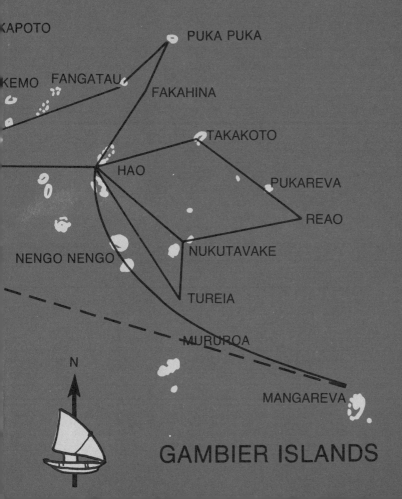

KAPOTO

PUKA PUKA

KEMO   FANGATAU

FAKAHINA

TAKAKOTO

HAO

PUKAREVA

REAO

NENGO NENGO

NUKUTAVAKE

TUREIA

MURUROA

N

MANGAREVA

GAMBIER ISLANDS

What Our Readers Have Writt

"The next time I go to Tahiti, I hope to spend more than a ni
there. I'll even take my wife if she's willing to carry McDermo
entertaining and informative guide. He tells you about places
stay in far away places, and good restaurants and bad bistros, fi
snorkling beaches and girl-watching."

Chuck Frankel, *Honolulu Star Bullet*

"Since I can't begin to relate all that there is to know for m
clients experiencing Tahiti for the first time, I always include you
book to help them seek the best there is."

Honolulu Travel Agency, manager/owne

"I now have sped through HOW TO GET LOST AND FOUND
IN TAHITI. McDermott makes me want to go there, a talent
lacking in too many travel writers. I also like the style of writing
very much. Punchy and wry. He's a readable writer."

Jerry Flemmons, *Travel Editor*
Fort Worth Star Telegram

"...a conscientious, painstaking, professional and, above all,
readable guide to Tahiti and the great expanse of French Polynesia. It captures the appeal, yet does not gloss over the short-
comings."

J.C. Graham, *Auckland Herald*

How To
Get Lost
And Found
In Tahiti

by John W. McDermott

edited by B. L. Hughes

ORAFA Publishing Co., Inc.
Honolulu, Hawaii, U.S.A.

First Published 1979
Second Edition 1986

Orafa Publishing Company, Inc.
1314 So. King Street, Suite 1064
Honolulu, Hawaii 96814
U.S.A.

© **1979 John W. McDermott**

Library of Congress Cataloging in Publication Data

John W. McDermott
  HOW TO GET LOST AND FOUND IN TAHITI
  Includes Index
  1. Tahiti — Description and travel — 1987 Travel Experience Books. II. Title
  86-62292

ISBN: 0-912273-13-5

Typeset by Crossroads Press, Hawaii
Printed by Fairfield Graphics, Fairfield, Pennsylvania

Books Of The Series
  HOW TO GET LOST AND FOUND IN NEW ZEALAND
  HOW TO GET LOST AND FOUND IN FIJI
  HOW TO GET LOST AND FOUND IN TAHITI
  HOW TO GET LOST AND FOUND IN THE COOK ISLANDS
  HOW TO GET LOST AND FOUND IN AUSTRALIA
  HOW TO GET LOST AND FOUND IN CALIFORNIA
    AND OTHER LOVELY PLACES
  HOW TO GET LOST AND FOUND IN NEW JAPAN
  HOW TO GET LOST AND FOUND IN OUR HAWAII
  HOW TO GET LOST AND FOUND IN UPGRADED NEW ZEALAND

How To Get Lost And Found In Tahiti

"It seems in retrospect," writes Mr. McDermott, page 164, "that several times in this book the subject of either bare-bosomed ladies or sharks has come up.

"The intention is not to lay undue emphasis on either subject but perhaps because of a Rocky Mountain youthful period of upbringing, they capture the attention faster than other subjects.

"You know, in Colorado Springs during my childhood, you didn't see many sharks or topless women."

The experiences of two Americans, John W. McDermott and his Lady Navigator, in French Polynesia going to every important island group are reported with humor and a delicate insight. As a result, the character of these charming islands and their people come into a new focus.

Continuing the pertinent and impertinent style set by the eight other books in the *Lost and Found* series, the new edition of *How to Get Lost and Found in Tahiti* offers the readers an updated, refreshing look at one of the most glamorous destination areas in the South Pacific, including hard facts and need-to-know information, sugar-coated with fun-to-read copy.

List of Maps

Contents

Two Preliminary Words

The first word is *geographic*.

A book entitled *How To Get Lost and Found in French Polynesia* would result in the question: "Where is that?"

However "Tahiti" substituted for "French Polynesia" is immediately recognized as to location and to spirit although technically Tahiti is but one island among 130 islands.

The islands are referred to in groups: the Society Islands including Tahiti, the Austral Islands 450 miles south of Tahiti, the Gambier Islands 1000 miles to the southeast, the Tuamotus about 250 miles to the northeast and the remote Marquesas 850 miles north by east.

All the islands are included in French Polynesia.

The second word is *economic*.

Prices in French Polynesia are high.

The official reason given is that there is no income tax, no property tax. To derive the income to run the government everything imported is taxed. The tax is passed on to the consumer in the retail prices.

An unofficial reason is that the French government's nuclear testing in French Polynesia has brought in thousands of military and technical staff, highly paid support personnel who pay no French income tax.

The result is an over-heated economy that produces some jarring bills.

Accept it before coming. French Polynesia is worth it. Once you've embraced the Tahitian attitude you too will be ordering champagne for breakfast.

It goes with the fruit.

Vahine (vá·he·knee)
1. Woman. 2. Wife. 3. Girlfriend.

Her name was Tua.

She had classic Polynesian hair, straight and glistening black, falling to her slender waist. Occasionally she braided it schoolgirl fashion and at other times she wound it in a crown over her head.

Her face was cosmopolitan with an acquiline nose, a full Tahitian mouth and huge, dark eyes that were signal lights for her ever-changing emotions: mischievous, sullen, sexy, giggly, pensive. At one moment the eyes were laughing and darting among her attentive audience. The next, deep, unfathomable, unreadable, animal-wounded. What produced one mood and what produced another was an unknown.

And her skin!

A setting sun had tinted her a luscious red-gold like a tangerine ready for plucking.

Her figure was twentieth-century perfect, that is, broad of shoulder, flat of tummy and slimly curved of leg. Everything was youthfully pert: the nose, the breasts, the derriere. When she danced, all parts twitched. And she was always dancing.

"You continue this line of research," said the Lady Navigator, *"and I'm going to stick my foot through your typewriter."*

Now about shell collecting . . .

1. The Magic Of Tahiti, The Reality Of Papeete

The Stuff Of Dreams . . . The Now Town

It is dawn.

A bedside radio starts its daily broadcast with the military sound of the *Marseillaise,* the French national anthem.

France?

You open an eye and take in a scene that includes a blue expanse of water broken by a white line of distant reef, and, beyond, the dramatic finger peaks of an island.

No, it's not France. It is Tahiti.

In the early hour of the morning the air is sweet with the scent of flower and sea. You inhale deeply.

The sun bounces a playful beam off the water up through your balcony deck boards. It darts around the ceiling of your thatched roof *fare,* the Tahitian cottage built on stilts over the lagoon.

It is your first morning in Tahiti.

The national anthem ends and the news starts in French.

What makes Tahiti so different in the South Pacific? The music and language are clues. It is the chic sophistication of the French combined with the charming insouciance of the Polynesian with an added spicy pinch of the Oriental and, *voilà, la différence.*

You will find this combination of cultures in dress and food, in manners and morals, and it is captivating.

Enough.

It is morning. Tahiti. Time to go out into the world.

Papeete is a helluva town.

It is as international as Paris . . . as local as a village store.

You can buy perfume next to papaya, silk prints next to bark cloth.

You can meet millionaires and the last of the remittance men. You can meet titled ladies and bar girls.

In Papeete you can shake-shake-shake or drink-drink-drink. Then

1

there is a surprisingly large number of people who pray-pray-pray for those who shake and drink.

The first look at Papeete gives a fairly accurate profile of the city.

Splashed across the waterfront is a solid line of worldwide yachts representing rich investments in return for rich adventures.

Across a calm harbor the more sedate shipping industry is centered and you can see rusty freighters, big tankers, and the sometimes-white interisland schooners discharging their copra cargos and taking on new cargos.

Over in one corner of the harbor is the no-nonsense grey of the French naval ships.

Papeete is a port town.

On land, opposite the yachts, a line of trees adds green and grace and shade to the wide boulevard and on the other side of the boulevard a line of buildings adds sparkle to the waterfront drive.

Behind the new waterfront low-rise architecture, dotted with steeples, is a sizeable acreage of commerce mostly Chinese operated.

There is nothing sleepy about Papeete anymore.

The little city of 35,000 jumps with traffic . . . you first think there must be 45,000 cars, trucks and velos. The traffic starts pre-dawn and continues until noon when suddenly the motor is shut off.

Everyone goes home to have a glass of wine, a large lunch and a small nap.

After two in the afternoon life returns to the streets.

Evenings a different rhythm takes over . . . it is a time for good eating . . . for having a drink or several . . . for dancing. Papeete is the only town in the Pacific where dancing till dawn is taken for granted.

Papeete is a swinging town.

The true profile of Papeete, the color and variety and excitement, is to be found in the people.

The tourists, the French military, the other islanders, the local businessmen, the shopping ladies merge to make a memorable canvas.

First of all you have to inspect the passing parade of the famous Tahitian women. They are entrancing.

Let me admit as a keen observer that there is a temptation to become enamored with one's own impressions of the women of Tahiti and having made a mental evaluation filled with lacy words and sexy implications . . . *and getting a foot through the typewriter* . . . I then

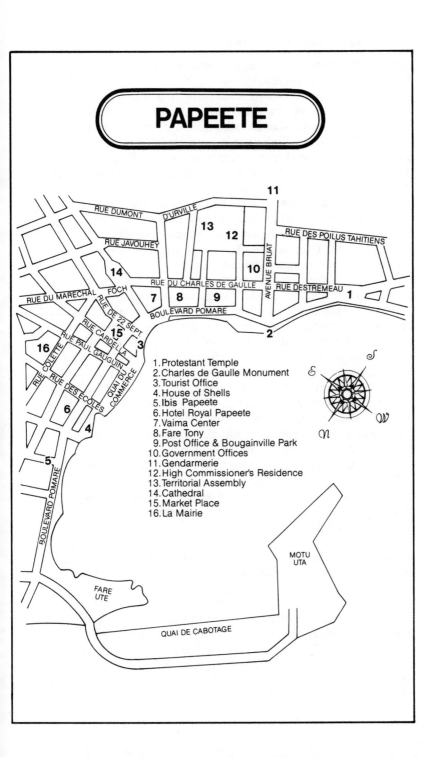

PAPEETE

1. Protestant Temple
2. Charles de Gaulle Monument
3. Tourist Office
4. House of Shells
5. Ibis Papeete
6. Hotel Royal Papeete
7. Vaima Center
8. Fare Tony
9. Post Office & Bougainville Park
10. Government Offices
11. Gendarmerie
12. High Commissioner's Residence
13. Territorial Assembly
14. Cathedral
15. Market Place
16. La Mairie

find in reality that the percentage of stunning women is not as large as first impressions conveyed.

The fact remains however that there is a high percentage of attractive women and that they tend to unbalance the scale.

There is the Polynesian girl who formerly danced and loved all night and slept all day. Today she is more educated, more avaricious and more likely to work as a secretary or clerk or office worker. She dresses very simply . . . but with an *elan* inherited from the French. And she walks like the river flows.

The Polynesian girls are really like the girls in Hawaii, a mixture of anything you can name but the all-important Polynesian blood gives that glamorous black to the hair and the gold to the skin.

Note also the Chinese girls. They tend to stay pure of blood and neat of dress and compact in figure. Lovely.

Then there is the young French matron looking like a sleek cat out of the zoo. Stunning to look at. Dangerous to touch.

Add a couple of dashes of the best-looking girl tourists and the best-looking passing-through stewardesses and you come up with a melange of femininity that is hourlessly beguiling to behold.

No, there is one more. The Polynesian matron. She tends to be larger and swathingly dressed and rolls when she walks but note that marvellous face full of humor and gentleness and love of the world.

There was a time when all of the *vahines* rode bicycles and velos, often in pairs, and the streets of Papeete were filled with charming things flying over the pavement with skirts hiked thigh-high and long black hair flowing in the airstream behind.

A law should have been passed to keep them out of automobiles.

But then that touches the theme of a veteran writer of the Tahitian scene, Ralph Varady, who wrote an article based on the line "you came too late." Whenever you came to Papeete, it was always a generation too late.

In Papeete there are those who still cry for the bedraggled waterfront and the raucous times of Quinn's Bar and the Lafayette nightclub . . . long gone . . . but the truth is that Papeete has never been better.

Cry not.

The redesigned, reconstructed waterfront, now a graceful two-way boulevard separated by trees and lawn is a visual source of joy.

The old Quinn's Bar where one could and did get smashed at ten o'clock in the morning is now a modern office building. A block away, once the location of the more genteel Vaima Bar where you didn't get loaded until lunch, is now the super multi-level Vaima Center shopping complex . . . with the only escalator in French Polynesia . . . a symbol of the new Papeete.

The infusion of vast amounts of military funding, and the subsequent prosperous fall-out, is seen on all sides. New buildings keep going up, government buildings get face-lifts, streets are repaved, sewers re-laid.

Papeete today is a pulsating, growing town which is exactly what makes people outside of Papeete say with obvious relish, "A dreadful place. Don't go there if you can avoid it. If you have to go, don't stay longer than is necessary."

Don't believe it.

Papeete is a helluva town.

Let's take a closer look.

Take A Walk

In every city and village in France of any tourist interest, there is a city tourist office, Syndicat d'Initiative. The first order of business for such offices is the compilation of interesting facts and facets of the town area for publishing a walking tour pamphlet.

For some reason, the Papeete tourist authorities do not deem this a needed tourist experience. However, you can pick up a detailed map of Papeete from the Office de Promotion et d'Animation Touristiques de Tahiti et ses iles, known in Tahiti as OPATTI and abroad as the Tahiti Tourist Board.

So come along and we will create our own hour-and-a-half tour.

Start early. The best walking time is early morning before the heat and humidity of the day rise to the drippy level. Humidity averages seventy-eight degrees.

Dress in your lightest cottons, the more ventilated the better. Don't go in bra top and shorty shorts. Bad taste in Papeete.

Let's start, arbitrarily, on Pomare Boulevard at Avenue Braut, the wide, shady street with a nightclub and bar on one corner and Le Tropicana, a sidewalk cafe on the other corner for a closer nose-to-nose look at the places of interest in the city.

On the waterfront side of the boulevard is the Charles de Gaulle monument (2 on the Papeete map). The monument duplicates the citation of the Freedom Cross given to the local marine and infantry battalion in Paris, 28 May 1945, by M. de Gaulle himself.

What lovely names!

The harbor itself is called Papeete Roads.

The water to the left is called Bay of Trees. Then Yacht Anchorage. To your right, with yachts tied stern or bow to the sidewalk dock, is called Port Pleasant.

Farther along in order is the Fleet of Fish, the Quay for Liners, the Quay for Schooners.

The Yacht Anchorage permits you do just that for a fee. You anchor and take your dinghy to and from the shore. (We saw a boat called Seaforth. Its little dinghy was called Back and Forth.)

The yachts on the right, tied to the Wharf, pay a token fee each day. Electricity is a luxury option.

Nearby is a Chinese junk that looks like it just sailed in from Hong Kong. It's a permanently docked floating bar called appropriately la Jonque. Opens early. Closes late.

Most yachties relate quickly to la Jonque because opposite the ship are the public showers and toilets.

Strolling along Port of Pleasure or Yacht Row you pick up the international flavor of Papeete. What an astounding selection of sea-going transportation. Here are huge, luxurious cruising ships. There are sleek, stripped down racing machines. There is a cross-section of tubs and scows, beaten, scarred and bedraggled.

No matter. Tahiti is obviously a holy grail for yachtsmen of the world as evidenced by the wide range of home ports registered on the fantails of the bobbing boats.

Doesn't it create a pang of wanderlust?

Doesn't it seem terribly dashing and romantic?

A friend of ours says that when you are standing on the pier staring at someone else's boat, you are enjoying the best of yachting.

We tend to share his opinion when he says he wouldn't get on one of those bitchy, soul-destroying, crew-destroying South Sea yacht cruises for anything in the world. The romance is brief when you're cramped, uncomfortable, banged against bulkheads day and night, pushed nose to nose with fellow deckhands who develop increasingly irritating habits.

No, no thanks. I'll join my friend and take a plushy Boeing 747 and meet you at dockside with a drink when you come sailing in.

Next to the fun-at-sea group is a dock section reserved for the fishing fleet. After five o'clock they'll all be back from the ocean, washing down, having transferred their catches across the street to the market or having put the fish on trucks to take to country stores or directly to customers from the truck tailgate.

Note in the same area, the small runabout boats with their uniquely designed forward cockpit, a singular, square well where the pilot stands with wheel in one hand and throttle in the other at the best position to keep a sharp eye out for coral as he swiftly takes his boat through lagoon waters.

Beyond the fishing fleet is the quay for cruise ships and, in between the dockside and the street, there is a cluster of buildings called Fare Manihini (3). Manihini means guest. Guest House. It is here that the headquarters for the tourist office, the OPATTI, is located. Here, you will find the best cross-section of information of what is going on in French Polynesia. Places to stay, yachts to charter, tours to take, dates of celebrations. Also, the offices are staffed with one of the prettiest collections of young ladies in Papeete. Make up a question, if necessary, and go take a look.

The exhibit hall next to the OPATTI offices frequently hosts art exhibits, cocktail parties, all kinds of public functions. It is also the headquarters for Fete tickets. That's in July.

Next to the Fare Manihini is the Customs House for yachts and ocean liners.

If you are going to take a boat to Moorea, you go along the dock to the Quai des Goélettes. *Goélette* means schooner in French and in Tahiti refers to the boats used within the islands for transportation. Just opposite the boarding dock for Moorea is the thatched-covered House of Shells (4) where the Polynesian ladies display and sell their shell handicrafts: necklaces, hat bands, earrings, home decorative items, etc.

After five o'clock in the evening the dock space is filled with eating vans known as Les Brochettes that feature inexpensive barbecued food.

You won't go any further because you've come to the iron gates of the French naval base.

Cross the street and you are in drinking country.

At the corner of Prince Hinoi and Pomare, in the new Ibis Papeete Hotel, you'll find the entrance flanked by three bars which draw a sizable military crowd. The Whisky-A-Go-Go is at the corner and the thumping you'll hear is a combination of the disco's music and, also, the turbines across the street in the city's power plant.

In the next block is the remodeled Royal Papeete Hotel (6) which retains a whiff of the oldtime Papeete. By day, its empty dance floor looks tired and forlorn but evenings it is filled with all sorts of characters and becomes one of the swingingest spots in the city.

Although the hotel has a slightly Sadie Thompson air about it, the clientele checking in and out is obviously put there by reputable travel agencies. Sorry we never experienced it.

The boulevard for the next three blocks is lined with restaurants, banks and the more expensive boutiques.

Back of the boulevard on the side streets you'll find the oldtime centers of commerce, the smaller Chinese shops, the snack bars and pool halls.

Note: the next two blocks of canopied shell counters are also frequented by local people buying leis to present to departing friends.

Vaima Centre occupies the entire block and is the hub of modern Papeete (7). On the top floor are furnished apartments and a swimming pool club which is also open to the public.

There is a bank, a French restaurant (excellent), a Chinese restaurant (expensive), two ice cream parlors, a delectable patisserie, a very good book store (Hachette) with a good stock of English language books, a one-hour photo developing service, jewelry, perfume and Duty Free stores, art galleries, a cinema with the most luxurious seats imaginable, a laundromat, and a super air-conditioned supermarket that flies in fresh New Zealand meats weekly and French cheeses under controlled refrigeration.

There are also a dozen dress shops selling clothes from Paris.

Air New Zealand has its offices in the Vaima Center, as do Club Med and travel and real estate agencies.

At the corner, there's a bar and restaurant; behind it, a disco. The taxi stand is on the same corner.

Next door is the shopping complex, Fare Tony (8). Aline's department store and supermarket anchors the center with small specialty shops surrounding it. It's dining trump is Acajou's.

At Vaima, there is validated parking underneath the complex. At Fare Tony, you park on the roof, free of charge.

At one time Fare Tony shared its block of space with the oldest hotel in Papeete, the Hotel Stuart, built in 1926. Over its portal was a sign: "Henri Matisse stayed here in 1930."

The mauve-gray building is gone now, along with the street level pool hall and bar that once was so popular with bare-torsoed locals. In its later years, it was never a place you wanted to take your Aunt Minnie.

At one time though, when Tahiti was reached only by steamers, the Hotel Stuart with its huge rooms and high ceilings and generous bathrooms with running water—cold running water, mind you—must have been the hotel of elegance.

We knew a family of three who stayed there in the mid 'Seventies and the bill was just $18 a night, a real bargain even then.

The next block is divided between the principal Post Office of French Polynesia and Bougainville Park (9).

The Post Office is a tall building with a glass facade which seemed to be under perpetual restoration; its scaffolding was a permanent landmark.

We were shocked when we returned this trip to find it had been finished, including a new annex.

The branch in Vaima Centre was closed and all operations moved to the air-conditioned new building. Much better.

Public telephones available here permit you to call home at much more reasonable rates than from your hotel room.

If you are tired of walking, Bougainville Park with its series of concrete benches on the perimeter is a pleasant place to rest and share the peace and quiet with the bust of Louis Antoine de Bougainville, the French explorer.

Bougainville Park forms a green link between Pomare Boulevard and rue du General de Gaulle. Behind it and in between the streets, a small stream flows. Once, a long time ago, the natives brought their baskets to be filled with fresh water, the genus of the name Papeete which means "water in a basket."

At the rue du General de Gaulle, the stream disappears underground, below what now are government buildings.

But, come with me back to Pomare Boulevard.

The all-in-one offices of Air Polynesie, Air France and UTA are in the next block. You might want to know that the offices are open during the noon period. Unusual.

Now we have reached Avenue Bruat again.

Turn left and you are facing a tree shaded avenue which once was known as Saint Amelie.

Halfway down the block on the right is the Librairie Hachette, the same as in Paris. There's a branch in Vaima Centre.

Ahead of you, across the rue du General de Gaulle, are the government buildings (10) on the left and the police station on the right where you pay your parking fines. Beyond, on the left and right, are military barracks and, at the end of the shady street is the *gendarmerie,* the constabulary.

Turn left at the rue du Général de Gaulle and walk back towards town.

On the right are two official-looking, Polynesian-style buildings. The one on the right is the new residence of the High Commissioner (12). The building on the left, which holds the Territorial Assembly (13), includes a modern convention auditorium.

We should stop here a moment, for this broad expanse of lawn we face and the buildings beyond are places of great interest, past and present.

For example, the area was owned by the Pomare family. In 1818, the Reverend Crook moved onto the hill just behind the Territorial Assembly Hall you are looking at. He was followed two years later by the young Queen Pomare, who moved her household from the district of Arue. Crook became the Queen's interpreter.

Thus, ship captains who wanted to converse with the Queen through the missionary interpreter had to go to Papeete. The harbor, though narrow of passage, proved a safer anchorage than the open Matavai Bay. Papeete became the place of power.

After the French became responsible for the Royal State, they built a pretentious two-storied palace with wide verandas and ornate cupola. It remained in place – slowly, disgracefully crumbling until it was torn down in 1966.

Today, the two buildings you look at represent the spread of government in French Polynesia. The Territorial Assembly's thirty elected members of the five island groups determine the economic policy and budget of French Polynesia.

The High Commissioner, whose residence is on the right, is appointed by France to represent the Republic and to administer the Territory. He is president of the government council, which is the executive branch of the government. His residence is named Tarahoi and his country retreat at Punaauia is known as Tarahoi Iti (Little Tarahoi).

The vice president is elected by the Territorial Assembly.

Representation in France is held by two elected members, one each to the French Assembly and the French Senate.

Pause at the huge old banyan tree near the sidewalk in front of the buildings. At one time the tree had stairs and tables on a platform in its branches and was the site of the old officers' club (Cercle Militaire) and here Gauguin enjoyed a drink shortly after his arrival.

A bit farther on and you are at the back door of Aline's and then Vaima.

Note the building across the street from Vaima, the James Norman Hall Building, and the historic mosaic "Mutiny on the Bounty" designed by the popular Parisian-now-local artist, Ravello. Worth a picture in the right light between two to three in the afternoon.

Next to the Hall building is the head office of the Bank of Indochina-Suez, an architecturally interesting building inside and out.

Across the street from the bank, in the geographic center of Papeete, is the Catholic cathedral (14) and if modern art attracts you, pay a visit.

The stations of the cross are executed in a primitive style by Yves Durand de St. Front. If you don't do anything else examine the first panel . . . the three sleeping figures. Delightful. Wouldn't you want to take the middle figure home?

Also look at the last panel near the altar.

My first visit to the cathedral was during a drizzly afternoon. The light was very poor. But at that panel the eyes of the large-headed Christ kept following me. It is an experience you've had with other paintings.

But when I inspected the panel at close range . . . *the Christ had no eyes at all.* Go and see.

Leaving the cathedral, Général de Gaulle gives way to rue Maréchal Foch. You go one block farther on and then turn left into rue du 22 Septembre.

In the middle of the block is The Market, the heart, soul and stomach of Tahiti (15).

We'll come back to The Market on Sunday morning when it is at its best. Sunday morning before dawn when it seems all of Papeete rolls out of bed . . . or before rolling into bed.

For the moment you should know that this is the center for *le truck* which is the island's chief means of transportation and if you want to take the cheapest transportation back to your hotel . . . or house . . . here is the depot.

Besides being cheap, it is fun.

The back streets of Papeete around The Market are filled with a hundred shops and restaurants, snack bars, cinemas and grocery stores, etc.

Explore them all. They will give you an excellent feeling of the true Papeete.

Above all don't miss the *mairie,* the city administration headquarters, just off the rue Gauguin (16). The largest building, the meeting room, used to be the schoolhouse. The second building with the signboard of Mairie is the administration building and the third building, Voirie, is the center for roadworks.

Look at the scalloped edges of the buildings and that true colonial-colored paint job.

And people would have you turn your back on Papeete!

Take A Ride

To appreciate all of the city of Papeete, we are going to need transportation.

We want to explore the entire harbor and we will want to go to the expanded boundaries of the city . . . perhaps about eight kilometers in each direction.

We need wheels. Take a rented car or buy a packaged tour or, if you are ingenious, plot several outings on *le truck.*

Regardless of what your means of transportation, you should have an early understanding of the Tahitian system of road signs and addresses.

First, there are red-and-white kilometer markers around the island. The tombstone-shaped distance markers, sometimes obscured by weeds, are always on the mountain side of the road.

Secondly, the island of Tahiti is divided into districts. There are no addresses as you are probably accustomed to addresses.

You may hear a person say, "I live at Arue, Peekay Five, ocean side."

You know he then lives in the district of Arue, five kilometers outside of Papeete on the ocean side of the road.

My first weekend in Papeete I had a rendezvous for tennis and my opponent said, "The courts are to the left of the first traffic light in Pirae. You can't miss them."

"Pier A," I thought not wanting to ask dumb questions. "Easy." I went driving around the docks for what seemed like hours until a

questioned gendarme pointed out the district of *Pirae* on a map.
Oh, well!

Learn the districts . . . and learn how to pronounce them.

Let's go see the harbor I saw that morning while looking for "Pier
A."

The Dock Area . . . Fare Ute And Motu Uta

When we stand in front of the yachts in Papeete and look across the
harbor, we see a long arm of land that comes around from our right
and ends in a dock area with a small cluster of trees at the end.

In earlier photographs and paintings of Papeete these trees grew on
a small reef island, Motu Uta, which was a playground for royalty
and in turn a military fort, a quarantine station, etc.

The elbow of the arm of land in those days was just a point of land
called Fare Ute, or a sacred house, a place where the children of
chiefs received their religious education.

As Papeete grew, the point of land became a place to repair boats
and then a dry dock and finally oil cisterns were added.

In the sixties as more accommodations for shipping and more
industrial land were required, much of the harbor was enlarged and
the lagoon land filled. A bridge connected the new land of Motu Uta
and Fare Ute so that it now looks like one piece of real estate.

A drive to the end of Motu Uta in the daylight – past container
yards, refrigerated cold storage houses, boat works, etc. – takes you
to one of the best photographic positions for a good across-the-harbor
shot of Papeete. Worth the trip.

The more romantic time however is to go at night to the dock area
known as the Quai de Cabotage where outer island bound copra boats
are taking on cargo for the little villages scattered through the vast
area of French Polynesia.

With spotlights playing on the small white ships, the winches
screaming and groaning, the swinging of the crates from pallets to
nets to the holds . . . it is a mesmerizing sight.

I was taken out to the docks one night by my local host, a travel
industry executive, and his wife. He was a man of trained patience,
meticulous, somewhat self-confined but the sight of the nighttime
dock activity seemed to unbutton his reserve.

"I could sit and watch the boats for hours," he said.

Gentle probe. "What interests you in boats?"

"The world they take you to, probably," he mused.

"The world?"

"Yes. When I was in my teens – no, you would have had to know my father. He was a barrister in New Zealand. In those days times were hard. We didn't have any money so if we wanted something, our father would say, 'Go and get it on your own.'

"I remember as a child my brother and I wanted a tennis court. Father said, 'There's a good flat piece of land down in the corner of the paddock, go and build it.' And we did. We were raised that way.

"So when I was in my teens and wanted to see the world, there was only one way. I packed a sack and took off. I walked across India. Worked the bush in Alaska and Canada and California. I left and didn't come home for three years. Went everywhere on the map.

"What did your family say when you left?"

"My mother said, 'I wish I were going with you'."

And we sat then in silence and watched the docks and recalled days of past travels.

A Drive To The East

Starting at the mid-town cathedral turn right onto the street of Maréchal Foch and head east, in the opposite direction from the airport.

To the east is a vintage suburb of Papeete. Shady wide lanes. Large homes with wide verandas, well set back so that the deafening noise of horse-drawn carriages on the dirt roads wouldn't disturb the family. If you look carefully you can still find them today.

To the east lies much of the cradle of the European development period.

For example, just beyond the roundabout on Avenue Georges Clemenceau is the major community hospital of Mamao. This site formerly was the first experimental agricultural station. Then a dump. Then a museum.

On the left after the hospital is a *patisserie-boulangerie* (bakery) in a blue building. Immediately after the bakery is a small road which takes you inland to an open Buddhist temple, the only such temple in Tahiti.

Next at 2.5 kilometers you'll come to two stoplights. A bridge is in front of you and a stoplight is on either side.

Interesting area this Fautaua River and the valley for which it was named.

At the first stop sign you'll see on the right-hand, opposite corner the Diadème Curio Shop. We thought that name was derived from the design of the building, an octagonal, diamond-shaped affair. We then learned that the Diadème is a spectacular mountain group of peaks looking like a rough set diamond ... or a bad molar ... set back at the beginning of Fautaua Valley.

If you have a clear day ... early morning is the best time ... you can see the mountains as you cross the bridge.

Fautaua Valley was also the location of the rendezvous pool of the famous French novel, *The Marriage of Loti*, a nineteenth century love story of unrequited love of an innocent Polynesian girl and her naval boy friend. The naval officer, Julien Viaud, who wrote the story, took the name of his hero, Pierre Loti, as his pen name. You'll find his name many times in Tahiti including on a bust to his memory located up the river. Not worth the visit.

Across the bridge the sign says *Pirae* ... ah, "Pier A" ... and at the stop sign are the tennis courts of Fautaua and the stadium. Turn right and you'll be at the larger Olympic Stadium.

You don't like stadiums but you like horses?

Drive straight ahead until the next stop sign. Market on the right called "Hippo." Turn to the right here and you'll find the stables where you can rent horses for riding. (Club Equestre de Tahiti. Phone 27041.) Continuing up the side road, you pass more stables and the usual just-teen-age girls who seem to find horses at this age. Opposite the stables is a simple dirt track set in the bowl of a large, quiet pasture. Quiet now but during the ten-day festivities of Bastille Day, the July Fourteenth French Independence Day, this is the scene of wild horse-racing activity.

You might want to know that in this general area, on the ocean side of the highway, are two hotels, the rebuilt Royal Tahitien which fronts on a black sand beach, and the Princesse Heiata. (Numbers 26, 27 on Tahiti map.)

At 3.5 kilometers if you watch on the right, you'll see an arched sign that reads: "Le Chemin du Repos Eternel" – the road of eternal rest. It leads to the Chinese cemetery built on a hill facing the sea. The wealthier Chinese build a tomb over the grave to protect the departed from the sun and the rain. The less wealthy plant a tree.

Just beyond the cemetery is a military barracks which holds members of the French Foreign Legion.

You'd rather go sailing?

Good. Immediately on your left is a sign pointing to the Le Tahiti

Yacht Club.

At 4.7 kilometers on the ocean side of the road is a turnoff to the Tombeau du Roi Pomare V.

The tomb of Pomare V is a curiosity. The undistinguished pile of stones is topped with what was supposed to be a Grecian urn. It looks suspiciously like a cognac bottle. According to history the bottle would have been more apropos because Pomare V was a heavy drinker. His boozing contributed to his death at the age of fifty-two in 1891.

Actually this point of land, Outuaiai, bordered by whispering iron wood trees has a nice air about it. Next to the tomb is a new church and that adds sanctity to the scene.

A bit farther on you'll find more Pomares.

On the left-hand side of the road under a restful umbrella of trees is Toanui. The Pomare family cemetery lies between the road and the sea.

This is the home district of the Pomare clan which ruled over the districts of Arue, Pirae and Papeete.

At the time of the arrival of the white man in 1767 the Pomares were not the most important chiefs in Tahiti.

But the white man landed in Pomare territory and with them the guns. Mercenaries made themselves available to the Pomares and were used successfully by the family for their ultimate recognition as the "Royal Family."

Two further landmarks of memory.

One at 5.4 kilometers on the mountain side of the road is the former home of James Norman Hall, co-author of the *Bounty* trilogy.

Second, on the right-hand side of the road just before starting up One Tree Hill is the remains of Lafayette, notorious nightclub of old. There are people left in this world who will stand and salute at the mention of the name, not in respect to the French general, but to the many long nights and early mornings they spent in this building.

Lafayette in yesteryears would stay open as long as there was anyone left standing, thirsty and with money. It was the destination of every party-goer in Papeete who didn't want to go home.

Edgar Leeteg, a former American movie poster painter, became rich in Tahiti painting nudes on black velvet and notorious for his brawling. One night going to Lafayette on the back of a motorcycle, the motorcycle crashed and Leeteg slammed his head into a concrete abutment. Very dead.

I remember being in the Lafayette a long time ago. It was barny and crude and full of loud music and slack-jawed, dull-eyed Polynesians and sloppy drunk Europeans. It was some unknown dreadful time in the morning and I wondered through the haze of too much beer what I was doing in this barn trying to do this dance with this girl. I shake my head at the memory and still wonder.

At the top of One Tree Hill is the Tahara'a Hotel, one of Tahiti's three luxury hotels. (Number 28.)

Glorious views. From the hotel lookout point you can look out over the Sea of the Moon to the romantic vision of Moorea. To the west you look back to Outuaiai and the Pomare tomb. To the east you look across Matavai Bay and Point Venus.

Historically, One Tree Hill was the scene of a murder of a too-powerful Tahitian priest by Pomare. Captain Wallis, the first arrival, bombarded the hill with cannon and called it Skirmish Hill. From here the *Bounty* mutineers kept lookout for the telltale sails that might signal British ships looking for the deserters.

The Tahara'a Hotel from its lofty position has rooms which descend down the hill. You enter the lobby on top. The hotel, besides having magnificent vistas, has a topside swimming pool, bars, dining rooms and two night-lighted tennis courts.

You can drive down a road marked Beach House Pavilion and find a black sand beach and a snack shop where you can eat and drink lightly.

A Short Drive To The West

Drive west on Boulevard Pomare towards the airport and the progressive areas of Papeete.

For example take the simple, white-steepled church on your left called the Protestant Temple of Paofai . . . Paofai being the district. (1 on map.)

It is interesting to learn that the Tahitians have established their own Christian sect with their own organization and pastors and churches. . . temples, as they say.

The first missionaries sent out to Tahiti by the London Missionary Society were interested only in converting the poor heathen to

Christianity no matter who did it. The missionaries had a difficult time deciding among themselves on the true doctrine and the proper rituals.

In 1963 the Tahitian protestants became an independent entity and the church was no longer run as a mission station from Europe.

Not surprisingly, the temple is well known for its music. For us it became the "Church of the White Hats" and an enchanting assortment of white finery.

One Sunday morning, after market, I went to the bottom of the church steps to listen to the singing. As the service began a tall Tahitian came down the steps and asked me:

"Français?"

"Non."

"Anglais?"

"Non," I replied. *"Americain.* Honolulu," I added. We had found earlier that the response was warmer if you were from Hawaii. Tahitians love to go to Hawaii and shop-shop-shop, row-row-row and shake-shake-shake. They go in big groups. All together. One big family. One big party.

"Come with me," my self-appointed host said in English. He guided me inside the church and up the staircase to the left. Males sat on the left-hand side of the balcony running down the length of the church, females on the right.

The main floor was reserved for the singing members of the congregation which was divided into groups. Each group consisting of about three rows of women backed by one or two rows of men and each group would sing one particular hymn between gospel and sermon and announcements.

They sang in French and Tahitian and that day they also sang in Rarotongan because a visiting pastor from the Cook Islands was in the congregation.

After the service the ladies in their graceful white-woven, wide-brimmed hats left the church looking like a covey of white pigeons scattering over the countryside.

Because the scene is becoming known as a charming visual picture of Tahiti on Sunday, the streets also held a growing number of photographer-tourists discreetly snapping pictures of the departing faithful.

Harbor-side of the church there are hundreds of racing canoes or pirogues beneath the trees lined up all the way to the end of the boulevard.

Visit the area in the afternoon after five to see the place come alive as the crews assemble to train for their week-end races . . . all pointing for *the* days . . . the days of the Fête when the most important races of the year are held.

At the end of the boulevard is a handsome set of buildings which look like an auditorium and cultural center complex. Right.

Next to the complex is the Olympic Swimming Pool.

The boulevard now blends into a three-mile section of Tahiti's super highway, the RDO (Route de degagement de l'Ouest) the quickest route over the hills to Maeva Beach.

We don't want to go that way. Let's go back and start all over.

Turn left at the Cathedral of Notre Dame and head west down de Gaulle. At Avenue Bruat, de Gaulle is succeeded by Commandant Destremeau as the street passes the Ecole Paofai, Lycée Gauguin and, on the left, the turnoff to Matavai Hotel . . . past auto sales and rental companies and then the public cemetery where Queen Marau, the divorced wife of Pomare V, is buried.

The road under the super highway takes you to the Hotel Tahiti, the first hotel—deluxe at that time—to open with the completion of the new jet air strip in 1961.

The Hotel Tahiti is a favorite site for Saturday night-until-dawn "galas" staged by local organizations as money-making events.

During the filming of *Mutiny on the Bounty* in 1961 you would see Marlon Brando here—young, vibrant, full of the animal verve he somehow gets across on a screen—playing with his colleagues.

You then pass through the districts of Pamatai and Faaa. Faaa's name is also given the international airport. It is a district of shops and snack bars and Chinese grocery stores, quieter now that so much traffic has been drawn off by the new RDO.

In a world of constantly expanding, dirty, unpleasant, crowded airports, the modern airport of Faaa gets good marks. It is open. Kept meticulously clean. Modern.

It has three bars . . . no, four . . . which is civilized.

On the ground floor is a post office where you can mail letters and buy stamps and even make long distance telephone calls at all sorts of good hours including Sundays.

There is a bank which, besides regular banking hours, is open one hour before international plane departures and one hour after arrivals.

In contrast with most international airports filled with Italian-made digital signs announcing plane arrivals and departures, there is only one clock in Faaa. It is located at the least used end of the terminal. And it doesn't have any hands.

Upstairs there is a pleasant coffee shop and bar. Not great food but beautifully air-conditioned and neat and modern. *Steak au poivre,* —wine. With green salad and French fried potatoes. You also get a pitcher of water and a bucket of ice.

At the far end of the coffee shop is a restaurant with ten white-linened tables. We never saw anyone in it.

Once I asked the only waiter present in the room: "What is the difference between eating in there," pointing to the coffee shop,"or eating in here?"

He replied with a shrug: "It is much more expensive eating in here."

On the restaurant walls are four panels of gracious young girls and white birds done by Carsalade in 1977.

Go inside and look. Free.

Eat outside. Much less expensive.

At the car exit end of the terminal, you'll find the counter for Air Polynesie. The local airline is going through a serious period of upgrading its equipment. Good pilots.

There is a bar nearby where you can have a soft drink or a sandwich, a cold beer or hard booze.

The traffic for Moorea is so heavy that its terminal and planes are set apart from the international and inter-island traffic.

Tahiti Air provides what is practically an air shuttle service between Papeete and Moorea every fifteen minutes. The flight time is about seven minutes.

As you enter the airport the Tahiti Air Terminal is straight ahead and to the right. A couple of minutes walk from the main terminal. Yes, there is a bar in the Moorea terminal . . . and if you are keeping count a dandy piece of information, in case you are thirsty, is that the fourth bar is found in an upstairs lounge beyond the customs and immigrations check-points, reserved for outbound international passengers.

One and a half kilometers farther along is the Beachcomber Hotel wrapped around historical Tataa Point. In Tahitian mythology it was from Tataa the souls of the deceased jumped into the lagoon on their return to the spiritual homeland.

Now Tataa Point holds a most pleasant deluxe hostelry, the Beachcomber. Its two hundred or so rooms overlook the majestic peaks of Moorea and the romantic Sea of the Moon. Fourteen *fares* are built over lagoon waters, the only ones on the island of Tahiti. Good restaurants. Best hamburger in Papeete.

Farther on is the Maeva Beach Hotel on a handsome spread of property, the third deluxe establishment on Tahiti. It advertises a white beach sand. The hotel spent a ton of money bringing the sand. Its swimming pool is huge and its night-lighted tennis courts are, perhaps, the best on the island.

Maeva is a highrise hotel, also with about two hundred rooms, each facing the lagoon and Moorea. Nice lobby filled with superb New Guinea artifacts.

Sandwiched in between Maeva and the Beachcomber is Te Puna Bel Air which advertises itself as a moderately priced hotel. Cottage. We think. The manager on duty was too bored with the idea to show us one.

Note: we wanted to established the boundaries of "Greater Papeete" early in the book because within these borders you find the majority of places to eat, drink and play.

2. About Eating and Drinking and Other Indoor and Outdoor Sports in Paradise

The Big Restaurant Scene ... Papeete After Dark ... Sunday Morning Market

French Polynesia is yummy.

The international dishes that flow out of the kitchens thanks to the cultural mix of the Polynesians, the French and the Chinese are gastronomically glorious.

The Polynesian feast, the *tamaaraa*, with most of the dishes cooked in the underground oven is the ultimate of Tahitian cooking. In addition there are other outstanding Tahitian specialties. A few have found their way onto restaurant menus but the majority are prepared in private homes. We'll come back to Polynesian cooking.

The French cuisine is accepted as a superior European art form. One of the happier results of the French residing in Papeete in military strength is the unusual number of excellent restaurants, restaurants which must face the test of the highly discriminatory, highly critical French palate.

The French enjoy dining in restaurants. In France only the family and intimate family friends are entertained in the sanctorum of the home. All others are entertained in restaurants. The French don't mind spending any amount of money on good food and good wine but the value had better be there or the tongues will wag and the *propriétaire* will find himself facing empty tables.

On the level with the French cuisine is the Chinese cuisine. Although only ten percent of the French Polynesian population is Oriental, most of that ten percent reside in Papeete. Their numbers are reflected in the number of good Chinese restaurants.

With such an international choice of foods and the critical attention restaurants receive, you would be correct in assuming that the debates on current restaurants are intense and passionate.

"It is the finest restaurant today in Papeete."
"Wrong. It has gone off."
"The service, for a change, is excellent."
"The waitress spilled soup in my lap."
"Worth every penny."
"For twenty-five dollars a person I expected better than paper napkins."
So it goes.

The Lady Navigator and I ate in over thirty Papeete restaurants, cafes, bars, street vans and came away with our own impressions. First of all remember the prices are high. Across the board, the Papeete restaurants will be about twice as expensive as your average restaurant bordering the Pacific, except in Japan.

As we said before, accept it going in and enjoy it.

Another word of caution.

Polynesian waitresses live in a world of their own. When you are ordering, they tend to be looking at far off clouds on the horizon.

When you ask how a dish is prepared, be prepared for a know-nothing shrug.

Al Prince, editor of the Tahiti Sun Press, recounts a story of lunching with a hotel manager, who, before others, is likely to get preferential treatment. He ordered French fries with his steak. The manager ordered spinach.

It was no surprise to the editor, an experienced Tahiti hand, that he was served the spinach. The manager received the French fries.

If, as a new tourist to Tahiti, you let it, this small incident could ruin your whole day.

Don't let it, was the editor's advice. Complaining about the service tends to backfire.

Whether it is the general lack of service capabilities or the lack of training doesn't matter.

This is Tahiti.

Eat your spinach and have a good day.

Being part of the French State, Papeete has a high proportion of experienced French chefs. The Maeva Beach Hotel, for example, maintains a minimum of five French chefs.

Once owned by UTA, the private French airline, the Maeva now belongs to the Sofitel chain whose management changed the decor of the deluxe dining room, the Gauguin Restaurant. It offers superb service, excellent presentation of dishes, and an upmarket

French wine list. (The Lady Navigator also had a plate full of profiteroles she wouldn't share and still salivates over.) Memorable but expensive.

Down the street, the Beachcomber has an excellent standard of dishes. We sought out the youthful French chef who reported that his Tahitian staff was very talented and easy to train, but just as easily bored. The "Tahitian" way would be to change the menu every month, completely.

My favorite meal at the Beachcomber was the steak, green salad and French fries in the coffee shop. You'll never find better French fried potatoes.

Beyond the Beachcomber and the Maeva hotels in the district of Punaauia, is a cluster of popular restaurants. (Remember that family dining-out-in-the-country at noon on Sundays is a popular European tradition that is kept alive in Papeete. If you are going "out into the country" for a Sunday drive and a long lunch, be sure you have reservations and prepare to be surrounded by ankle biters and babies in cribs.)

A popular spot is the Lagoonarium if only because it has an underwater observatory which gives the kids something to do.

Fish is featured on the menu and three types of *poisson cru:* Tahitian, Mexican, Chinese. Mild, hot and sweet. Good Tahitian floor show Saturday night and guaranteed fresh lobster. You know they are fresh because they live in a view tank.

The Baie des Pecheurs we remember with pleasure because of its fresh fish and al fresco ambiance—blue umbrellas and red-checkered tablecloths. A surprise on the menu is the choice of Alsatian dishes. The house wine is Sylvaner and the proprietor looks as if he needs a drink. So grim for such a delightful place.

The white facade of Auberge du Pacifique looks more like a Mexican restaurant than a classic French one but, in our exhaustive first research trip, it had the only pressed duck in Tahiti. And, upon departure, a rose for your lady.

Friends of ours from Honolulu, Lee and Barbara Grey, returned from Papeete raving about Coco's, at P.K. 15, where they had cocktails on the lawn, excellent French food at an *intime* table on the verandah, and a gracious host. Take an extra roll of money, they cautioned. Dark on Sundays and Mondays, and you must have a reservation.

One unique restaurant is Le Belvedere in the mountains behind

Papeete. Free hotel pick up and a wild ride, we are told, to the alpine setting from which you'll get different panoramic views of Moorea. On the other end of town is the plush Tahara'a Hotel. Until it changed hands, it had the best reputation for food in Papeete. After its reputation went to hell, the new owners have worked hard to re-establish the good name of the Captain Cook Dining Room.

People staying at the Tahara'a without a rental car find that they are so far out of town they have no choice.

Downtown is loaded with restaurants.

Our newest discovery was Lou Pescadou, a pizzeria with a brick oven presided over by the owner-proprietor who is a study in motion—baking, cashiering and usually jovially shouting to his waitresses, his clients and to the world at large. Good food. Steaks and chops grilled over wood in the oven are succulent.

Very popular locally despite its lack of air conditioning. On a back-of-town narrow street two blocks behind Vaima Centre.

A similar restaurant, the Italian Pizzeria on the waterfront, didn't attract the same degree of activity the last time we were in Papeete. It used to be a favorite of ours.

Le Retro is popular because of its location in Vaima Centre and its open-air restaurant-bar, a nightclub that blasts until 2 a.m., and a bakery that is the place to go Sunday mornings for croissants after touring the Sunday morning market. (Our favorite bakery behind the Cathedral burned down.)

Opposite Le Retro in a corner location of Fare Tony is Acajou. A noted chef at a popular restaurant that closed after he opened his own place, Acajou has a fine culinary reputation. We felt a personal loyalty to Acajou because we had been in Papeete the day he opened for business, had attended the grand opening festivities as part of the Fete that year.

We left the comfort of a Royal Viking dining room on a boat stop in Papeete a few years ago to enjoy Acajou again. It was a terrible experience. Terrible food. Indifferent, indolent service. But on our last trip, a couple we met said they had eaten breakfast, lunch and dinner at Acajou, and it was all marvelous. They said they'd return to Tahiti just to eat at Acajou.

The Petiti Auberege is still there and recommended by friends who also told us that the Bougainville, one of the oldest restaurants in Papeete with yesteryear's atmosphere, was closed. We found it open.

The Chinese restaurants are concentrated downtown except for

Dahlia on the road to One Tree Hill where we had a fine lunch. The roast pork with a coconut milk dip was particularly good.

Two of the better Chinese restaurants downtown are the Mandarin and the Le Dragon d'Or.

We used to prefer the Mandarin which was frequented by a healthy cross-section of local people. (The Chinese kids order steak and eat with knifes and forks. The Europeans order egg rolls and sweet-and-sour pork and eat with chopsticks.) Good fried noodles. Excellent roast pork.

The Dragon d'Or on rue Colette we found on the last trip to be superior. Authentic Cantonese cooking or French cuisine and air-conditioned. A place we'd try again.

The oldest Chinese restaurant in Papeete, now modernized and air-conditioned, is La Soupe Chinoise operated by the Chan family since 1914. Worth a try.

Another dingy looking restaurant with plastic tablecloths, Waikiki, was a "try-it" recommendation of Papeete friends who said to forget the atmosphere and order the crab cakes. Delicious.

(A Pacific jet-setter pal from Honolulu who never eats bread—except in Papeete where the French bread slathered with butter is too good to resist—noticed his waistline was expanding. He decided to try a Chinese restaurant for a change. The first thing the Chinese waiter did was to put half a loaf of French bread and a pile of butter in front of him.)

One of the dining bargains of Papeete is "Les Brochettes." After five o'clock, vans pull into the now-empty parking places on the waterfront around the House of Shells, lower side panels for counters, put stools beneath them and light outside charcoal fires where steaks and chicken legs and shrimp are barbecued. You can depend upon delicious *pommes frites* being served with them, but no beer or wine is available. After the main course, you walk to another van and order a huge crepe—plain, sugared, with Grand Marnier or chocolate or jam.

The vans are most popular after the nightclubs close, when partying "way-wayers" seek a nibble before heading home. Accordingly, the vans stay open until about midnight during the week and until three or four a.m. weekends.

During the Fete they never close.

There are no identifying signs on the vans. You can't say to a friend, "Go to Lola's for the best steak on the waterfront."

The lady at our van explained, "We are known by our faces."

Tahitian cooking is basically in the underground oven and takes time to prepare—usually a Sunday—and therefore "Tahitian restaurants" are not listed.

The traditional *tamaaraa* however is a weekly event at many hotels and should be tried.

We think the pig done in an underground oven becomes particularly tasty and succulent.

Fresh fish is a protein staple of the Tahitian diet and besides baked fish and grilled fish found on most Papeete French and Chinese restaurants you will find *poisson cru*, raw fish.

Actually it is not raw. It is marinated in lime juice which cooks the fish just as if you had boiled it on the stove. The first time I tried *poisson cru* in Tahiti I thought I was eating a delightful chicken salad.

To make *poisson cru*, cube raw tuna or bonito and marinate it for ten to thirty minutes in lime juice, but not too long or the fish will become mushy . . . over-cooked. Then mix with minced tomato, grated carrot and chopped onion. Blend with coconut milk. Optional ingredients, according to spirit and taste: bits of cucumber, hard boiled egg, green onions, all chopped.

Poisson cru is usually a first course.

Fowl is common in Polynesia and the following is a Tahitian dish from the Beachcomber chef. Chicken with *fafa* or young taro leaves. Spinach is a good substitute.

For four people, cut one large chicken into eight parts . . . remove bones if desired. Brown one large, chopped onion. Lightly brown the chicken parts and then add onion. Cook ten minutes. Add pre-cooked *fafa* or spinach. Strain off any liquid and fry at a low heat for another ten minutes and then add two cloves of finely chopped garlic. Before serving add half a pint of warmed coconut milk.

The traditional Tahitian dessert is *poe*, (pronounced "poy") a pudding made with cooked, pureed fruit and sugar, and thickened with tapioca flour *(manioc)* then baked for forty-five minutes and covered before serving with warm coconut milk.

Papaya also makes a delicious dessert when baked with a pat of butter, a dash of rum, an inch of vanilla bean and a sprinkle of sugar. Just a bit fattening.

The French love to make love. The French love to eat. The French love to talk.

The ability of the French to cleanly destroy a meal while talking incessantly has always been a source of distant admiration for me. Indeed if the French were paid by the word, they would own the world.

One night, alone, I went to the Pizzeria for dinner. I was seated at a table built to accommodate two parties. I sat at the end of my section to give myself enough room for my dinner companion, the notebook.

Facing each other at the other end of the table were two Frenchmen, with knife and fork in each hand, their arms between the wrist and the elbow resting against the edge of the table which they used at a fulcrum to reach the food on their plates.

They didn't hunch over their food but angled cleanly over the table with their noses close to each other . . . intense and earnest and always talking.

From my host-position observation point, I came to realize that they performed a graceful ballet of words like two natural dancers: one led, the other followed. One inhaled food while the other exhaled words.

Frenchman A	*Frenchman B*
(Exhale) "Let me tell you what happened. Now the story you won't believe . . . it is incredible."	*(Inhale quick bites of this and that on the plate)*
(Inhale one quick sip of wine and a snatched morsel of bread)	*(Exhale)* "Yes. I listen."
(Exhale) "But it happened not too long ago to my grand-mother who lives in Aix-en-Provence and who is very wealthy. It is incredible."	*(Inhale food)*
(Inhale snatches of various morsels on the plate, assenting responses made with his fork because his mouth is full.)	*(Exhale)* "I know what you are going to say because I think the same thing happened to my Aunt Felice . . . she is my mother's sister and lives in Normandy I think."

(Exhale) "Alors . . . just when the whole family thought she was going to die and they took her off to the hospital."

(Inhale a fast rhythm of bread, wine and food from the plate, like a good fighter with lightning jabs.)

And so the ballet of food and words continues forever and forever . . . until the check is paid. That's how the French take three hours for lunch and it should be remembered that they have excellent digestions.

The mannerisms of the French have always held a fascination for me.

Carlisle said that we model our lives on the worship of heroes. But the French?

Sometimes in the isolation of their splendid superiority you have the impression that the French aren't playing any role for anyone because there is no one out there in the audience good enough.

You can understand the Japanese playing the role of the grand *samurai.*

The American switches his hero worship from movieland cowboys and Indians to television cops and robbers to football celebrities.

The Englishman emulates the throne.

The eloquent Latin—stage center, house full, in the hot spotlight—plays to himself, his best audience.

The German directs his actions toward his bank account.

But the French?

Working and living among the French has moved the answer further away instead of closer.

The only answer, true in part but unsatisfactory in total, is that the Frenchman is playing to his mistress.

Eh, *voilà,* it will have to do.

Papeete After Dark

"I'm going to *ueue* (pronounced "way-way") until four o'clock in the morning," says the Tahitian *vahine.*

Run for cover. She means it.

As you would suspect there are several places where you can shake ("way-way") until four o'clock in the morning, although the more serious nearly-to-dawn partying is usually reserved for the weekends.

All the major hotels have orchestras but only the Maeva Beach

Hotel has a disco, Cafe de Paris.

Working your way across town, you will come to the Hotel Tahiti with its big weekend happenings. Can be wild.

We leaned on our favorite source of information in Papeete, Acajou, brother of the restaurant owner with the same name but a different occupation. Our Acajou offers a limousine service with his own Mercedes-Benz and is a highly sought after tour chauffeur.

He told us that the raunchy Tiki Room with imported strip teasers at the old Holiday Inn—now the Matavai Hotel—is gone.

The most popular disco is Club 106, located above the Moana Iti Restaurant on Pomare Boulevard.

Opposite Club 106 is the Mayana Disco. Another new one is Peup. You pronounce it anyway you like.

Vaima Centre concentrates on after-dark action at Le Retro, a gathering place for the casually dressed, and, upstairs, in the *tres chic* Roll's Club which is *tres popular*.

Weekend dancing is one of the sports at the Royal Papeete Hotel in La Cave. Go early. Stay late.

Farther down the street, flanking Prince Hinoi, are the Whisky-A-Go-Go and the Zizou Bar.

If you are feeling quirky, you can go to the Bounty Club or the Piano Bar on rue des Ecoles and see pretty boys playing as if they were pretty girls.

Lastly, Acajou said, there was a Las Vegas Nightclub in the Ariana Hotel and a Saturday night "way-way" at the Princesse Heiata.

Partying—loooong partying—is a French Polynesian vocation.

Note: if you want to be a gracious gentleman for your Friday or Saturday night outing, go to the corner of Pomare Boulevard and rue Cardella and buy a *couronne*, a crown of flowers for your lady's hair.

The local ladies sit on the corner making fancy and simple, white and multi-colored *couronnes* and it is worth a visit.

Buy one while you are sober. The ladies will be cruising the night clubs later with the *couronnes* strung on the out-stretched arm. They want *you*.

What Else To Do In Papeete

Besides the excellent eating and drinking and girl-watching, Papeete is primarily ocean-oriented.

Charter a yacht.

Go deep-sea fishing.

Snorkel. Scuba dive.

Swim.

There is only one eighteen-hole golf course in all of Papeete. The humidity does not encourage this kind of activity. Atimaono (P.K. 45) is open from 8 a.m. to 5 p.m. every day. Modest greens fees. Clubs can be rented and also carts. The course takes up lots of country. Just short of 7,000 yards. Play early in the morning.

The Beachcomber and the Tahara'a have pitch and putt courses which are never used and might be gone by your next trip to Tahiti.

Tennis is easier. Each of the deluxe hotels has two night-lighted tennis courts. Again try to sign up for early morning or late afternoon or even better play tennis in the evening and take a night off from eating and drinking. Your liver will love you. There are also public and private courts around the island.

There is a hiking club and there are interesting parts of the interior of Tahiti and Tahiti Iti but you are advised not to go without a guide.

Horses, as has been said, can be hired at the stables near the race course.

If you are serious about deep sea fishing, contact the Haura Club de Tahiti, P.O. Box 582, Papeete, Tahiti, French Polynesia.

Dave Cave, a tall, grey-haired American who went to Tahiti on a vacation many years ago and never went home, founded the Haura (meaning "marlin") Club in 1962.

In his office next to the Hertz main office, a Papeete franchise he started and recently sold, he dabbles in selling new yachts from Florida ($100,000) and pre-constructed homes from New Zealand. Not seriously. I was told earlier, "Don't go looking for Dave Cave if it looks like good fishing weather."

His office is filled with mounted fish and fishing mementos. There's a 1930 colored picture of Zane Grey with his first one thousand pound marlin taken with line and reel. The monstrous fish was missing a couple of hundred pounds taken off by hungry sharks.

A *colored* picture in 1930?

Yes, Cave said. *National Geographic* gave the writer experimental colored film and asked him to use it in his South Pacific fishing journeys. In another picture in black and white of the same scene you can see the color camera off to one side.

Zane Grey went to Tahiti in search of his prize and set up a basecamp on the south side of Tahiti Iti at Vairao. He carried with him a fleet of boats, automobiles, prefabricated houses and a staff. He was *serious*.

Today the entire site is for sale. Who is selling it? Dave Cave.

Game fishing in Tahiti is at its best from the end of November until July. In other months you can still get mahimahi and wahoo.

One place to find details on charters boats is at the tourist office. Another is Le Yacht Club de Tahiti, (P.K. 4) in the district of Arue.

The yacht club is an informal organization. You can wander in and buy a drink from the bar or lunch at their restaurant without any trouble. Very Tahitian.

An entrepreneurial source we found along the waterfront, in an office-boat, was Mer et Loisirs which had a list of boats available for cruises with or without crews.

Several of the boats are anchored in the Leeward Islands.

A fully equipped yacht with crew and food included ranged from $345 a day for a two-passenger 40-foot boat to $1,400 a day for a six-passenger sloop-length yacht.

The company can also arrange for game fishing on different types of boats, or scuba diving, or speed boat rentals, among other nautical activities.

Write Mer et Loisirs, Boite Postale 3488, Papeete, French Polynesia.

Surfing?

On one of the outer island airports we talked with a bleached-blond young man, twenty-six-inch waist, legs coral-scarred, ragged shorts, no shirt. A surfer.

His name was Richard Brassard and he was a Malibu Beach-Lahaina wanderer who traveled the world looking for waves, never without a surfboard or without a pretty girl.

He said that there isn't any great surfing in Tahiti but that the sport is growing anyway. He estimated there were about six hundred surfers in Tahiti. One surfboard shop.

The most *consistent* surfing is at Papenoo, the first point after Point Venus.

The *best* surfing is at Taapuna at the entrance to Punaauia Lagoon but it is dangerous because of the coral and the strong waves.

"Any sharks?"

"Oh, yeah, but they aren't harmful. You just scare them away."

The biggest sport in Tahiti is outrigger canoe racing . . . an all-Polynesian sport.

How seriously the Polynesian takes this sport can be judged by the fact that he'll do *road running to get in shape.*

That gesture alone moves the sport to an exalted plane.

But listen to this: before the all-important races of Bastille Day in July, the crew members will abstain from smoking and drinking for three months . . . *and* for two weeks before the races will abstain from women!

It used to be that Bastille Day was the only race of the year . . . now races are held almost throughout the year as part of a training program which must include literally thousands of Tahitians.

One of the prettier sights in the islands is during the training hours of early evening when large canoes with six or sixteen paddlers glide across the golden waters of the sunset, their paddles rhythmically synchronized, the sun reflecting from water to flashing blades and bouncing off their dripping shoulders.

Late Friday night and early Saturday mornings, canoes move from all directions towards Maeva Beach, the locale of most of the training races. (The Bastille Races are held in Papeete Harbor.)

Canoes are towed through lagoon waters from Papeete in long continuous lines. They come by land behind jeeps. Occasionally you'll see an outrigger strapped to the top of *le truck* and sitting precariously on top of the canoe will be one or two crewmen.

On racing day Maeva Bay is filled with Polynesia paddlers, men and women and their relatives and their friends . . . and children by the dozens.

There is a palm-frond shack selling cold beer, soft drinks and plate luncheons. A larger group of men stand around drum barrels, evidently gambling in some game which can't be seen because of the crowd.

The starters' stand, narrow and bursting with people, also covered with palm fronds, is a scene of organized confusion.

On each side the racing canoes—hundreds of them—are being assembled by the different racing clubs.

The paddlers wear *pareus* of a club motif in color and design.

This is strictly a Polynesian sport. There are no Europeans in the canoes and the barest sprinkle of Europeans among the spectators.

The Polynesian is not hostile but he and she will often simply ignore your presence. You'll note this in French Polynesia and when you ask why, you are sometimes told it is because the Tahitians are basically shy. Perhaps.

Swimming on the island of Tahiti is surprisingly limited. The black sand beaches of Matavai Bay offer the most open swimming.

White sand beaches don't appear until you are well around the corner to the luxurious beachside homes at Punaauia and the Tahiti Village Hotel.

There is a shallow lagoon at the Beachcomber and also a water taxi service—$2 round-trip—to three pontoons anchored well inside the reef.

During dinner at the Beachcomber an employee of the hotel, at a reference to the swimming rafts said, "Oh, yes, the nudie pontoons."(!)

The next day, just by happenstance, there was a break in the research and I said to the Lady Navigator, "Well, time for a swim."

"Want to go to the rafts, eh?"

"Hey, that's a good idea. Let's."

And we did. The outdoor motor runabout zipped us in a few minutes out to the pontoons and . . . *my!*

The scene was one of well-oiled seals lolling on the rocks only in this case it was mostly women, some men, a few children. The children, interestingly, all kept their clothes on. A few of the men. None of the women.

Now, whether it was because it was Saturday or the luck of the draw but the bodies were beautiful. Nothing that good in a stage show. There were Polynesians and French women and maybe a couple of tourists. Hard to tell. No name tags. Nothing to pin them on.

We quietly took a corner of a raft, stayed in our swimming things and started a game of backgammon. The Lady Navigator's imitation of her shifty-eyed opponent playing backgammon on the "nudie pontoony" is now one of her favorite party charades. (Really, they were gorgeous.)

We went snorkeling and the purple coral and the variety of fish were interesting but not great.

Where it was great was above the water.

That night the Lady Navigator said, "You picked up a bit of color today."

"Yes! Yes, as a matter of fact perhaps tomorrow we should . . ."

"You go back to the raft and I'll slit your waterwings. One trip makes you a researcher. Two trips make you a dirty old man."

That's bad . . . isn't it?

Sunday Morning At The Market Place

If you like food . . . all kinds of food . . .
If you like people . . . all kinds of people . . .
If you like theater-in-the-street . . . honest, colorful dramatic . . .
You'll be enchanted with the Sunday morning Papeete Market.
The only price of admission is a few hours of sleep. You have to get up early. Pre-dawn early.

Before five ayem you should be at the marketplace. Although it will stay open until ten ayem on Sundays and six peeyem on other days, by six thirty Sundays as the sunlight begins to filter down on tops of *les trucks*, the show is over.

Located one block east of Vaima Center and one block off Pomare Boulevard between rue 22 Septembre and rue François Cardella, the four, rusted, corrugated iron roofed Market sheds that keep off the sun and the rain are not the most attractive.

But be assured that this is probably the cleanest marketplace in the South Pacific. Looks neat. Smells clean.

Sunday mornings all the best products come to the Market . . . and all of Papeete and many from the country come to market to buy for the entire week.

First of all there exists a nicety about the division of sales. It is strictly ethnical.

The Tahitians sell the things that are traditionally Tahitian. The products that grow underground. The fruit that grows on trees. The fish that come from the sea.

The Chinese, in turn, have selling rights to produce that grows *on* the land. Non-traditional products. Meat. Poultry. Bakery products. Vegetables.

In the first shed on the harbor side of the marketplace the Chinese are selling fresh pork and fresh beef. Big crowds of people around booths selling smoked pork (*char siu*). Pork pâte. Pigs feet.

Other booths in the same shed are selling coconut bread and a figure-eight type doughnut, sometimes dusted with sugar, called *firifiri*. (Buy a whole bag-full for a hundred francs but if you want to walk and munch, eat only one. Heavy on the stomach.)

In the second shed the Tahitians sell a cornucopia of products.

Like a piece of fruit? Banana, pineapple, orange, papaya, lime, mango, avocado, lychee, coconut. Other exotics you've never seen!

Or root products: taro, *manioc,* sweet potato, yams.

You'll also see breadfruit and gorgeous grapefruit.

On the Tahitian tables you'll see old Scotch bottles filled with a brown liquid. This is scented coconut oil used as a body ointment.

In the third shed the Chinese are selling non-traditional vegetables: tomatoes, lettuce, wombok, beans, artichokes, cabbages, potatoes, onions and carrots.

Shed number four is the Tahitians' fresh fish market. A large blackboard swings from the roof listing the ceiling prices of the fish on sale. Bonito, mahimahi, carangue, lobster, shrimp, tuna, etc.

In the fish section you'll see Polynesian ladies stuffing coconut sauce mixed with bits of raw shrimp into cellophane bags. The fermented delicacy is known as *taioro*.

The pale liquid in recycled bottles is fish-enriched water used in making a highly smelly fish stew called *fafaru*. (When *fafaru* is served at a party, it has a special place in the corner, far removed. It is understood that those who eat *fafaru* will not mingle with the other guests.)

Don't confuse it with the bottles of *mitihaarii*, coconut milk mixed with salt water, a favorite sauce that Tahitians put on almost any dish like Americans use ketchup.

Also in the fish section you will see a glistening purple or blue product being sold off of a plate. This is the tridacna clam, another delicacy, and is known as *pahua*.

In the same area desserts are sold. *Poe* wrapped in taro leaves and grated breadfruit cake. I saw a man selling sections of filled bamboo and was told that it was either stuffed with *poe* or with wild pork, killed and cooked in the mountains and packaged and sealed in bamboo lengths on the spot.

Outside, more Tahitians sell their products from alloted spaces on the ground. A municipal officer goes around with a little book and collects a sales tax from each of them.

On the east side of the shed an officer weighs the incoming fish, another notebook entry and the fisherman is also taxed.

The west side of the shed is like a zoo. Live chickens. Live ducks. Live rabbits. Guaranteed fresh produce. On the west side the vegetables are weighed and taxed before they enter the market place.

At one corner there is a fresh flower and plant market and behind the marketplace the beautiful cantaloupe and watermelon from Huahine.

That just gives you a rough idea of what is being sold.

The best part of the scene is the crowd.

You'll see the party-types, slightly red-eyed, slightly weavy, who are shopping before going home to bed . . . or home to continue the party.

You'll see proper French types concentrating on the job to be done because food to the French is a proper, serious business.

You'll see Chinese restauranteurs doing their heavy marketing with keen, scrutinizing eyes.

You'll see the camera-carrying tourists pointing at strange alien objects and tittering to each other.

Best of all you'll see the happy Tahitians, greeting each other with kisses, gossiping, comparing shopping, laughing.

Great cross-section of people.

The ideal breakfast after touring the marketplace is a pot of rich Tahitian coffee, a pile of croissants from Le Retro bakery, and a sweet cantaloupe from Huahine.

End of the beginning of a good day.

3. Tahiti... Its Geography And History...

A Prelude To A Tour Of The Island

Tahiti is by far the largest island in French Polynesia.

Although the 130 islands of French Polynesia cover an ocean area as large as Europe, less Russia, only 1,500 square miles of land stick above the sea and of this total land mass Tahiti covers more than 400 square miles.

In population, this single island holds 71% of the total 167,000-plus, and 16% of all French Polynesians call Papeete home.

Physically, Tahiti is a most satisfactory island to see. As a beginning promise you will have spectacular vistas, waterfalls, beaches, wave-crashing coastlines, a glimpse of towering mountains and submerged reefs. Rich foliage will constantly border your route.

Tahiti's two mountain peaks, Orohena (7,337-feet) and Aorai (6,786-feet) are more than twice the height of other volcanic peaks in French Polynesia.

The island is shaped like a turtle. Tahiti Nui is the body and Tahiti Iti the head, pointing to the southeast. The road doesn't go completely around Tahiti Iti. But you can drive around Tahiti Nui in two hours without stopping and without knowing any background or history and have a pleasant, eye-filling tour.

Despite its physical size Tahiti has not always been the capital island. It was not even the first island found either by the ancient Polynesians or the sixteenth-century Europeans.

To appreciate Tahiti's history we have to go back to the beginning of the Polynesians themselves.

What Happened And When

The origin of the Polynesians has long been a subject of hot debate among scholars.

One school said their heritage was directly connected to the North American Indian. Another said South America. A group said

38

Micronesia. Still another group claimed Melanesia.

A singular scholar said that the Polynesians were the remains of a race from a lost continent like Atlantis, which has since slipped beneath the waves.

According to Dr. Kenneth Emory from the Bishop Museum of Honolulu, a recognized authority on Polynesian history and culture, the evidence presented by findings of physical explorations, carbon dating, linguistic heritage, botanical and zoological specimens traces the forefathers of the present day Polynesians to a gathering place in Tonga and then in Samoa where over a period of generations the unique physical characteristics, culture and language of the Polynesians evolved.

At some time before the birth of Christ, the era of about 100 B.C., the first new "Vikings of the Sunrise" moved east to the Marquesas.

From this base point the spread of the "Eastern Polynesians" was comparatively rapid. As far south as the Society Islands and Tahiti by 500 A.D. As far east as the Easter Islands about the same period.

Hawaii and New Zealand were first reached about 850 A.D.

The most powerful center of Polynesian activity by this time was in Raiatea, largest of the islands of the Society's Leeward Group.

Raiatea's ancient name was Havaiki and the inhabitants of both New Zealand and Hawaii claimed they came from this island.

It was not until the arrival of the white man that the island of Tahiti became the center of what is today French Polynesia.

The First Europeans

In the nationalistic rush for glory, the English credited the discovery of Tahiti to Wallis and Cook. The French to Bougainville.

The visitor has to remind himself that the Spaniards as early as the 1500's considered the South Pacific as "Our Sea" as they plied a trade route passage from Peru to the Moluccan "Spice Islands" although there was no record of their landing until 1595. The only "calling card" was a cannon dated 1526 found on a Tuamotu reef.

In the Marquesas, the Spanish colonizer Alvaro de Mendana first set foot on Tahu Ata in 1595.

In 1606, another Spaniard, Pedro Fernandez de Quiros, sailed through the Tuamotus.

The Dutch also came through the waters of French Polynesia on voyages of exploration and discovery.

A century and a half later, Captain Samuel Wallis—in command of the English effort to find what was generally thought to be a massive land area in the South Pacific to counter-balance the massive land area of Europe—first saw the shores of the island of Tahiti on June 18, 1767 and, sailing up the coast, put into Matavai Bay on June 23.

Wallis called the island "King George III's Island." (Wallis, who never recorded a native name, ranks low on the list of efficient explorer-discoverers. From a distance he named Moorea "Duke of York Island." He never bothered to go there.)

When Louis Antoine de Bougainville arrived in Tahiti within the year, assuming that he was the first to discover the island and charmed by the Tahitian girls and the freedom of their sleeping habits, he called the island "New Cythera" after the goddess of love, Venus.

Between the glowing reports of Wallis and Bougainville the spark was lit under the sex-appeal reputation of Tahiti, a reputation which lives to this day.

If for no other reason the "discovery" of Tahiti by Wallis was most fortunate for Captain James Cook.

Wallis returned to England just as Cook was in final preparation for an expedition to the South Sea to measure the transit of Venus. Cook had only two known destinations on his map to set up his base: the Marquesas of Mendana or the New Zealand of Tasman. Mendana did not land on Hiva Oa, had spent only ten days on Tahu Ata and Tasman hadn't landed at all in New Zealand. Information had to have been sketchy.

The Wallis report with information of food and water and friendly natives must have influenced the Royal Society. Cook was ordered to Tahiti.

He landed at Matavai Bay in 1769 and spent three months.

In 1772 the Spanish responded to the English landings with a feeble effort at establishing a mission at the farthest end of Tahiti. It was a failure.

On October 26, 1788, the next European character appeared on the Matavai stage. Enter Lt. William Bligh, captain of the *H.M.S. Bounty.*

Bligh's mission was to collect breadfruit seedlings as a potential staple food for the slaves in the West Indies. The subsequent mutiny in Tongan waters resulted in the return of the *Bounty* to Tahiti but now under the command of Fletcher Christian and his mutineers.

The *Bounty* was to return a third and last time after the mutineers failed to establish a colony on the island of Tubuai in the Australs. Some stayed behind as mercenaries and aided a local chief, Pomare, to conquer most of Tahiti. The remainder of the mutineers sailed on to

Pitcairn, never to return.

In 1797, the first missionaries from the London Missionary Society landed on the same piece of beach which Cook had named Point Venus. The struggles of the missionaries paralleled those of the Pomare chiefs and eventually both factors had to abandon Tahiti to save their lives. Some missionaries went to Moorea with Pomare. Others retreated to Port Jackson in Australia.

In the battle of "Fei-Pi" in 1815 Pomare regained his kingdom and the missionaries, with Pomare now professing to be a believer, started gaining their first converts in significant numbers.

In 1817 the missionaries were augmented by a new wave of European colleagues and in the same year they set up the first printing press and began growing cotton and sugar cane.

In 1836 the Catholics responded to the English Protestant success by trying to establish a Catholic church on Tahiti but the two missionary priests were expelled by Queen Pomare under the advice of the English businessman-cleric, George Pritchard who was appointed the British Consul the following year.

There followed a religious-politico tug-of-war between the French and English culminating in a French admiral arbitarily establishing a protectorate over Tahiti and Moorea in 1842 and then annexing the islands by naval force in 1843.

The French government at first disapproved but then re-established the protectorate in 1844.

George Pritchard was expelled by the French at the same time and the Tahitians revolted only to be subdued in a three-year series of formal and guerrilla battles.

In 1880, the protectorate of Tahiti and Moorea was transformed into "French Oceania," a formal French colony, and in a gradual process all of the other islands were tucked under the same tent by 1909.

The first World War saw peaceful Papeete visited by two German cruisers, the *Gneisenau*, and the *Scharnhorst*, which were after coal stored in Papeete. In what was a serious error of judgment the French fired on the Germans. The German warships promptly sank a French ship and Papeete, in the line of fire, received considerable damage.

In World War II the local population voted to become "Gaullists" and sent off a seven hundred man troop of Tahitians to fight for their "homeland."

The Americans arrived in Bora Bora in 1942 to establish an airfield on an adjoining reef. For three years, 5,000 military troops were stationed on the island.

In 1957 in the first steps towards decolonization, French Oceania became French Polynesia with a more autonomous form of government and in 1958 a referendum upheld the population's desire to remain with the French government.

In 1961 the new international airfield at Faaa was completed, introducing French Polynesia to the jet age.

The atomic age was also introduced to French Polynesia two years later when the nuclear testing program of France was programmed by the Centre d'Experimentations du Pacifique. The first detonation occurred in 1966 in Moruroa 850 kilometers away. The program continues today although all explosions are confined underground.

4. Tahiti Nui And Tahiti Iti

The Circle Island Tour . . . The Big And The Little . . . Places Of History . . . Places Of Beauty . . . Places Of Museums.

When you make the tour in person, you really should be armed with *Tahiti, Circle Island Tour Guide* by Bengt Danielsson. The guide is complete with maps, photographs, drawings and kilometer-by-kilometer points of interests including titillating historical background stories.

Our "Greater Papeete" tour left us on One Tree Hill looking left towards Pomare V's tomb and right across Matavai Bay to the black sands of Point Venus, probably one of the most intriguing historical sites in all of the Pacific. Here Western civilization in the South Seas began.

Fortunately the Point is satisfactorily preserved. No hotels or apartments or Captain Cook condominiums.

You can stand on the unsmothered site where it all started and imagine yourself in other times.

To reach Point Venus we slide down One Tree Hill for about two kilometers. At the P.K. 10 marker you will see on the left a Venusstar Supermarket and, on the right, a Mobile Service Station. Turn left. The directional sign is usually gone, a Tahitian habit.

Drive straight ahead past churches on the right, military housing on the left to the end of the road. There, directly in front of you, is the only highrise lighthouse in French Polynesia.

Beyond the parking area—filled with tour buses at the predictable hours—there's a pleasant park, a native marketplace, the beach, and remnants of history.

Take a picnic lunch. Go for a swim. Some days the beach is practically empty.

At one time there was a small museum here called the Museum of Discovery dedicated to the exploits of the first navigators, both the Maori and the later Europeans who came ashore in Tahiti.

It added a beneficial layer of knowledge and we hope the rumor we heard about its being rebuilt is true.

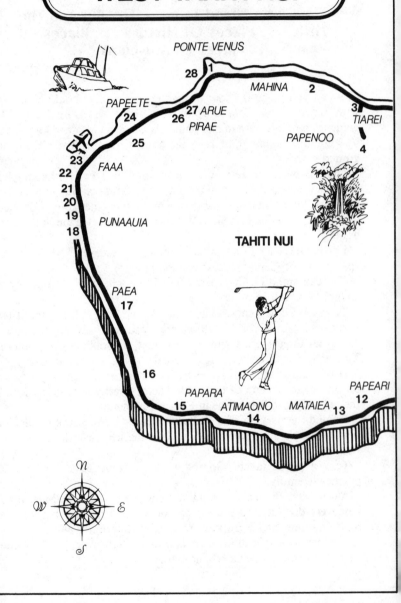

EAST TAHITI NUI & TAHITI ITI

1. Historic Site
2. Leper Village
3. Blowhole
4. Waterfalls (Cascade de Fa'arumai)
5. Bougainville Camp
6. Military Training Camp
7. Te Anuanua
8. Tautira
9. Plateau Lookout
10. Hotel Puunui
11. Auberge de Pari
12. Botanic Garden & Musee Gauguin
13. Restaurant Gauguin
14. Golf Club of Atimaono
15. Mahaiatea Marae
16. Le Petit Mousse
17. Marae Arahurahu
18. Former Tahiti Village
19. Musee de Tahiti et des Iles
20. Maeva Beach Hotel
21. Te Puna Bel Air
22. Beachcomber Hotel
23. Faaa Airport
24. Hotel Tahiti
25. Matavai Hotel
26. Royal Tahitien Hotel
27. Princesse Heiata
28. Tahara'a Hotel on One Tree Hill

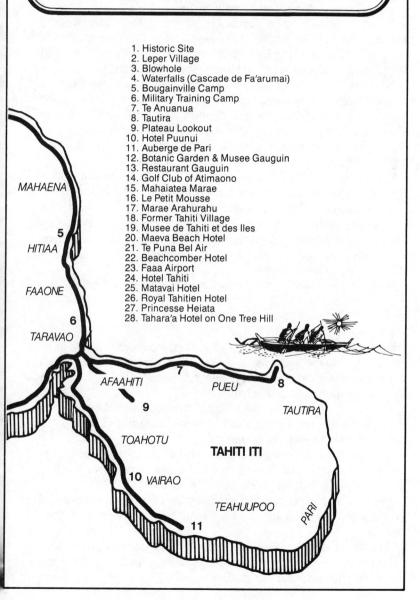

MAHAENA

5

HITIAA

FAAONE

6

TARAVAO

AFAAHITI   PUEU   **8**

7

9   TAUTIRA

TOAHOTU   **TAHITI ITI**

10 VAIRAO

TEAHUUPOO   PARI

11

The museum helped visitors put Point Venus into proper perspective, recalling the first Europeans' arrival to Tahiti and remembering that it was the intrepid Polynesians who were the early explorers, who sailed incredible distances navigating only by sea currents, winds, clouds and celestial bodies.

If you want to read an engrossing adventure that recaptures the navigational abilities of the Polynesians, seek the December 1974 copy of National Geographic and read "Wind, Wave, Star, and Bird," by David Lewis, the run-away medic. Fascinating.

Near the door of the museum was the calling card of history: a cannon dated 1526 found on the reef of Amanu Island in the Tuamotus, a reminder that the Spanish and Portuguese sailed in these South Pacific waters 250 years before the English and the French arrived with their botanists and journal keepers, artist and map makers—the public relations men of their era.

On the park side of a little stream that leads to the beach, stop at the monument commemorating the work of the first missionaries.

Keep going over the foot-bridge of the little stream . . . it used to be much larger according to eighteenth century drawings . . . to another monument of modern sculptured wood. The names on the monument read Wallis, Cook, and Bougainville. Bougainville never landed at Matavai Bay but no matter.

You are now standing on a spit of black sand beach. This is Point Venus.

Imagine it is June, 1767.

The English ship, the *Dolphin*, has been ten months at sea in an attempt to find the land mass in the southern hemisphere. The ship is under the command of a naval lieutenant, Samuel Wallis. Like most of his men he is sick and exhausted.

On June 18 the ship sees land, Tahiti, and slowly works its way up the east coast trying to find a safe anchorage. At last on June 23 at Matavai Bay the ship drops anchor.

Imagine the delight of these scurvy-riddled, sex-deprived sailors the next morning when the ship is surrounded by over five hundred canoes bearing fruit and nude young women!

Imagine their surprise when suddenly the charade is dropped and young warriors bombard the ship with hurled stones from their canoes.

The shocked sailors are hit, injured. They counter-attack with cannons sinking Tahitian canoes and killing hundreds. It is the Tahitians' first exposure to gunfire.

Evidently believing that the cannons were a one-time weapon the Tahitians repeated their attack two days later only to be repulsed again by gunfire. The *Dolphin* pressed its counter-attack with a land force that burned a number of large war canoes on the beach.

That was enough.

The Tahitians sued for peace.

The *Dolphin* sent a landing party ashore and, still wary, set up a fort where you now stand. A site ideal for protection – wedged between the river on one side, Matavai Bay on the other and the ocean behind.

Wallis' priorities were to resupply the ship and restore the men to health. The men's idea of restoration was to be with the Tahitian women. The encampment on the Point to keep the Tahitians out was a mere hindrance of keeping the English sailors in. They were over the walls and into the bushes. The price for favors was a piece of iron and the *Dolphin* nearly fell apart from the men pulling nails from her bulwarks.

The *Dolphin* stayed in Matavai Bay a month.

Eight months after Wallis, Bougainville arrived at Tahiti and landed on the east side of the island at Hitiaa. He stayed less than ten days.

Both explorers paled in the shadow of Captain James Cook who followed them to Tahiti in the spring of 1769.

In command of the converted coal collier, the *Endeavour,* Cook landed at Matavai Bay and immediately saw that the black spit of land described by Wallis was as ideal a location for his celestial observations as it was for natural protection. Here he built a veritable fort and named the area "Point Venus."

It is amusing to stand on the Point now and imagine the sizeable encampment with moats, spiked palisades and mounted cannon, not a bad exercise in protecting the valuable equipment from curious Tahitians, but that was the only thing that needed protection.

The English sailors didn't want protection from the *vahines*. Once again it was over the wall and into the bushes.

The serious business took place on June 3, 1769, the day when Venus was to transit the sun.

It was an important day internationally and in many places throughout the world the Germans and French and Russians were making their own observations and measurements. The reason was simple. The distance from the earth to the sun was unknown but if an astronomer could successfully triangulate a body of known distance, Venus, passing before the sun, then the astronomer could successfully compute the distance to the sun.

The Venus transit to the Royal Society in England was important because a previous attempt had failed in 1761 and the next transit of Venus would not take place for another hundred years.

Cook, in order to assure success of the sighting in the South Pacific, even established a second observation station on a small island off the east coast of Tahiti.

The day came bright and clear. The transit hour approached and the observations began . . . and were completed.

The scientists would not know until they returned to England that the measurements made by the available instruments were not precise enough to be of value.

The primary objective of the voyage was a failure.

Biologically and socialogically however the Tahitian trip was a great success. Joseph Banks, a wealthy young botanist who helped finance the voyage and really considered the expedition to be his own private party – he brought seven personal servants and two hounds aboard the overloaded little ship – collected myriad specimens of new plants and wildlife and fish.

Cook made invaluable observations of the native life and he and Banks made a trip around Tahiti by boat and on foot.

The transit of Venus was also a springboard for the adventures of Cook which were to follow. On completing his scientific assignment he opened sealed orders which instructed him to search for new lands which led him on this first expedition to New Zealand, landing the first white party on its shores and surveying the country in detail.

Two following voyages of Cook took him back to Matavai Bay in 1773, 1774 and on the last trip in 1777. Aboard the *Resolution* he had as his ship's master the able twenty-three-year-old William Bligh.

On October 26. 1788 Captain William Bligh in command of *HMS Bounty* set up base camp at Point Venus to collect breadfruit. The men collected women. When the time came to leave the happy life of Tahiti five months later, the seeds of discontent had been deeply sown and the famous mutiny erupted not long after in Tongan waters.

The irrepressible Bligh returned the next year with another breadfruit expedition.

Point Venus became the focal center again on March, 1797 when the first missionaries from the London Missionary Society were landed by Captain James Wilson in command of the mission ship, the *Duff*.

It is easy today to shrug away the role of the missionaries but in reading the books of William Ellis, *Polynesian Researches*, himself an early missionary, you can't help but be caught up in the drama, the heartbreak, the resolution; to admire their ability to face, again and again, failure and personal tragedy . . . and still carry on.

The missionaries were but a handful of men and women, some with wives, a few single. They went years without hearing from families. Years without any moral and physical support. They lost their clothes. Their belongings. They eventually lost their houses and precious gardens at Matavai Bay and had to run for their lives.

They lost each other. Some ran home. Some gave up and died. Others gave up to women.

The worst of all was the lack of success. They were ignored. Scoffed at. Laughed at. They converted practically no one.

Listen to Ellis writing about the beginning of 1809:

> *"The ravages of diseases originating in licentiousness, or nutured by the vicious habits of the people, and those first brought among them by European vessels, appeared to be hastening the total devastation of Tahiti.*
>
> *"When the Missionaries spoke to them on the subject of religion, the deformed and diseased were sometimes brought out and ranged before them, as evidence of the efficacy of their prayers and the destructive power of their God."*

That would make a very tough audience.

Before leaving the Point, turn to the mountains.

On a clear morning, you have your best view of Orohena on the left and Aorai on the right. Although Mount Orohena looks like a Sunday morning hike to the top, it was not successfully climbed until 1953. The climbers found an ancient Tahitian shrine on top. (New Zealanders will recognize Aorai as being almost the same name as the Maoris gave to Mount Cook: Aorangi.)

Cross back over the bridge and stop at a metal pyramid to

commemorate the arrival of the mission ship, the *Duff*, and a low wall with stones set in to denote islands in French Polynesia and the dates the islands received the first missionaries.

There are two plaques, one in French, the other a poor English translation that says:

> *"Even as these stones once scattered far and wide over the island groups of the Pacific are this day brought together into this monument, so the churches for which they stand on in hope, one in faith, will one day be gathered together into the Kingdom."*

The black sands of Point Venus in the lee of the small peninsula is a favorite bathing beach with semi-nude swimmers.

(Japan sailors come in small herds and surreptitiously take pictures of the swimmers. Tee-hee-hee.)

Unfortunately, the site is badly littered with leftover paper plates, cellophane food wrappers, plastic bottles . . . the debris of alfresco snacking. Like Hawaii, it is not the tourists who create the litter but the local residents. A shame.

Near the site of the former museum are now souvenir huts with the usual offering to tourists: shells, bright pareus and Tahitian shirts.

Between the shops and the sea is a curious monument which, in past years, caused a bit of knee slapping and snickering.

Danielsson wrote that it was the biggest joke this side of the equator.

Surrounded by a hexagonal iron railing is a white concrete plinth with a white ball on top.

Today, no marker reveals what it represents, or why it was erected. On our original visit, there was a plaque that read in part:

> Monument Erected by James Cook
> June 3, 1769
> Replaced and Restored
> by the Royal Society and
> Royal Geographic Society in 1901.

Erected by James Cook! Out of concrete!

Danielsson, in his *Circle Island Tour Guide,* pooh-poohed the errors in the plaque so fiercely that, undoubtedly, he played an important role in its removal. In truth, he points out, the whole thing was conceived and executed by the local Public Works Department. Nearby is an eighty foot lighthouse erected in 1867, according to its plaque. Could this be another plaque project of the Public Works Department? The lighthouse was not really completed until 1868, according to Danielsson.

One of the reasons for going around the island clockwise, said my pretty lady guide from the Office of Tourist Development on my first of many round-the-island trips, is that you have the inside of the road going around the cliffs of the east coast!

From One Tree Hill to the point of Papenoo (surfing) you are in the district of Mahina.

One kilometer past Point Venus you come to the closed gates of the CEA, the French Energy Commission, (Commissariat à l'Energie Atomique), the civilian arm of the nuclear tests in the Tuamotus. In 1975 the heavily secured base was closed and moved to Moruroa.

At 13.2 P.K. in Mahina you come to an eastern turn in the road. If you keep your eyes on the road, you are apt to miss the Orofara Valley which became a settlement for lepers in 1914 and is still active as a hospital. (2)

Although the disease exists in French Polynesia, it can be controlled and most inmates eventually return to normal lives.

At Papenoo, you pass over the longest bridge in Tahiti. (Not very long.) The Papenoo River is to be damned at its source according to present plans, and a hydro-electric plant built. The authorities are still looking for the money.

At P.K. 22 you see a sign warning that high seas ahead might present danger to automobiles. Here is the *Trou du souffleur,* or blowhole. (3) Park your car a hundred yards beyond it and walk back. Don't go down on the platform. High waves in the past have swept people into the ocean.

A little farther along is a well-marked sign to the *Cascade de Faarumai* . . . a series of three waterfalls which are about a mile up a pretty valley (4). Take insect repellent and wear tennis shoes that you don't mind getting wet. If you are going beyond the first waterfall, *Vaimahuta,* you need good hiking shoes. Apt to be muddy.

At the end of the road up Faarumai Valley you might pass Tahitian ladies with wheelbarrows of watercress. At the end of the road there is a small parking place. Follow the footpath over a bridge and up the righthand stream to the pretty cascade. The stream waters are inviting and are a source of fresh water shrimp, eels and even small perch.

On the east side of the island you feel that Papeete has fallen away and you are in the country. It is not as heavily populated as the western coast. It is quieter. More peaceful. Somehow the croton and the *tiare* and the flowers seem more in their place, lusher, more colorful.

Here you may see boys bathing in a fast flowing river jumping into the turbulent water from a bridge and being swept away laughing. We stopped our car and two little boys, with only the slightest of sidelong glances, climbed a high riverside tree and made magnificent, look-at-me jumps into the river.

At Mahaena you drive through an area famous as a battlefield between the French and the Tahitians who in 1844 objected to the arbitrary annexation by a French admiral. At Mahaena, they fought from mile-long trenches which couldn't serve as protection from the French naval war guns. After their seaside defeat the Tahitians took to the hills and fought guerrilla fashion for two years until they were finally subdued.

Off of Mahaena is a small islet of Teaaupiri where Cook set up his second observation post for the transit of Venus.

At the turn of the century the island was used as a quarantine station.

Farther down the road is Hitiaa. Here, the chief of the district greeted Bougainville when he first came to Tahitian shores. Bougainville dropped anchor off this coast (5) for reasons only he knew. Why he chose the often stormy east coast anchorage is curious. In addition to losing six anchors, he almost lost his ships.

His stay in Tahiti could hardly be called a success, except for the crew's enrapture with the islands and their tales back home of the natives' friendliness and of their charming habit of sharing house, table, wives and daughters.

The views through the district of Hitiaa become more appealing for the photographer. There are waterfalls, swelling surf, panoramics of Tahiti Iti appearing on the horizon as a distant island.

At Taravao, you are almost halfway around Tahiti Nui. Once a French fort, Taravao is a training camp for the army (6). The Polynesians, because they are French citizens, must do one year of service. Half of the trainees are Tahitians and half are European French . . . or, as they say, *Metropolitan* French.

You are on the isthmus facing Tahiti Iti.

Because the road doesn't go all the way around Tahiti Iti, you are faced with a problem of choice.

The branch of the road to the north side of Tahiti Iti goes through Pueu and ends at Tautira.

The southern branch takes you past Vairao, Zane Grey's old fishing camp, and ends at Teahupoo.

A third seldom taken road, traverses the middle and leads to the plateau of Tahiti Iti (9) passing cattle, vegetable gardens and abundant fruit trees, with beautiful views of Tahiti Nui.

Tahiti Iti

Once upon a time there was a good reason to take the north coast road because, at Pueu, halfway to Tautira, there was a small family-run resort called Te Anuanua (7) with twelve bungalows and a restaurant which a newspaperman in Auckland, a real rascal, described to us thusly: "The first thing you do is to tear off your clothes and dive into the clear water and shake hands with all the exotic fish.

"Then you wrap yourself in a *pareu* and order a bottle of wine and stick your feet up in the air.

"The third thing you do is to tear up your ticket home."

Te Anuanua cast its spell on most guests.

We once went to a *tamaaraa* at the little resort. The wine flowed freely, the dancing was wild, the High Commissioner "way-wayed" the *tamure* with a local school girl, and the newly elected governor of American Samoa danced cheek-to-cheek with the proprietress. I think there was swimming, with and without clothes, as well.

Alas, the Te Anuanua suffered a serious fire and had to close.

But all is not lost.

The only other hotel built on the island of Tahiti in the 'Eighties, besides the Ibis Hotel on the Papeete waterfront, is on Tahiti Iti. The Hotel Puunui (10) is located on the side of the mountain overlooking the ocean. Its facilities include junior suites with kitchenettes that accommodate up to four guests, or separate bungalows and deluxe suites with full kitchens to house even more. There is a restaurant, bar, swimming pool, and tennis courts on property.

A regular shuttle service takes guests down to the beach, a mile-and-a-half away, where there is another restaurant, a marina for twenty-five boats, and a water sports center.

Horseback riding, billiards, archery are to be added to the activities menu shortly.

You are invited to spend the day on the white sand beach.

You'll find showers, changing rooms and lockers.

Eat in the restaurant, relax, enjoy the best of French Polynesia without leaving Tahiti.

A travel writer told us that his four days at the Hotel Puunui his was the highlight of the Tahiti experience. Removed from the traffic and congestion of Papeete, its isolation is one of its greatest assets.

Pueu is only half way to the end of the road. Go on to the village of Tautira (8). Another good reason for the north coast drive. The drive is picturesque and soothing because there is little traffic and not too many human beings. Only the sea and the coconut trees and the rich flora and fauna by the side of the road.

Tautira is interesting historically because in 1772 it became a focal point of the Spanish effort to establish Tahiti under the Spanish flag. From Tautira a Spanish ship took four young men to Peru to teach them, by example, the awesome power of the Spanish Empire. The two who lived came home unimpressed.

Spain, again from Peru, sent two priests and a prefabricated house to Tautira in 1774 . . . twenty-three years before the Protestant missionaries were to arrive from London. Evidently the priests lacked fervent missionary zeal. They never left their fortress house for fear of the natives and departed gratefully when the first ship came with fresh supplies a year later.

Cook, on the other hand, was the English answer to the Spanish thrust. He anchored at Tautira and carved the English dates of English visits on the reverse side of the cross left by the Spanish.

In 1773 Captain Cook nearly lost the *Resolution* and the *Adventure* in the same waters when the ships struck a reef. He was able to kedge himself off the coral but the *Adventure* lost an anchor doing so.

When we were at Te Anuanua there was a documentary film crew making a film of the discovery and the recovery of the anchor.

Robert Louis Stevenson aboard his chartered yacht the *Casco* spent a month at Tautira in 1888 and although his book *In the South Seas* relates in detail his experiences in the Marquesas and the Tuamotus, his visit to Tahiti is not reported. Letters to friends however were glowing in praise of his temporary village home. Danielsson's Tahiti tour book shows a picture of Stevenson and his wife Fanny lolling in a coconut grove with a Tahitian couple.

At Tautira you can also charter a canoe with an outboard motor and a steersman guide to take you inside the lagoon for a very different sightseeing trip. Take your own food and drink, or arrange with the chief to have it brought. Catch a fish and grill it over coals. Have one of the more isolated and unusual picnics of your life.

The rowers of Tautira are the heroes of canoeing in Tahiti. At the annual Courses de Pirogues, canoe races, during the days of the July Fête the Tautira teams are those to beat.

Perhaps being at the end of the road at Tahiti Iti puts them in closer touch with the sea.

I never return to Taravao and see the building of the Gendarmerie that I don't recall the time I was being escorted around the island by a pretty girl from the tourist office. At the Gendarmerie she stopped and went inside with a piece of paper.

She came out a few minutes later and I asked her, "What did you do there?"

"I had my paper from the office stamped."

"Why?"

"It's to prove that we went around the island."

I frowned about that for a couple of miles and finally concluded that it was flattering.

On the southern coast of the peninsula of Tahiti Iti you'll find, unlike the northern side, white sand beaches and calm lagoons. Families frequent Toahotu's gentle sandy beach particularly on Sunday outings. Toahotu is the site of Zane Grey's fishing camp, Flower Point. His adventures in pursuit of the one-thousand-pound marlin are described in *Tales of Tahitian Waters* . . . if you can find an old copy.

At Toahotu is also the beginning of a huge deep-water harbor. During his first three-month stay in Tahiti, Cook made a trip around Tahiti on foot and by small boat and he reported that the harbor here was inferior to none but for some reason he never utilized it.

The French, during the first atomic tests in the Tuamotus in the sixties, used it as a base fleet anchorage, which included immense aircraft carriers. Before it was taken out of service the French luxury liner *France*, on world cruises, spent several days in this harbor.

At Vairao (10), there is a sizeable French government oceanographic research station which large signs announce as being CNEXO, Centre National pour l'Exploitation des Oceans.

Here you'll pass by large outdoor ponds which look like reservoirs and which in reality hold experimental shrimp-breeding projects.

The road ends at Teahuupoo. From here you can walk into the bush of Pari which at one time was a refuge of the runaway disciples of Rousseau. The hippies of many parts of the world who wanted to get back to mother nature tried to camp here but were flushed out by the French police and sent home.

A couple of hundred yards from the end of the road is a pleasant touch of gastronomic civilization. The Auberge de Pari (11.) is a favorite week-end destination of local families and is an attractive, inside-outside restaurant with thatched- roofed pavilion and tables covered with clean white and red linen and napkins of woven cotton. Nice.

The Lady Navigator tried the shrimp from the nearby oceanographic station and she mopped up the last of the oil and garlic sauce with a morsel of fresh French bread and sighs of satisfaction while I finished off a huge steak with the last glass of imported Tavel rose.

Cigars and candies were proferred by our angelic Tahitian waitress. You could easily make Auberge de Pari an all-afternoon eating experience.

Back again at the isthmus and only about one kilometer along you will be at the 60 P.K. marker which is the half way point.

In the district of Papeari you reach a combination attraction: the Botanical Gardens of Motu Ovini and at the end of the garden the Gauguin Museum (12).

First the garden.

Its history is unusual because its founder was far from typical.

His name was Harrison Smith and he was a professor of physics at the Massachusetts Institute of Technology in Boston with a hobby of tropical botany.

The inheritance of a small fortune changed his hobby into a lifetime occupation and he moved to Tahiti in 1919. In the district of

Papeari, he started buying property, lot by lot.

Eventually he became the owner of about three-hundred and forty acres and into those acres he created a working laboratory of international tropical trees and shrubs and flowers.

Harrison Smith was more than just a nature lover. He was interested in adapting foreign trees and plants which would have a useful place in the Tahitian economy. The rambutan is one example. Another is the sweet Tahitian grapefruit which really has to be eaten over a sink it is so juicy.

He busied himself with the welfare of the surrounding farmers and took pleasure in grafting plants for them and giving them seeds and cuttings and lending them money.

At his death in 1947 at the age of sixty-five he left the gardens to a friend and fellow botanist but the gardens fell on hard times. They became part of the residence of Cornelius Crane, the inheritor of an American industrial fortune who was also a philanthropist. Following his death the gardens were opened to the public by a botanical association.

If you'd like a thorough history of the gardens and a plot plan of its many plantings, you can buy a booklet at the entrance. The cost is only one hundred francs. If you are a botanist and a nature lover you can spend timeless hours wandering. If you are professional you'll note that the plants are mostly non-Tahitian but are imported from other parts of the Pacific and from Asia and Africa and America.

In any case the gardens are worth a stroll through even though your only botanical experience has been mowing lawns for mother.

At the entrance to Cornelius Crane Alley where there is a sign posted "Allée, Cornelius Crane, 1905-1962, Donateur du Jardin" there is a turtle pen with two mammoth turtles which were brought from the Galápagos in 1930 as a gift to the children of Charles Nordhoff. (The pamphlet says that they could date back to the time of Captain Cook, which proves how gullible and careless pamphlet writers are.)

Stroll up the paved walk through the varieties of stately palms, breadfruit, bananas. Giant elephant ears from Samoa. Flowering white jasmin from Thailand. Golden bamboo.

Left of the turtle pen is a banyan tree startling in its size. The branch-to-ground roots are as big as telephone poles!

The peaceful walk eventually brings you to a shingled resthouse where you could sit and enjoy the quiet—except for the noise of the highway and the cars going over the bridge behind you.

By angling to the right on your return to the entrance road you can pick up a series of paths that wend through a forest of *mape* or Tahitian chestnut trees with their strange above-the-ground roots shaped like waving elephant ears.

At a spot in the middle of the garden is a wooden plaque commemorating the six plants brought back to Tahiti from Hawaii on the *Hokule'a*, a replica of a double hulled Polynesian sailing canoe which retraced in 1976 the voyage of early ancestors made over one thousand years before. The *Hokule'a* made the voyage without modern navigational aids in thirty days.

Bringing plants to Tahiti was an important part of Tahiti's development.

It is difficult, having gone more than half way around Tahiti and having been overwhelmed by its lushness and growth and the variety of trees and shrubs and flowers, to remember that when the first explorers and missionaries arrived they were struck by the paucity of vegetation!

Tahiti must have been very bare before the arrival of the Polynesians who brought the coconut and banana and the breadfruit trees to provide food above the ground. To grow below the ground they brought taro, yams and, the botanical mystery because nobody is sure how it arrived in the Pacific, the American sweet potato.

The missionaries introduced sugar cane and corn and cotton. They also brought lemon trees, tamarinds, pineapple, guavas, figs, coffee trees and a variety of vegetables.

A French marine lieutenant in 1847 was first charged with experimental agricultural development and he successfully grew cabbages and tomatoes and leeks and melons and parsley.

Forty years later a pharmacist-botanist, Edouard Raoul, as passionate about growing plants as Harrison Smith, arrived in Tahiti under the sponsorship of the French government with a cargo of "forty greenhouses containing 1,500 plants."

Raoul's experimental gardens grew never-seen-before trees: hundreds of fruit trees, kauri from New Zealand, red cedar and eucalyptus from Australia, rubber trees, gum trees, jack trees.

By the end of the century the Raoul Gardens were providing plants without charge to farmers from a variety of one-hundred and fifty species.

The new hospital of Mamao now occupies the site of Raoul's nursery, the origin for much of French Polynesia's present richness in trees and flowers and plants.

This was the tradition that Harrison Smith found in Tahiti and to which he added his own measure.

He lies buried on a terrace three kilometers above Motu Ovini in a peaceful spot overlooking the lagoon and his beloved gardens.

The Gauguin Memorial Museum

If you'd really like to get the most out of the Gauguin Museum, buy another Danielsson pamphlet, *Gauguin in Tahiti,* and review the life of this strange, twisted man who gave up wife, children, business, country and comfort to pursue the conviction that "primitive art is truth, the purest form of celebration."

Gauguin was one of few who believed in his own artistic talents.

The museum offers a full documentary of his life, particularly as it pertained to his three periods of residency in French Polynesia: three years at Mataiea (1891-1893), six years in Punaauia (1895-1901)—both on the island of Tahiti—and his last two years in the Marquesas (from 1901). He died May 8, 1903 at age fifty-five.

Like the missionaries on Point Venus, he never knew material success. And, like the missionaries, perhaps the work was success in itself, and the material never mattered.

Clockwise from the entrance to the museum, you approach the air-conditioned, humidity controlled and secured Henri Bing Room, the gift of his widow as a memorial. She gave the money to build the separate *fare,* in part, because there was no suitable exhibit room for paintings in Tahiti. She also contributed twenty canvases by contemporary artists.

At the time of our visit, the Bing Room contained two minor Gauguins. While the museum is diligently negotiating for the loan of Gauguin works and that of his peers, its benefit now is as a backgrounder on one of the twentieth century's great artists. It is a most satisfactory experience.

Also, the setting of the museum is superb, sited along the lagoon and surrounded by the same lush vegetation found in Gauguin's canvases.

The buildings form a large quadrangle separated by a broad green lawn. They flow into one another with planned architectural variation to keep you interested and alert. You step up into one building, down into another. A tower presents a refreshing panorama.

The exhibits flow in the same varied manner. Here, in photographs, you see Gauguin and his family. Gauguin as a child. As a mariner. With his buxom Danish wife. With his companions, Van Gogh, Pissaro, Manet, Laval, Bernard, the disciple who thought himself the teacher.

Here, through personal possessions, are Gauguin's early days in Papeete. His guitar, an easel, all of his painting gear, a carving, his work as a journalist, his engraving tools.

You can't like him. Gauguin gave up his wife and children, and his job to follow his own selfish interest to be "an artist." He squandered money when he got it. He caught syphilis from a Parisian cabaret dancer. He battled authorities almost automatically. He "married" thirteen-year-old girls.

You can feel sorry for him. His talent was his torture chamber.

We learn that, once, at his Punaauia residence—racked with physical pain, broke, starving—he planned his final canvas—his final cry of creativity—and his suicide. In a near mad, blind, savage rage, on coarse copra sacking, he painted "Where do we come from? What are we? Where are we going?"

Then he swallowed a bottle of poison and crawled up a hill and waited to die, in agony, and in vain.

He threw up the poison. And returned to painting.

You have to admire him, if only for his courage.

The museum takes you with him to Bretagne in 1886, to Panama in 1887, to Paris in 1888—searching, seeking—and, finally, to Tahiti.

In Tahiti, Gauguin's subjects, color, and light came together.

He had found home.

In thirty years Gauguin finished 649 identified paintings. One exhibit is a letter from a government official warning persons to whom the dead artist owed money that they would be lucky to get anything back because "the artist's work has no chance of selling."

At his death in 1903, a Gauguin sold for 150 francs. Fifteen years later, the price was 14,000 francs. By 1942, one million francs.

In 1984, a Gauguin sold for $3.8 million.

"Where do we come from? What are we? Where are we going?" is now in the Boston Museum of Fine Arts . . . and it is priceless.

Gilles Artur, director of the Gauguin Museum since 1965, is optimistic about the future.

Through a New York-based foundation started in 1985, The Gauguin and Oceania Foundation, he foresees the day when there will be enough money to acquire five or six originals for a permanent collection, and to underwrite periodic loan exhibits including other artists of Gauguin's era.

"It all started with the critical Henri Bing Room, and our twentieth anniversary, also in 1985. The Jeu de Paume Gallery in Paris loaned us the famous 'Femmes de Tahiti' and we obtained 23 other Gauguin originals of lesser importance on loan.

"We plan to add a new wing and create an artists in residence program, bringing well known artists to work in Tahiti and, simultaneously, work with our local artists.

"With the support of our 600-member Friends of the Museum and a board of influential people, we are working toward making Papeete a free port for art with no tax on artwork coming into the country, or going out.

"We are moving forward. It just takes money."

The Gauguin and Oceania Foundation, a tax-deductible organization; 3 East 77th Street, New York 10021. Your donation could help return some of the over 600 works of Gauguin—if only temporarily—to the land of their inspiration and creation.

In Peter Buck's excellent book, *Vikings of the Sunrise,* a photograph shows the author beside a large, grim, ominous stone carving taken from Raivavae Island in the Australs in the '30s.

The *tiki* has had an interesting history.

It was moved to the museum in Papeete many years ago and it was said that everyone who was involved in the move died inexplicably.

The old museum then was on the site of Raoul Gardens and when the site was designated to become the new hospital, the *tiki* was to be moved to the location of the present Gauguin Museum.

Of course no one wanted to move the *tiki* because it was "alive."

Finally, a foreman and two helpers agreed to the job. They all died, the story goes, shortly thereafter.

My around-the-island guide said that a German girl took a sunbath in its shadow and fell ill of an undiagnosed ailment and had to be brought back to the *tiki* to be cured. She said it was true because she read it in the newspaper.

Anyway, the *tiki* of Raivavae reigns over the Gauguin Museum. You go touch it if you like. I'll stay over here. When we asked Gilles about the *tiki,* he said, "I have my Western security system, and, with my *tiki,* I have my Polynesian security system."

Around the corner from the Gauguin Museum is the Gauguin Restaurant, (13) a popular luncheon spot for tour bus passengers.

Another kilometer and a half and you come to the Vaihiria River.

You can drive up the dirt road in good weather and then hike into the Vaihiria Lake which is appreciated among the locals for its huge eels. Want to go swimming?

In the village of Mataiea there is nothing left of the famous men who once lived here. Gauguin's native hut has long since gone to ashes. Nothing remains to remind you of Rupert Brooke, the English poet who fell in love with a Mataiea girl and immortalized her in his poem *Tiare Tahiti*. William Somerset Maugham lived near here researching *The Moon And Sixpence*.

At Papara a large sign identifies the Atimaono Golf Course (14). At one time it was a flourishing cotton plantation with a resplendent residence. The owner, William Stewart, was responsible for bringing in one thousand Chinese laborers to work the cotton fields. The end of the American Civil War restored southern cotton to the market place and the local venture collapsed.

There was not enough money to fulfill the contract of sending the Chinese back to their homeland. They stayed and prospered.

The drive through Atimaono and the district of Papara is extremely pleasant, often driving through peaceful tunnels of trees. On a Sunday morning particularly when the traffic is the lightest and the ladies in their broad-brimmed hats are on their way to and from the many churches which border the highway it is a most tranquil scene.

One of the true wonders of Tahiti was the massive temple pyramid of Mahaiatea at P.K. 39.2 (15).

Cook and Banks were told that the grand *marae* had only been completed within the last ten years before their arrival and, incredibly, constructed in only two years.

Without mortar to hold the coral blocks and stones together and without iron tools to shape the material, the Tahitians nevertheless built a temple two hundred and sixty-seven feet long by eighty-seven feet wide at the base—almost the size of a football field—and then eleven platforms each about four feet high but progressively shrinking in size until the top-most rectangle was one hundred, seventy-seven feet by seven feet.

It was the largest structure seen by Europeans in French Polynesia.

Today it is only a pile of rubble overgrown with trees and bushes and hardly worth the mile-long detour off of the highway.

What happened to the great *marae* of Mahaiatea?

When it was abandoned with the advent of Christianity, like almost all temples in history, it became the easy source of building materials and in this case was used for roads and structures built by the cotton king of Atimaono and his army of coolies.

You can't help but notice the yesteryear Victorian structure on the sea side of the highway at P.K. 36.8 with a sign saying "Vahine Moena." It is a restaurant serving baked-in-the-ground Tahitian foods on Sundays, the only day it is open.

Le Petit Mousse (16), a full restaurant with sleeping accommodations available, borders the lagoon at P.K. 32.5 between Papara and Paea. For folks who want to put-put around the lagoon, maybe catch a fish and have the chef prepare it, there are small boats for hire. A rather pleasant way to spend a day.

A couple of miles closer to Papeete is the Paroa cave, a large hole in the cliff filled with water and it is a matter of pride for some to say that they have swum in the cave of Paroa. There is a small space where you can pull your car off the road but you have to keep a sharp lookout or you'll miss it.

Six kilometers farther along is the *marae* of Arahurahu well marked by signs (17).

In contrast to the *marae* of Mahaiatea the *marae* of Arahurahu has been restored by Dr. Y.H. Sinoto, archaeologist of the Bishop Museum, and it is worth a visit particularly during the days of the Fête when the old ceremonies are re-enacted including the "sacrifice" of a human body. In this case the body will be alive and not left to rot on a wooden platform along with the pigs, dogs and fruit which make up the other offerings.

The tour guides are accustomed to answering the questions before they are asked and they volunteer the information that 1. the human victims were not sacrificed alive on the temple altars but were banged on the head quite unsuspectingly in the bush and 2. they were not eaten.

Although cannibalism was practiced in many parts of Polynesia — Fiji, The Cook Islands, New Zealand, the Marquesas — it was also unthinkable in other parts of Polynesia — Hawaii, Tonga, Tahiti.

The setting alone of the Marae Arahurahu amid the green forest and underneath the surrounding cliffs is worth the visit.

The districts of Paea and Punaauia, especially ocean side of the road, have become a European suburb of Papeete. The weather on the west coast is protected from the rain-bearing southeast trades and the beaches are often of white sand and the lagoons are calmer.

If you think that cluster of Tahitian *fares* facing the water on that perfectly curved white sand beach should have been a hotel instead of a residence, you think correctly. It *was* The Hotel Tahiti Village. It has one of the best beaches on Tahiti, and was a great luncheon spot.

Historically the area has a significance as the location of the major battle of "Fei-Pi" in 1815 between Pomare who was returning from exile on Moorea with an "army" of eight hundred led by European mercenaries and the forces of Teva, always a stubborn crowd. Although Pomare had come at the invitation of the chief of Punaauia, the leaders of Papeari, Mataiea and Papara had other opinions which they backed with combined forces. Unfortunately they went into battle without waiting for the entire force to arrive and when an important chief was killed by the gunfire from the mercenaries, the opposition broke and Pomare returned to rule.

Musee De Tahiti Et Des Iles . . . 15 P.K.

Just past SuperMarche Tamanu and the Total Service Station is a small sign on the left hand side of the road pointing to the museum (19). Don't miss it.

If I were advising a new visitor to French Polynesia as to the best way to fully enjoy the history and culture of the islands, I would send them to two places at the beginning of the visit . . . to Point Venus . . . and then to Pointe des Pêcheurs where the new museum opened in 1978.

At Point Venus the student stands physically on the spot where the modern history of French Polynesia began.

At Pointe des Pêcheurs in the Musée de Tahiti et des Iles is a fascinating exhibit of all that makes up French Polynesia . . . the geographic-oceanographic explanation of the islands . . . the life in the sea and the life on the land. The progressive stages of its history . . . the pre-European artifacts . . . a collection of memorabilia of the times and the political and cultural and social leaders. It is all in the Musée and it is superb.

The small cost for admission has to make it one of the best

bargains in the islands.

The Musee is open nine-thirty mornings to six in the evening daily except Mondays. One word of caution. As it should be, the museum is used as a teaching tool for the school system and can be over-run with mobs of curious children who might be more interested in you than in the exhibits. Go first thing in the morning or late afternoons or the weekends. We found so many highlights in the museum that we couldn't absorb them all.

The museum was worth repeated visits.

On an initial visit let's look at a few of the most outstanding exhibits.

In the entry hall there will be revolving exhibits of interest. It will be worthwhile.

In the first room on the left is a self-service slide presentation in French using multiple screens visualizing the growth and life of the two different types of islands, coral and volcanic. It is so well done graphically that French is not necessary for understanding the ten-minute show. There are poof cushions for reclining on the floor and relaxing during the presentation.

Nearby, under a plastic bubble, is a three dimensional map of the islands of French Polynesia which tells you with one glance not only where the different islands are located but how they are built up underneath the ocean floor. Excellent exhibit.

The rest of the room deals with oceanography, coral formations, shell collections, geology.

The next rooms deal with pre-European history and the artifacts of earlier times.

You have to pause a moment and remember that the first explorers and traders and missionaries were also zealous collectors. The treasures of Polynesia were sent and carried home in vast quantities with the result that the Polynesian collections in Leningrad and Boston and London and New York are far superior to those few objects that remain in the islands of their origin.

When the missionaries finally succeeded in winning the natives to the new religion, the converts, undoubtedly encouraged by the missionaries, destroyed most of the stone *tikis* of their old religion and burned the wooden carvings. Few sacred objects remained.

One famous private collection in England, the Hooper Collection, became available for sale in 1978. The local authorities responsible for the museum were able to raise about $400,000 to buy fifty-two pieces out of the collection.

You'll see several of the purchased articles in the Polynesian rooms. For example find the tapa cloth robe and appreciate the delicacy of the color and the material. This mantle worn by a priest looks like soft, brown silk. Notice also the delicate fern motif imprinted in the bark-based fabric. Bloody marvelous.

Look for another robe, or part of a decoration, worn by an official funeral mourner. It is a breast plate made out of a thousand tiny pieces of mother-of-pearl sewn together with coconut sennit.

In another case you see carved canoe paddles and paddle-club combinations, Polynesian wood carving at its best so delicately and lovingly sculptured that they look like pieces of intricately spun lace.

As a matter of future interest also note the bows and arrows. Archery was a royal sport in pre-European days; the bows and arrows were not instruments of war. In the archery contest of old, it wasn't who could shoot the most accurately but who could shoot the farthest and on the island of Moorea you'll visit temples where there are restored archery platforms.

You'll see in the Musée how the adzes, the early hatchet heads, were made. You'll see examples of the daily life of early Polynesians, the food utensils, the house structures, the different types of poi pounders.

Examples of plaiting rope, beating out tapa cloth, tatooing, making of fish hooks; examples of medicines. All are found in the Polynesian section along with a rare wooden *tiki* and a collection of stone *tikis* . . the wide-staring eyes of the Marquesian *tikis* . . . and the narrow eyes of the Australs.

The next rooms recall the history of the first European explorers and missionaries through primitive art wall murals. There is a copy of *The Discovery of Tahiti* by the master of Captain Wallis' ship, *Dolphin*. There is a familiar painting of Captain Cook.

On another wall is a copy of the famous Polynesian girl painted by Cook's artist, John Webber. She looks remarkably European.

A curator explained that the illustrators on such voyages were primarily responsible for recording technical information such as the precise dimensions and conformation of war canoes. The rendition of people such as the Webber girl, he said, was often done after their return to Europe where the paintings were completed from memory and with romantic imagination.

We commented that the chiefs shown in paintings were of huge proportions and the curator said this was often true. Eating was one of the royal prerogatives. Many foods were forbidden to commoners.

The chiefs who had probably won their initial titles through physical prowess sustained their superior warrior physiques with the balanced diets that were available only to them.

Two cases near each other hold portraits of the leading characters in the drama which led to the eventual take-over by the French. In one case is the picture of George Pritchard, 1796-1883, the missionary-businessman-English Consul whose expulsion from Tahiti nearly led to an international war.

In an adjoining case is a picture of his great friend Queen Pomare, Tahiti's Queen Victoria. She ruled for fifty years dying in 1877. The Tahitian people feared that with her death an era of history would end. They were correct. Only three years later the protectorate would change into a French colony.

A quick stop before a couple of other displays.

In one is a fascinating rarity, a wooden tablet found on Easter Island known as a *kohau rongorongo* or "talking board." Legend says that King Hotu-matua brought sixty-seven tablets with him from the islands of Marae-renga. There are twenty known to be in existence in the world today.

One of them is before you.

If you are a student of communications you would have to be enraptured with this piece of dark brown wood, no more than six by four inches, because it was believed at one time that the detailed carvings on each side constituted evidence that the Polynesians indeed had a *written* language.

On a subsequent visit I expressed my interest in the "talking board" and the young man in the office said they didn't have a picture of it but would I like to take my own? I didn't have my camera but he volunteered to show it to me anyway. We went to the case and he unlocked and opened it, removed the plastic box cover over the *kohau rongorongo* and handed it out to me.

The officials at the Bishop Museum would have died! An article such as this would have been guarded by laser guns and security police.

In the light of a nearby window I inspected it reverently without understanding the little stick figures and their postures and the fish and other symbols. I had never seen an example of boustrophedon writing, that is writing like an ox plows, continuing the left to right inscriptions by turning the tablet upside down and continuing from left to right.

Fascinating stuff.

(Later I was told the Musée's *kohau rongorongo* was a replica!)

One more exhibit in the category of communications is that devoted to the writers of the South Pacific legend: Herman Melville, Pierre Loti, Robert Louis Stevenson, Victor Segalen, a French poet, and Rupert Brooke.

Somerset Maugham, James Norman Hall, Charles Nordhoff, Robert Dean Frisbie, James Michener, Louis Becke are not mentioned.

Give the museum the time it deserves.

As the entrance is the following greeting:

"Polynesia past and present is alive in this museum.
"How the islands were born, how fauna and flora took possession of land and lagoon, how the first inhabitants came and lived and worshipped, how other men came from all parts and made their mark here, how this world lived through history, invigorated and ruled by the ocean."

On the ride back to Papeete there is one curiosity.

It is a primary school at Punaaiua and over the entrance is written in large letters and numbers: L'ECOLE 2+2=4. The French planter who donated the land for the school insisted on the inscription because he had serious doubts about the ability of the local students to learn the French curriculum and was determined they would learn at least one thing: two plus two equals four!

Marvelous.

Fifty yards up the road is a sign saying that Gauguin had his last house on Tahiti at this location. Nothing to see.

In a few minutes you are back to the airport (23) and, hello noisy Papeete!

5. Tubuai . . .
A Hideaway Island

Shady, Peaceful, Noiseless . . . A History Of Runaways . . . Colony Attempt Of Bounty Mutineers . . . The Empire Of Chung Tien

Papeete is part city, part village. Part carnival. Part market place. It is the Big Papaya of French Polynesia.

The contrast in the streets of easy flowing Tahitians to the industrious Chinese is as strong a contrast as is the precise, short-cropped French military to the loose, long-locked yachtsmen.

In Papeete there is a constant mixture of the naughty and the mighty.

Added to the mixture are the 120,000 annual tourists who must come to Papeete because it possesses the only international airport.

Suppose you wanted to get away from all the people, the tourists, the military, the cars, the trucks, the air-conditioned hotel room, the whole homogenized twentieth century scene . . . where would you go in French Polynesia?

Ah, so many choices.

One such place is Tubuai.

Tubuai is the principal island of the Australs. Four hundred and sixteen miles due south of Papeete.

Tubuai has no hotels. No discos. No taxis.

The population is sixteen hundred. The annual tourist count is about one hundred.

Tubuai has a long history of attracting runaways. It was the first stop of the mutineers on the *Bounty* and they liked what they saw so much that they voted to return to set up a permanent base.

The twice weekly flight to Tubuai leaves at eight-thirty in the morning. Flight time: one hour and fifty minutes. On Fridays the jet-prop, twin-engine Friendship-27 of Air Polynésie makes a triangular pattern from Tubuai, over to the sister island of Rurutu and then back to Papeete. On Mondays the pattern is reversed and the flight goes to

Rurutu, Tubuai and back to Papeete.

The other four islands of the Australs are Marie, Raivavae, Rimatara and Rapa.

One Friday morning at the airport I knew immediately I was headed off the tourist track.

When the flight to Bora Bora was announced, the line of passengers was made up of pink, bi-focaled and bubbly Americans in white shorts or checkered-country-club golf pants and white shoes.

When the flight to Tubuai was called a moment later, the line was made up of women in *pareus* carrying cardboard packages of food delicacies from the Papeete Market, and dark men in dark trousers with black shoes. All pleasant but somber commuters.

With my Air New Zealand flight bag and portable typewriter, I didn't need an identification badge.

Another passenger, a returning pastor, wore a white, delicately woven hat which I coveted. What a beautiful hat. I was to learn that this was a *chapeau niau* made from young palm leaves boiled in water and bleached in the sun. The leaves were then cut into fine strips, filed individually to a perfect thread and then hand woven.

It is a craft special to Tubuai and the hats are only made to order. Even if you are able to place an order the delivery may take two weeks. It may take two months.

The airplane landed on a sunny strip and we disembarked at a large, open-aired, pandanus-thatched building crowded with people, many of whom came out just to see the airplane land and see the passengers disembark and see the Papeete-bound passengers get on board and see the airplane take off again. They didn't have anything else to do and the twice-weekly airplane was one of life's little diversions.

Since the tourist office had sent a telegram to the Administrator I had expected to be met but when no one approached I asked a khaki uniformed *gendarme* if there were anyone present from the administration.

No one.

The airplane left. The crowd dwindled. It was evident that Tubuai was going to be a make-do situation.

A young man offered me a ride into the village and I accepted but the *gendarme* said I should come with him as it would be less crowded and he would drop me off at the administration offices.

His vehicle was a jeep. I crawled in the back, and he in the front next to his uniformed driver and we left for Mataura, the principal

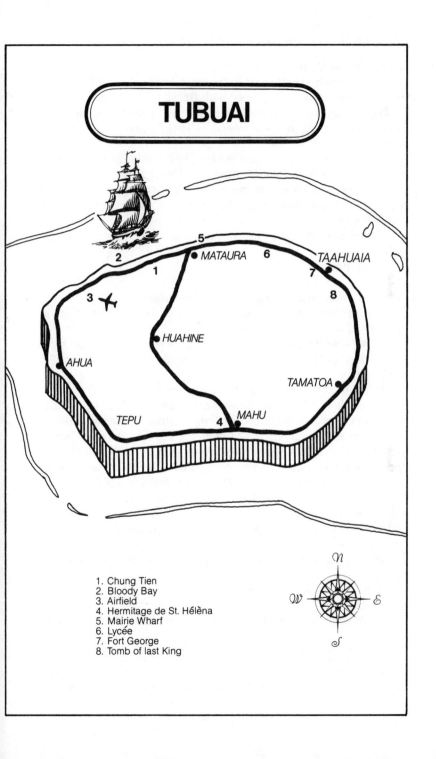

TUBUAI

1. Chung Tien
2. Bloody Bay
3. Airfield
4. Hermitage de St. Hélèna
5. Mairie Wharf
6. Lycée
7. Fort George
8. Tomb of last King

village on the island.

He turned in his seat to chat on the ten-minute drive into the village over a narrow paved road lined with trees.

The Gendarme Commandant of the two-man force, naturally, wanted to know where I was from, how long I was staying and why I was there.

In stumbling French I gave him a brief background and, remembering the two *Lost and Found* editions I had brought as a present to the Administrator, showed him the books. They serve, I had found, as big calling cards having the advantage of being instantly self-explanatory.

He looked at the title, the portrait on the back cover, riffled the pages.

"Vous avez ecrit ces livres?"

"Oui."

Lifted eyebrows. *"Tiens."* He was impressed.

In turn I asked him how long he had been on Tubuai. How long was his tour of duty.

By this time he was French-charming. A witty Frenchman has a special kind of Gallic gaiety and my conductor was overflowing with good humor.

He had been there about a year and it was peaceful and beautiful. However there were few amusements, few distractions, without which unimportant things became large irritants. That was bad.

His work was minimal. Children getting into mischief out of boredom. And family domestic quarrels. "Oh, la, la, la," he shook a hand like it had touched a hot stove, the stories he could tell me.

Before I could get him to tell me we had passed three small buildings, made two right-hand turns and stopped in front of the administration building.

I unloaded my single bag and asked my new found friend for his name.

He dropped his head and then slyly looked up from underneath his *kepi*.

"You want to put it in the book?"

"Perhaps."

Thank you very much for the lift, Commandant Paul Dupuy.

The white, low-lying building of the Australs Administration was modern, neat, tidy. Inside, the furniture was sparse but military neat and gave the impression of a no-nonsense, efficient operation.

The Administrator had people in his office and I was taken over by a young Frenchman with the face of a choirboy who wanted to know what I wanted.

They'd never heard of me. No telegram.

Back to square one. Staying three nights. Taste of the Australs. Doing a book on Tahiti. Gave him the books to give to the Administrator.

Ah. I needed a place to stay?

Yes.

There was only one place to stay and that was at the Chinaman's.

Would I stay there?

(There wasn't any other solution.) Yes.

There was only one place to eat and that was at the Chinaman's.

Would I eat lunch there?

Same reason. Same answer.

He thumbed my travel books and he asked me travel questions. I in turn learned that he was doing his obligatory year's service by doing civil work instead of military.

As it became obvious that I wasn't going to see the Administrator before lunch, he took me in a rust-eaten car around the corner to Chez Caro, part of the empire of Chung Tien.

In a motel cluster of concrete block structures, I was deposited at a duplex cottage, separated from the next unit by a garage. There must have been a half a dozen such duplexes. Only one served as a transient rental unit. It had three bedrooms. One bedroom already had a bag, making it apparent that the single bathroom and the kitchen were to be shared.

For a modest charge you get a bedroom, including electricity, and quite possibly, a cabin mate. There was no communal electricity but Chung Tien's generator slapped away in the distance, serving his economic empire.

He then took me around to the ramshackle corrugated-roofed grocery store belonging to Chung Tien and left me for lunch.

I was shown to a back room with a half dozen tables of chrome and plastic. Under my table a large dog enjoyed the coolness of the bare concrete floor, his tongue dripping, his eyes half closed.

The generator was just outside of the glass louvered windows. In a corner was a sink where you could wash your hands.

Four Frenchmen from the airplane entered. They were also somewhat stunned by the appointments but bravely ordered an aperitif.

The meal consisted of bits of beef over macaroni, vinegar and oil over lettuce leaves, fresh bread and butter. The dessert: half a papaya. I had a large bottle of cold beer.

After lunch I met the Administrator, a dark-haired gentleman, probably in his late thirties, who had worked in the administration offices of Paris for ten years before getting his foreign post, the Australs.

Sitting in his large, well-appointed office he explained the meager economy of the islands. A little copra. A private enterprise endeavoring to establish a sizeable potato farm. A bit of coffee. Very minimal.

Through the windows was the Administrator's gracious house with wide porches and comfortable furniture. He had been in Tubuai for almost four years and was in his last year of duty. A long way from Paris but not too bad . . . not too bad.

His teen-age daughter thought there was no world beyond Tubuai and was facing a cultural shock when his tour was finished and he was transferred to some as-yet-unknown destination.

He was gracious, rather at odds at what to do with me since press relations was never on his agenda, and promised me help if I needed it. I had brought my tennis racquet because I had understood from friends in Papeete that he was a tennis player. Perhaps we could play tennis before I left. End of interview.

I was on my own.

The island of Tubuai is an oval about six miles long and three miles wide and surrounded by reef. Mt. Taita, at 1300-feet, is the highest point on the island. A second peak, Fanareho, guards the west side of the island. From a distance Tubuai has been mistaken for two islands.

Captain Cook first spotted Tubuai in 1777 and the missionary ship, the *Duff*, passed by twenty years later.

In between the two dates the island had its most interesting visitors ....the mutineers of the *Bounty*.

After unloading Bligh and eighteen others into a long boat in Tongan waters on the 28th of april, 1789, the mutineers sailed southeast for a month before landing at a harbor at Tubuai on the 28th of May. The landing was greeted with hostility from the natives, hostility that led to bloodshed. The mutineers called the harbor Bloody Bay.

Even so, Christian was so impressed with the isolation and the potential of the island that he wanted to establish a colony. The mutineers voted to go along with the effort although James Morrison, mate of the *Bounty* who kept a journal wrote: "...*the Natives of Toobouai (sic) could not gain favour of any Man in his senses.*"

The mutineers continued on to their familiar base at Matavai Bay, Tahiti to stock up for a permanent settlement. They gathered four hundred and sixty hogs, fifty goats, a quantity of fowl, a few dogs and cats and, in exchange for a few red feathers, a bull and a cow.

By June 23rd they were back at Bloody Bay, and this time found the natives friendly.

In trying to find a settlement location, Christian aroused the jealousy of the chiefs and it never went smoothly after that.

The mutineers stayed until September, then fled for their lives.

The only entrance through the reef for ships of any size is into "Bloody Bay." Once inside the reef boats anchor off the village of Mataura and off-load their cargo onto small boats.

Mataura is a sweet village. *Mata*-eye, and *ura*-red or sacred. It is the "sacred eye" of Tubuai. Sleepy might be a more accurate description.

The pier of Mataura leads into the village square. The Mairie forms one side and the Salle de Fête forms the other.

In the center of the square is a flagpole flying the French tricolor and around the flagpole are four shade trees. Peaceful.

In front of the Salle de Fête is a triangle of roads. One road goes around the island. The intersecting road goes across the island. At the intersection is a giant shade tree, Protestant temple, meeting hall and Chinese store.

To the east of the intersection is Mr. Taro's petrol station where you can charter his fishing boat.

To the west, towards the airport, is the complex of Chung Tien. The rusty store has food, general merchandise, restaurant and, most important, beer on ice. Next door the large shed holds a bakery. Mr. Chung Tien's bakery. Next to the bakery another shed protects the island's single piece of public transportation . . . Mr. Chung Tien's truck driven by Mr. Chung Tien's son-in-law.

The motel units are behind the bakery.

Next to Chung Tien's is an elementary school, a playground, a broken-up tennis court and an open-air assembly hall.

Hard by the school is a small white post office building for communications traffic. There are fifteen telephones on the island.

The government complex is just off the road that intersects the island: the Administrator's *fare,* the head office, housing for minor officials and a small hospital.

That's Mataura.

Normally it would be somnolent. Shady. Peaceful.

During my trip however there was a major sports festival in progress involving the soccer, volleyball and ping pong teams of the other Austral Islands. Mataura was comparatively jumping.

At the store I tried to hire a car so that I could tour the island but this was not possible. Instead one of the family would drive me around and across the island in a figure-eight loop.

The cost, after much family discussion, was fixed at about $25.

The Chung Tien Circle Island Tour was set for the next morning after breakfast.

With nothing better to do I took a long walk passing a young Frenchman – I had seen him on the plane – frantically pedaling a tiny-wheeled bicycle rented from Chung Tien for $3.50 for a half day! We waved at each other not knowing that we were sharing the same bungalow.

I strolled back to the village and out the west side for another mile or two before I became aware how calm everything was. There was little or no traffic on the road. The trees cast cooling shadows over my path and the lagoon waters almost next to the road looked refreshing and tranquil.

Two busy weeks in bustling Papeete had been preceeded by four frantic weeks of travel and action: Los Angeles, Aspen, Suva, back home to Honolulu, to Auckland, Wellington and Christchurch. Interviews, parties, writing, researching, working, playing and people, people, people. Frantic.

Now ambling down the empty road on Tubuai in perfect weather with nothing to do but flick the odd stone alongside the road with a walking stick or watch the occasional bird or glance across the lagoon to the white line of the reef beyond, I felt the peace and grace of life on a small island.

Exactly the reason for going to Tubuai.

Now and then there was a house on the mountain side of the road and inevitably on the lagoon side would be a small outrigger canoe usually parked on stilts to keep it out of reach of stormy waves.

What do you do on Tubuai on the week-end? You go fishing in your outrigger canoe.

On the stroll back to Mataura, a small truck stopped and a brown-haired, curly-haired Polynesian offered me a ride. I didn't need the lift and certainly was in no need of saving time but still it was an unexpected gesture of hospitality.

We introduced ourselves and he said his name was Taro.

Ah, the man with the boat. Would it be possible to charter his fishing boat and go out to one or more of the little islands?

It was possible.

I was to go around the island Saturday morning and Taro's religion forbade him to work on Sunday so we fixed the time for one o'clock Saturday afternoon. We would visit three or four islands and still get back in time to see the inter-island soccer game finals – the biggest sporting event of the year. Couldn't miss that.

The excursion would cost another $25.

There were no options.

On returning to the bungalow I found an exhausted but amiable young bicyclist, Jeanfrançois Mignon, an antique dealer *(antiquaire)* from Aix-en-Provence. I was in luck. He was an excellent source of information.

He knew, for example, that there was no meal that night or *any* night in the "restaurant" and that the store closed Sundays at midday.

I hurried to the store and bought a can of tuna and a loaf of bread for dinner. There was no mayonnaise to buy to put on my tuna sandwich dinner but the pretty young daughter went to the family kitchen and brought back a small saucer of mayonnaise. I wondered if it would go on my bill.

Mr. Mignon who had made trips to French Polynesia before said he never booked a reservation, even in the Marquesas where he had spent three weeks the year before.

"You arrive at the airport and always someone will take care of you," he said.

He wasn't interested in the Chung Tien Circle Island Automobile Tour because he had done much of it on the Chung Tien Circle Island Bicycle Tour. He planned to climb one of the two mountains but would join the boat trip in the afternoon.

After splitting my cabin-mate's can of peaches for dessert, I went for a pre-sleep stroll down to the village square.

The Friday night film in the Salle de Fête broke the silence with the whine of ricocheting bullets. It had to be a Spaghetti Western. It was. When I peeked in the audience, packed to falling-out-of-the-window capacity, was loving every shooting minute of it.

The next morning after breakfast standing next to a red, four-door Datsun was my tour driver. Surprise, Chung Tien himself.

He was an always affable, moon-faced man probably in his sixties but looking more like late forties. His hair was still jet black and his solid bulky figure was always moving, working, busy despite the danger of his gunnysack pants losing their preferred position.

He spoke Tahitian and Chinese and pidgin French. My French to him was about as incomprehensible as his Tahitian was to me.

The road around the island is twenty-six kilometers or about fifteen miles.

We drove in the direction of the airport.

Halfway between the village and the airport is the single entrance through the reef to Mataura and I had been told that here was the best swimming beach on the island. This was Bloody Bay where the mutineers had landed.

In an attempt to start a conversation with Chung Tien who was smiling affably but silently, I tried to confirm the reputation of the beach.

"C'est la meilleure plage dans l'île?" I asked.

"Ah – bateau." He said. (Boat!) He cut the air with his hand to signal a boat going through the channel.

Silence. We both smiled affably and bounced along.

Occasionally we would pass a church and, breaking the affable silence, I would point and ask, *"L'eglise?"*

"Oui," would respond my chatty tour driver and add, *"Protestante"* or *"Catholique."*

Inquiry later confirmed that there are six different Christian denominations on the island each striving for the privilege of saving the sixteen hundred souls on Tubuai! We also were told that the people take this variety of salvation very casually and it is not uncommon to be a Catholic one year and a Seven Day Adventist the next and a Mormon after that. It all depends on where your friends are at the time. Religion is social in addition to being spiritual.

We passed small wooden or concrete-block houses . . . always with the status-conscious corrugated roofs. Even on this remote island there are no *fares* of bamboo walls and thatched roofs.

We passed a horse-drawn, two-wheeled produce cart. Called a *charrette*, this vehicle was at one time — and not too long ago — the principal form of transportation on the island. As late as 1957 there was only one car on Tubuai and it was a war-beaten jeep. All other transport was by bicycle or by *charrette*.

We passed patches of coffee trees, taro fields, many breadfruit trees and banana and citrus trees.

Silently.

Halfway around the island we stopped in the village of Mahu in the shade close to the sea and my guide motioned me to a white wooden gate on the other side of the road beyond which I could see an impressive tomb.

I started to walk in but C-T held up his hand and asked a little boy to get his mother. The little boy's eyes were sullen, his mouth set in a permanent pout. He wasn't about to move. The sense of Tubuai hospitality starts early.

A young girl came down the drive behind the entrance. Her expression was not that of a professional receptionist either but she waved us in.

I approached the large tomb reverently and translated the inscription:

> *In memory of Noel Ilari*
> *Born in Rennese, France*
> *11 September, 1897*
> *died faithful to his God*
> *to his family and to his ideals*
> *to his grateful country*
> *after long years of moral suffering*
> *within isolation and solitude at this place*
> *Passerbyers, think and pray for him.*

"Who was he?"

Mr. C.T.'s response was to put his arms stiffily to his sides and lift his chin stiffily in the air. He was *dead*, that's what he was . . . his pantomine was telling me.

From Mahu and the tomb of Hermitage St. Hélène, we cut through the middle of the island passing two more churches. Up a small ridge we passed plantings of carrots and cabbages and then sizeable acreage being prepared for potato planting.

A syndicate had been organized, I was told later by a friend in conspiratorial tones, by an Italian Count to grow potatoes commercially in the cooler climate of Tubuai.

The first crop had proved disastrous for one of two reasons. One report said that the potatoes were too small. The other reason was, because imported potatoes were banned by the government, the Chinese wholesalers in Papeete rebelled at the restraint of trade with the result that the Tubuai potatoes went to rot in warehouses or had to be given away.

At the top of the rise halfway between Mahu and Mataura the still affable C.T. stopped the car. We were not more than four hundred feet in elevation but we could see fields of agriculture in all directions and beyond the green water lagoons, the reefs and the deep blue of the ocean. C.T. waved happily in all directions.

Two mountains on either side interrupted the landscape. To the east Mt. Taita and to the west the five peaks of Fanareho.

We then went past the few houses of Huahine and soon re-entered the shady streets of Mataura.

Instead of starting the second part of the figure eight, C.T. headed toward the safety of his empire and after climbing out of the car, he turned and, smiling, pointed to himself and then made a motion of eating, holding up his hand for me to stay where I was. We had been gone an hour.

I nodded my understanding.

It was to mark the final deep conversation that C.T. and I ever had.

His son, George, took over as relief driver. A relief to C.T. and a relief to me.

Just beyond town center, we stopped near a service station and George, who was positively chatty compared to his father, pointed out young palm leaves drying in the sun. We went into the yard to examine them closer. They were dried a lovely white.

The yard and drying palm leaves belonged to Mr. Taro who appeared and we reconfirmed our boating rendezvous for the afternoon.

I expressed my desire to own a *niau* hat but both shrugged. There wasn't one to buy.

George and I pushed on past the meteorological facility in a series of small buildings and then past a long pile of concrete jutting out into the lagoon.

"The new municipal wharf," explained George. It had been five years under construction and still needed to be extended another forty meters into the lagoon in order to reach deep enough water for a ship to tie alongside. Also in the blueprints for completion was a cold storage facility.

On the right we passed the buildings of the Rural Economic Service which supplies advice to local farmers and also conducts experimental efforts including the forestation of the mountains with pine trees.

We passed a small sailing club which was part of the school and then the French *lycée,* the only secondary school in the Australs. Two hundred and fifty boys and girls between the ages of ten and eighteen from the other four islands attended the school. They boarded in dormitories on the property.

George, my guide, was also a supervisor who looked after the students and was responsible for their discipline. To look at these charming, attractive, budding young adults, wild with spring energy, I felt sympathy for him at the size of his job.

Our next stop a few kilometers along was Taahuaia where a site sign, erected by National Geographic Society, reminds of the settlement which the mutineers tried to establish after leaving Tahiti.

FORT GEORGE
Built by the mutineers of
HMS Bounty
under the command of Fletcher Christian
July 10th, 1789

It took the mutineers two weeks to kedge the *Bounty* through the coral heads and over the shallow bottomed lagoon. It was almost one-third a way around the island from Bloody Bay to this location.

They immediately started to construct a quadrangular fort one hundred yards on each side surrounded with a ditch eighteen feet wide and twenty feet in depth . . . the thickness of the fort walls was eighteen feet at the base and twelve feet at the top.

A drawbridge was built on the northside facing the beach. On each corner of the fort a four-pounder cannon was mounted.

Throughout August the mutineers worked on the fort.

By September tenth, tired of being without friendly women, they voted to go back to Tahiti where part of them wanted to stay but others, in fear of the long arm of British naval justice, voted to press on in search of a hiding place which they eventually found on Pitcairn island.

When they began to round up their livestock, however, they met with fierce resistance.

On the thirteenth of September a party from the fort was ambushed by seven hundred Tubuai natives. In the following battle Christian wounded himself on his own bayonet. Tahitians, who came with the

Bounty, took spears from the fallen Tubuai warriors and carried on the battle which the *Bounty* men won, killing sixty Tubuai warriors plus six Tubuai women who went along to provide their men with stones.

Christian was responsible for killing the brother of Chief Tinnarow and he was warned he would never be safe again on Tubuai.

The *Bounty* sailed for Tahiti on September seventeenth.

Morrison's final comment on the natives of Tubuai in his journal was: *"seem rather Serious than lively and appear to be always ruminating on some Important business."*

Today nothing remains of the mutineers' sand castle. We walked over the area recreating it in our mind, thinking how desperate men can get escaping from the law.

A few kilometers along we came to the tomb of the last king of Tubuai, a ten-by-twenty-foot concrete vault, well worn by time . . . the king's name barely legible. Tahuhuatama A. Tahuhuatama. He lived from August 9, 1845 until October 31, 1897.

At the time of the *Bounty* there were three chiefs on Tubuai according to Morrison who said their names were Tinnarow, Heeterirre and . . . Tahoohooatuma. (His spelling wasn't too reliable.)

Buried underneath the vault was the old chief's son or grandson.

As the road continued around the eastern circumference of the island, all signs of building and farming ceased. George said that too many land boundaries were in dispute which prevented the investment in farming.

Alongside the road he waved at a fisherman friend who had just come in from the lagoon and was putting his *pirogue* on wooden blocks.

We stopped to visit.

George said this was one of the last of the sailing *pirogues* on Tubuai. The outboard motor had become the means of propulsion for the local fisherman.

His friend the fisherman with his broad Tahitian hat full of holes and his broad, toothless grin, made his living by fishing with net and line inside the reef in the broad lagoons surrounding the island. Or he would anchor inside the reef and climb on top of the reef wearing three-inch high shoes made of sennit to protect his feet from the razor sharp coral. Here, he would spear the larger fish that came to feed on the small fish that fed on the reef.

A tough way to make a living.

We visited a local sculptor who carved simple plates and ornamental daggers from a tree with red wood. Crude carving and high prices.

A little later we were back at Mahu and, again crossing the island, returned to the Chung Tien complex.

In the cottage I ate a fast lunch of French bread and peanut butter and Perrier water thinking that it was time to meet Mr. Taro. My roommate had not appeared.

I hurried to the front of the store to wait not knowing that I had misread my watch and I was an hour early.

It was a good hour.

Sitting on the bench in front of Magasin Chung Tien at noon puts you in the mainstream of Mataura village life.

A constant flow of fascinating people swept in and out on velos, bicycles, in trucks, in jeeps . . . stocking up for the week-end with canned ham, canned fish, fresh bread by the armload and cases of beer.

Others arrived just to drink beer copiously at $1.90 for the large bottle. *Amazing.*

Several customers detoured from their route to approach my bench and shake my hand. Friendly. Others just looked over at the stranger and gave that quick upward nod of the head which is a Polynesian "hello." Others, more in the spirit of Tubuai, didn't acknowledge that the stranger was there at all.

I could have sat outside the store all day and watched the passing parade.

Promptly at one o'clock Mr. Taro appeared. It was then I knew I had made my mistake. He was right on time.

Mr. Mignon appeared . . . limping. The mountain he had tried to climb looked easy from the distance but turned out to have a vertical face half way up. He had tried the climb in thonged slippers! His feet were bloodied and blistered.

Mr. Taro said he would like to bring his daughter-in-law. I said that I would like to bring Mr. Mignon.

We visited four *motus.*

We tramped through coconut trees, picked up shells, threw away shells and swam . . . at one point swimming a short distance between two islands.

We also picked up survival tips.

The most dangerous animal in French Polynesia is the *guepe*, the wasp. If you stumble on a nest of wasps you could be in trouble. Don't panic. Stand still until they settle down. Also at the bottom of coconut trees you could find an occasional scorpion but you don't stop underneath coconut trees anyway because a coconut could fall on you.

In French Polynesia they say the same thing that they do in Fiji: the coconut has two eyes and can see what it falls on and only falls on the wicked!

The boat zipped between the islands over depths that varied from fifty deep-blue feet to five foot shallow-green and the white sanded bottoms that were cleanly visible. From time to time coral heads appeared with halos of tropical fish. Occasionally the shadow of a larger fish would be seen and quickly disappear. Fascinating traveling.

On the way back to Tubuai I was reminiscing over my morning round-the-island trip and with congenial companions I inquired about the details of Ilari the hermit who was buried at the Hermitage St. Hélène.

"Buried?" the young daughter-in-law hooted and slapped her knees.

"Yes, buried."

"He's no more buried than you are."

"What!"

"No! Ilari is eighty-four years old, runs around every day, drives his own car. He'll bury you."

"But why the tomb?"

"He just wanted to make sure it was going to be built the way he wanted it built and to say what he wanted it to say."

"But – but –" the vision came of Chung Tien pantomining a corpse – "that's *dishonest!*"

Mr. Mignon, my roving reporter, the next day marched half way across the island, stopping off at the Hermitage St. Hélène, and talked to the future tomb occupant whom he found to be an intelligent, talkative, senior citizen still enjoying all of his faculties.

Six years before he had a serious malady of the mouth, perhaps malignant, and he thought he was going to die and, indeed, he created his tomb just the way he wanted it to be and even had the inscription carved in marble in Marseille.

Obviously he got better.

Mr. Mignon also reported that Mr. Ilari had an excellent cabin to rent, well appointed with two double beds. Modern. With a refrigerator. Its rental, he said, was very modest and included in the price were three meals a day.

Thinking the daughter-in-law might be a possible link to a *niau* hat I asked again and got the same response. They weren't available.
"If I could buy one, how much would it cost?"
"Forty dollars . . . fifty dollars . . . depending on the weaver."
Did the high price – and scarcity – make it more desirable? Probably.
Mr. Taro deposited us on the beach in front of the playing field where the inter-island soccer final was about to begin.

If the villagers turn out on Fridays and Mondays just to see the airplane land and take off, you can imagine the crowd at the inter-island soccer match between the home team and its rival island Rurutu.

There were people sitting solidly on the shady sideline of the field. Crawling babies, the bent-over elderly, girls in *pareus,* the Administrator and family, the Commandant and his assistant, the French teachers and meteorological employees, all of the young students and young bucks. All were there sitting on jeeps, sprawled on mats, in branches of trees.

The home team carried the attack. Much cheering. The home team scored the first goal. Wild cheering.

Rurutu charged back. Scored the second goal. Polite cheering.

What soon struck an observer was the good manners of the players. This was a semi-contact sport . . . an emotionally charged championship game . . . but there was never any dirty playing and no one ever got mad. A thrown fist would have been unthinkable. It would have been bad form, bad manners.

At half time there was a burst of sideline activity. The players huddled on the ground and thirstily devoured sections of grapefruit.

There was ice cream, crêpes, cake.

We bought iced coconuts. The tops were hacked off and we drank the chilled sweet water. The coconuts in far-away Tubuai, on an island where coconuts drop from every tree, each iced coconut cost fifty-five francs or about sixty-five cents.

In the second half Tubuai scored the single, winning goal. The local people went home in that glow of post-victory contentment.

Sunday in Mataura was naturally celebrated with church first. The women's and men's championship volleyball would be celebrated in the afternoon.

At the village square I sat in the shade of the Salle de Fête to watch and listen to the *himene* (hymn) singing and played catch-up with my notebook which invariably drew little boys to peek closely over my shoulder. Once at the airport at Faaa while waiting for an inter-island airplane, I unzipped my portable typewriter and put it on my knees and tapped out a long letter and it drew a crowd. Could have sold tickets.

The church flow at the Protestant temple was almost casual with the coming and going of people but the songs on the morning air were lovely, sweet in their easy, natural harmony without any superficial backing of organ or other musical instrument.

A peaceful time.

After church I changed into swim trunks and strolled down to the white sand beach at Bloody Bay attracting a friendly dog as a companion.

A car stopped.

The Administrator leaned over and asked how it was going and would I like to play tennis at, say, four-thirty? Agreed.

The beach was deserted. I went into a coral-less patch and was enjoying the cool, clear, clean water when suddenly I heard a splashing behind me. There was my companion dog!

I swam away from him and he faithfully paddled after me, much over his head, until I finally stopped and he paddled into my arms.

Damn. Here I was in romantic Polynesia and did I have a lovely black-haired, golden skinned *vahine* in my arms? No, I had a slathering, wet, paw-scratching puppy.

At the volleyball games were girls, boys, crawling infants. A group in one corner playing guitars and a tiny ukulele with what looked like a coconut shell for the base of the instrument.

A crowd full of color in dress and sound and actions.

The Tubuai girls won their match.

The Tubuai men lost the championship to Raivavae.

After tennis we sat on the Administrator's *lanai* with a cool drink. He said there was no written history of Tubuai although there was a book written about the southernmost island of Rapa.

He didn't feel isolated from the world. There was the radio and shortwave. French magazines and newspapers from Paris that were decently current could be had *par avion*. His annual leave was extensive and he and his family traveled to other countries going to and from France.

But the daily news became less and less important until, he felt, it was of no importance whatsoever.

He graciously asked me back for lunch the next day with his family and volunteered to take me to the airplane afterwards.

Mr. Mignon and I were having a Sunday night dinner of cold salmon, the remains of a canned ham, lots of left-over apricot jam and lukewarm beer when a knock at the open door announced Mr. Taro's blond daughter-in-law.

She held a glorious, white *niau* hat!

She gave it to me and I put it on reverently and went into the bedroom to the mirror. Was it too small?

Back in the living room.

"How much is it?"

"Five thousand francs."

Sixty dollars! Much more than I had in mind.

"Tilt it back some. Turn down the front of the brim."

Back to the bedroom. It was handsome. But $60?

You don't argue price with a Polynesian. You pay it or you don't. To discuss the price of the hat would be to demean the pride of the seller and the workmanship.

A Polynesian will do anything for nothing if he likes you. He won't do anything for any price if he doesn't like you. But you never argue a price.

Back in the living room.

Daughter-in-law: "You look like a movie star."

That's when I bought it.

Undoubtedly in Papeete there was a man who fussed, "Oh, those people on Tubuai can never do anything on time."

I bought his hat.

Monday morning I was at the Mairie early to confirm my return ticket to Papeete. Airplane reservations are taken very seriously because space is limited and officials have priority and can bump passengers even with confirmed space.

In the window reserved for the airline was a sign:

"I ask you to please reserve your place and recon-
firm your tickets at the office and not at my house. I
ask you to respect the days and hours which are the
following and not after:

Monday   8:30 - 9:30
Wednesday   8:30 - 11:00
Friday   7:30 - 8:30

Tubuai hospitality. Then she was a half an hour late showing up.

After securing our airline reservations Mr. Mignon and I went to the other Chinese store, Areni, and had a small ice cream cone (50¢) and talked to the proprietor. There were a few tables in the back of the store which served as a restaurant but not now, he said, because the meat wasn't in. He also had a small bakery.

Paying my bill at Chung Tien was an exact exercise. The large notebook came off the shelf and was opened to a page with my name on it and item by item was ticked off, put on a separate bill and the amount recorded on a pocket calculator. The total bill was $73.10. (No, the mayonnaise was not charged.)

Luncheon with the Administrator on the *lanai* with his charming wife and teen-age daughter and pre-teen-age son was a colonial joy.

The luncheon, served by a winsome Polynesian girl, consisted of ham and melon for a first course, chicken in a mushroom sauce for a second, an excellent cheese and fruit for dessert. Red wine.

Besides myself as a guest there was the cherubic administration assistant plus a grey one-eyed cat and a black and white kitten.

The conversation was mostly about travel punctuated by getting the black and white kitten off my lap and the behind-the-napkin giggles of their son at my often desperate French.

At parting, madame presented me with multiple strings of fine shell leis. In French Polynesia you receive flower leis on arriving and shell leis on leaving. Shells because they last forever.

The Administrator said I could count on the airplane being an hour late. However it was a plane I didn't want to take any chances on missing because it would also have meant missing a flight to California and back to Honolulu.

He took me by the bungalow to pick up my bag and also Mr. Mignon who reported that at the Chung Tien restaurant, opened for Monday business, he had had an excellent lunch of ham and melon, chicken in mushroom sauce and cheese and fruit!

At the airport I said goodbye to the Administrator and hello again to Mr. Taro.

Mr. Taro was not there to wish us *bon voyage*. Mr. Taro, the charter boat operator, the service station owner, the professional fisherman, the raw material supplier of *niau* hats, was at the airport as the cargo loader for Air Polynésie. A hard-working Polynesian.

A group of local ladies sat in a circle with their handicrafts—mats and gourds and baskets. One had a *niau* hat wrapped in an immaculate white cloth. I kneeled to admire the hat and she complimented mine. As she unwrapped her hat she confirmed it was not for sale. It was made to order, you understand. Someone in Papeete was not going to be disappointed.

Commandant Dupuy was at the airport. He thought that Tubuai was too crowded to serve as a true example of the real lifestyle of the Australs. For instance on the island of Rimatara, when you got off the boat, you still had to pass through the smoke of a fire to be purified before stepping on the island.

Too crowded he said! After only four days, most of the faces at the airport were familiar to me.

Not too crowded with tourists. When Mr. Mignon and I left, the tourist population would be reduced to zero.

Would they want more tourists? If they turned in their velos and motorcycles and trucks and cars and returned again to the *charrettes,* they would create a tourist appeal which could make them all tourist-rich.

But then again that would mean disrupting a lifestyle, bringing in electricity and telephones and buses and television and hordes of strangers.

Strangers!

The people who threw out Fletcher Christian and company would probably say they were at the airport to see that the two tourists who had been inundating their island got away.

Good-bye, pretty island. Keep the fists up!

Note: The first three weeks in Tahiti were spent without the Lady Navigator and the observations suffer accordingly.

It is remarkable how a good woman adds extra dimensions to your life. There is salt and pepper sprinkled on every day. You see more. You appreciate more things in more ways. You relax and laugh more.

Also, you stop sucking your thumb at night and sleep better...

6. Beautiful Moorea

The Sister Isle Of Tahiti . . .The Restored Temples of Opunohu . . . Once Around The Island . . . The Formidable Lady Builder . . .The Happiness Boys, Kelley, Jay and Muk . . . The Island Of Tetiaroa

After a period of time on Tahiti, the profile of Moorea becomes as familiar as a painting on the living room wall.

The peaks of Tohivea, Mouaputa, Rotui, frequently haloed with clouds, profiled in the glorious sunsets, are part of the evening ritual of sunset viewing in Papeete.

The ocean passage between the two islands is called the Sea of the Moon and takes but a few minutes to cross on one of the airplanes which constantly fly between Faaa and Lake Temae on Moorea.

Given good weather and a calm sea, the better way to approach Moorea for the first time is by ship.

In bad weather the gentle Sea of the Moon can be a hellish roller coaster and if you are a poor sailor...we won't go into details. Go back to the airport and take the plane.

Two small passenger ferries are available to take you from Papeete to Captain Cook Bay or to the small port of Vaiare.

The newest boat is the *Keke III* which leaves for Moorea three times a day. It takes thirty-five minutes to get to Vaiare, fifty-five minutes to Captain Cook Bay. The trip to Vaiare costs a little less. At each debarkation point there is public transportation *(le truck)* and cars to rent at the pier.

Another older and slower but cheaper boat leaves from the same pier in Papeete, destined for the same ports.

It is better to be out on deck and take a little splashing, in our opinion, than face the queasy atmosphere of the inside of the cabin.

The Sea of the Moon sounds as if it is always tranquil but, unfortunately, that is not so. Be prepared.

The first boat to Moorea leaves at nine-thirty in the morning...nine on Sundays...and returns in the late afternoon.

Even at nine-thirty the waterfront dock is alive with activity.

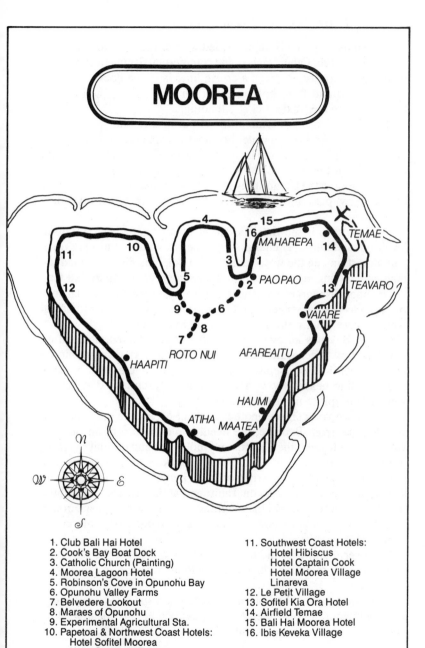

MOOREA

1. Club Bali Hai Hotel
2. Cook's Bay Boat Dock
3. Catholic Church (Painting)
4. Moorea Lagoon Hotel
5. Robinson's Cove in Opunohu Bay
6. Opunohu Valley Farms
7. Belvedere Lookout
8. Maraes of Opunohu
9. Experimental Agricultural Sta.
10. Papetoai & Northwest Coast Hotels:
    Hotel Sofitel Moorea
    Hotel Climat de France
    Residence Les Tipaniers
    Club Med Moorea
    Residence Tiahura
11. Southwest Coast Hotels:
    Hotel Hibiscus
    Hotel Captain Cook
    Hotel Moorea Village
    Linareva
12. Le Petit Village
13. Sofitel Kia Ora Hotel
14. Airfield Temae
15. Bali Hai Moorea Hotel
16. Ibis Keveka Village

A large fishing boat is being loaded with crushed ice to bed down the coming catch. Other boats of the commercial fishing fleet prepare their day's activity. Perhaps a cruise liner is at the dock.

The interisland ferry boats create their own swirl of action with tourists, baggage, taxis, tickets, loading.

It is hot and you are grateful to get out in the water.

Leaving the harbor the water becomes a deep blue and, on a good day, the swell in the channel is soft rolling and the passage is peaceful as you watch the peaks of Moorea come closer and closer.

Near Moorea the ocean spray splashes over the bow and members of the crew pass up rain jackets to protect the forward riding passengers.

The first stop is the Bali Hai Hotel. Entering the lagoon the sea levels out and the water changes from the lapis blue to the aqua green and almost on cue the water erupts with dolphins diving around the boat and playing tag with the bow underwater. Welcome to Bali Hai.

The boat discharges passengers, stops again for the convenience of Ibis Kaveka passengers, and then proceeds on to the municipal wharf where trucks and rental cars are available.

Cook's Bay has an awesome beauty. It is a cathedral of nature enveloped by sheer walls of towering, jagged, god-guarding mountains and its floor of deepwater blue is dotted by the relief of white yachts riding peacefully at anchor. When "yachties" die, here is where their spirits must go. It is heavenly.

From here you can see another angle of Mouaputa and what you couldn't see from Papeete, the needle hole in its top, an obvious subject for a legend: the Tahitian mythological god of thieves, Hiro, plotted to steal the mountain of Rotui and take it to Raiatea. Pai, the hero of the legend, was warned of the evil intention by the gods and kept vigil from Point Tataa on Tahiti and at the precise moment the thieves attempted to steal the mountain, Pai threw his spear through the top of Mouaputa awaking the roosters who sounded the alarm and drove off the robbers.

However the thieves did manage to heist a piece of the mountain and with it the *toa* trees which are now found isolated on a mountain in Raiatea.

In another legend the hole was created in a spear-tossing contest and the winner not only pierced the mountain but his spear went on another hundred miles and split the island of Huahine!

A true story makes an even better tale.

Hugh Kelley, one of the Bali Hai "Happiness Boys," climbed the peak of Mouaputa one day at the risk of everything breakable and, inside the hole, he left a note under a rock offering the finder a reward of a case of beer, or a bottle of booze, upon presentation of the note at the Bali Hai Moorea Hotel.

"There," congratulating himself, "it'll be some time before I see that paper again."

One week later—six days precisely—two clean-shaven bright-eyed Mormon missionary lads came into the hotel proudly bearing the note!

And Mormons don't even drink.

They were happy with a substitute case of soft drinks instead.

Kelley was crushed.

Just above the municipal dock is a time-sharing hotel called Club Bali Hai, a development of the early 'Eighties, with neat bungalows, a swimming pool and bar.

The site formerly belonged to the Hotel Aimeo, the first hotel on Moorea which Matson luxury liner passengers of the 'Fifties may remember as the focal point of shore excursions. "Aimeo" was the earlier name of the island and was alternately spelled "Aimeho" or "Eimeo."

It was operated by the Winkelstroeter sisters, Christa and Verra.

Christa Winkelstroeter, the younger sister, reminded me of the Dutch Queen Wilhelmina, except that she dressed in shorts and halter top and wore a *coronne* of flowers on her head instead of a crown.

She was a commanding woman, always supervising some kind of construction work, pointing, talking, demonstrating physically what she wanted done.

At the time I stayed at the hotel, she had just completed the new combination meeting house/dining room which she pointed to proudly, "You don't see craftsmanship like that anymore."

Have a meal in the Club Bali Hai's dining room and judge for yourself. It's a handsome legacy of the Hotel Aimeo.

Across the street is a new tourist center; the owners call it a museum but it is more souvenir shop than museum although there are exhibits pertaining to the history of Moorea.

Driving toward the head of the bay, on the right hand side of the road is the gallery of Aad van der Heyde. We were scolded by Nissen and Susan Davis of Manhattan Beach, California for leaving van der Heyde out of the first edition. They spoke highly of him, his talent, his gallery.

The Dutch painter arrived in the islands over twenty years ago and built a simple *fare* with a thatched roof and a sand floor. For furniture, he used packing crates.

He painted during the daytime and fished at night and picked fruit off of the trees.

Today, he has a pleasant house, the largest gallery in French Polynesia, we're told, his canoe and nets, and a huge coconut grove.

The idyllic life is one often dreamed of by artists and others. Free from cares, from stress, from crowds.

But most people, including artists, can't stand it. For some people freedom from stress creates stress and they rush back from their Polynesian paradise into the mad stream again.

Which is one thing that makes van der Heyde unique. He stayed.

His peace with himself and with the world shows up in his face and his manner and in his paintings which reflect a fluidity of nature, a motion of lights and shadows.

The outside of his garden serves as his gallery and on the enclosing wall are hung his works and those of other island artists.

His gallery, also known for its wide selection of quality black pearls and a notable collection of votive and primitive art, is often a meeting place of yachtsmen, old friends and new friends.

It is a good place to stop, particularly if you have a chance to chat with the artist. (Don't ask him if he gets bored.)

At the head of the bay is the Hotel Ibis Kaveka Village Moorea.

Originally, there was a group of *fares,* and a restaurant over water called Kaveka Village. It was gathered into the new adjacent Ibis Moorea which opened in 1986 with seventy-six rooms and twenty-four bungalows. The neo-colonial styled buildings rising no higher than a coconut tree—that's the law—are oriented to the bay, as are its two restaurants and three bars.

There is a large swimming pool where, when we passed by, a gorgeously built girl was doing her morning exercises unencumbered by clothes. In addition to this outstanding attraction, an activities pier juts into the bay, tempting you into the clearest of waters imaginable to swim, snorkel, water ski, sail or scuba dive.

Very seducing scene, the pier . . . and the pool.

Jean Noel, a French-suave, French-handsome manager, with an

attractive French accent, was proud of the restaurants and their French chefs.

Next door, as mentioned, are the bungalows and the seafood restaurant with a lobster tank.

Eventually, Ibis plans to have a shopping center.

In the classification of Accor, the hotel holding company, Ibis ranks as a modestly priced facility.

Around The Island

The island of Moorea covers fifty-three square miles and has a population of about five thousand.

You can zip around the thirty-seven mile perimeter road in something over an hour. Or you can take your time. Swim. Lunch. Have a drink at a hotel, or two, or three, and take all day. There are a dozen hotels along the coastal route.

Your circle island tour will take in the remnants of the generations.

Pre-European history is shown in well restored religious *maraes*, which you can visit.

Colonial day reminders are colonial houses that date back to pre-World War II days when Moorea was a successful agricultural island of vanilla plantations and copra.

You'll see twentieth century Moorea: modern hotels, petrol stations, boutiques by the side of the road. If you walk down the road at night, you'll see houses lighted by a single flickering light; no, not by candle or gaslight, but by the light of the family television set.

But let us go back to the municipal pier at Cook's Bay and start our tour of the island counterclockwise.

At Paopao, you have the choice of going around the peninsula that separates Cook's Bay and Opunohu Bay or traversing the peninsula at the base of Rotui Mountain on a narrow dirt road.

We'll keep to the coastal road. A mile and a half beyond Paopao you will see a relatively new church. Peek inside and view the warm scene of the Holy Family, Polynesian in countenance, painted by Pierre Heyman.

The Moorea Lagoon Hotel sits at the tip of the peninsula on one of the best white sand beaches on Moorea. It has a most scenically satisfying stop-for-a-beer bar.

Coming down the banks of Opunohu Bay you can appreciate the serenity of this calm anchorage and understand the yachts stopping in Robinson's Cove at its south end.

The alternate route from Paopao through the gentle Opunohu Valley is pastoral and particularly pleasant in the first hours of the morning when everything is fresh and sparkling.

The traffic-less dirt road takes you through a green hodge podge of agricultural settings: pineapple fields, groves of bananas, papaya orchards, patches of taro and fields of coffee berry bushes.

In less than two miles you arrive at a junction. The road on the right rejoins the circle island main road. The road on the left—up the mountain and beyond a governmental agricultural experimental station— will take you to Belvedere, a lookout point with one of those views that is so breathtakingly beautiful it almost makes you ache inside.

Below you is the Opunohu Valley and beyond is the peninsula. You get a different perspective of the twin inlets bays, Cook and Opunohu, and of the Rotui Mountain.

Claim it at its best during the first morning hours when you have the lookout all to yourself.

The green blanket on the right side of the road is a forest reserve of Tahitian chestnut trees called *mape*. Hidden among the protected trees is a cluster of restored temples which you must visit.

About halfway down the Belvedere Lookout Road, just above the agricultural station, you may have noticed a wide shoulder of the road obviously used for car parking. Return to that spot, park the car and walk a few meters only to the rather large *marae* known as Afareaitu. It was restored by Dr. Yoshiko Sinoto, the Honolulu anthropologist associated with the Bishop Museum, a foremost authority of Polynesia.

You will discover, if anthropology is of interest to you, that wherever you go in French Polynesia, Dr. Sinoto has been there before you.

Flanking either side of the *marae* are two restored archery platforms. Archery was a royal sport, reserved for men of high rank. Women were not even allowed to be present.

Imagine yourself in an earlier era. An archer comes forward, kneels and lets an arrow fly high over the trees. Distance being the criteria of competitive superiority, a small boy marks the ground with a white flag where the arrow came to rest.

A simple game in a more simple time.

I was alone at the *marae*. The day was still new. Sun filtered through the branches of the mape trees and touched the ancient stones of worship and there was a sense of another time and departed spirits.

I was alone, but I did not feel alone. Yet, the only sound was the questioning cry of an owl from deep inside the forest.

There was a hint of the supernatural in the air which I was not reluctant to leave and went back to my rented car, drove a kilometer downhill to a turnoff just above some concrete water tanks. You can see the larger *marae*, Titiroa, from here.

Actually, there is a compound of *marae*s clustered in this forested area. There is a small pile of stones that once was a meeting place for the council en route to Ahu O Mahine, a well formed *marae* that post-dated the visit of Cook, and two small *maraes*, probably private family temples, beyond it.

Let's pretend—again—to be present when these sacred stones had an *ahu* (altar), *turui* (stone backrests for the gods), *faoa-tu-marae* (upright stone backrest for the priests) and *ofai-manava-arii* (memorial stones for deceased chiefs).

The altar would have been decorated with carved boards *(unu)*, a sacred drum *(pahu)* would be heard in the distance, and a sacrificial platform would be burdened with fish, fowl, pigs . . . perhaps, even a man.

Why did the Polynesians need human sacrifice as a step ladder to their gods?

Robert Louis Stevenson, reviewing the culture of the Polynesians, said he could always find corresponding examples in the mores of the European culture.

Even human sacrifices?

Oh, yes.

D. H. Lawrence knew. In criticizing Melville's repugnance of cannibalism, he wrote: "Melville might have spared himself his shudder . . . no doubt he had partaken of the Christian sacraments many a time hearing these words, 'This is my body, take it and eat it.' And surely their sacred ceremony was as awe inspiring as the one Jesus substituted."

The mind reluctantly reviews the means of sacrifice by the evolving civilizations.

The hemlock of Athens.

The crosses of Rome.

The bloody altars of the Mayans. The Aztecs. The Incas.

The fires of the Inquisition.

The stakes of Salem.

The gas chambers of Hilter.

The guns and bombs of today's terrorists.

What dark corner of the human mind finds a subconscious relief in the murder of fellow man? What guilt or burden is expiated by the death of the sacrificed? Very strange.

Standing on the *marae* of Titiroa, there was no feeling of superiority. Only sadness. Titiroa was the temple of another time, other customs.

From the depth of the forest, I once again heard the owl hooting.

The Polynesian in Hawaii accepts the owl as a symbol of good luck. I welcomed a happier thought and moved off downhill to connect to the circle island road.

To resume the counterclockwise tour of the island, take a left to Papetoai. Its citizens have built a Protestant church on the site of an ancient temple.

Here, in Papetoai, are excellent examples of the old plantation houses, well set back from the road, their wide verandahs often elaborately trimmed with scalloped balustrades. These were called *fare vanira* (vanilla house) or *fare metua* (family house), and were the abode of the prominent and prosperous.

The most common modern home architecture is a square concrete block building with corrugated metal roof and glass sliding windows.

Still, such houses retain touches of gracious Polynesia. The neat yards set off by masses of bright flowers, floral patterned splashes of color draped across windows and *pareu* printed streamers barring access to the flying insects at every door.

Typically, a table covered in bright prints and bearing a vase of flowers or a bowl of fruit has been placed just inside the open door. French Polynesia's symbol of hospitality. A pretty, warming sight.

The inhabitants seldom wave at visitors, or even look up, for that matter.

"There was a time, of course," said one hotel oldtimer, "when you would have been pulled in off the street and made to eat and visit . . . but, then, that was a time when one seldom saw a stranger on Moorea. Now, there is a constant stream of foreign people looking in your windows, taking photographs of your house, your children. It wouldn't encourage you to be too friendly either."

Understood.

"How would you like it," she continued, "if your wife liked doing her family laundry in her underwear—even in the nude—and a stranger came in without permission and took her picture?"

"I'd bash him in the teeth."

"Exactly. That's how the local people feel when the passing tourist stops at a river, laughs and points and takes a picture of the local ladies washing the family clothes."

The northwest corner of Moorea is awash with tourist accommodations.

Head of the list is the luxurious Hotel Sofitel Moorea with its mix of fifty bungalows built over the water, fifty beachside bungalows and fifty conventional hotel rooms. With its opening in 1987, is an exciting new watering hole overwater and two land-based bars, if you like your drinks straight.

Two restaurants, three boutiques, tennis courts, swimming pool and volleyball are tossed in.

An aside triggered by the question: "Where is all of this development money coming from?"

In 1984, French Polynesia became autonomous. The new government, committed to increasing the economic base of tourism, adopted as their first objective the doubling of the existing one thousand hotel room inventory in the shortest possible period of time. To do so meant offering a protected package of development incentives to investors, to draw in not only local but outside money.

Accor is a French national hotel holding company. Under the Accor umbrellas are a series of hotel chains serving different economic brackets of travelers: Sofitel is four star, Novotel and Mercure—not yet in French Polynesia—are three star, Ibis is two star. There are new—or refurbished—Ibis Hotels in Papeete and on Moorea.

Accor, now a dominant hotel chain in French Polynesia, also took over the management of the Kia Ora hotels.

Down from the new Sofitel complex is Hotel Climat de France (forty rooms), and then the Residence Les Tipaniers (twenty-one bungalows, eight with kitchens).

Next, and the largest pleasure factory on Moorea, is the Club Med complex which, in 1985, reopened for the pleasure of 700 swingers instead of the 500 swingers it formerly accommodated. That is a lot of swinging, even on Moorea.

Before its renovation and expansion, we tried to get past the guards at the gate, but couldn't. However, we were told by a French guest—male—that it was big, organized, and a bit touristy for him.

The quality of the feminine companionship depended on what arrived on the last airplane. The girls who are part of the rotating hostess staff were great, he said.

On the next visit we had the name of the manager and were able to get in. (The entrance, unfortunately, has all the charm of a concentration camp. I fear I would have a feeling, if I had signed on for a Club Med stay on Moorea, that I was being incarcerated.)

Once inside, however, we were surrounded by gardens, acres of tennis courts, a vast reception area, and an open-air theater where a group of new arrivals were receiving the general rules and routines of the camp.

We strolled a nice beach where a group was taking setting-up exercises at the water's edge. We visited the two restaurants and the cocktail bar where classical music is played at sunset.

We liked that.

Offshore, there was water skiing, part of the free-for-the-taking package, along with snorkeling, scuba diving and sunbathing of any persuasion at private offshore islands.

Friends of ours from New Zealand, who are in the over-sixty age group, have spent vacations at Club Med Moorea and report that age is no barrier. They had a wonderful time.

Southwest of Club Med is a series of smaller hotels: Hotel Hibiscus, Hotel Captain Cook, Hotel Moorea Village and Linareva which advertises itself in the Tahiti Sun Press as a scuba diving center with all equipment furnished and diving twice daily in the lagoon or ocean.

Along this coastal area called Haapiti you'll find snack shops, rental car and moped establishments, and even a riding stable.

You'll also find that the paved road runs out. Dirt. Close the windows.

You pass Nuuroa, Haapiti and a church made of coral block one kilometer outside of Haapiti.

From Vaianae Bay, on the south end of the island, the fishing village of Atiha is framed by the lagoon and the dramatic peaks of the island. Get your camera cocked and ready to take more photos. Fishing villages mean fish nets drying in massive swags from tree limbs bordering the lagoon.

As a matter of curiosity, we have always wondered what excites a cameraman, amateur or professional, about the sight of fish nets

drying in the sun? Show me a coffee table picture book of the South
Seas and I'll show you a handful of four-color fish net photos.

At the village of Maatea there is supposed to be an important
waterfront *marae*. We never found it. Unmarked.
"They've all been bulldozed over," volunteered one person.
"They are no longer important," another said.
Hard to believe.
Afareaitu, the second missionary base on Moorea, is an important
village today because of its port. Boats carry cargo and people to and
from Papeete. Also, it is the chief administrative town on the island.
Because of these factors, the road is paved.

It is a short drive to Vaiare, the closest port to Papeete, and the
beginning of a footpath that crosses the mountain to Paopao.

The coast road to Teavaro is lovely, skirting a white sand
beach—another dandy picture taking spot. Before the road reaches
the airport turnoff, there is a discreet sign pointing down a narrow,
jungley road to The Sofitel Kia Ora Hotel. Highly recommended as a
liquid spot stop, if that's all the time you have to spend at this
gracious hideaway.

The thatched-roofed hotel facilities are spread out over green lawns
facing a beautiful beach, possibly the most beautiful hotel beach in
Tahiti.

There is a relaxed air in the large, open-air reception *fare* staffed
by young pareu-draped men and women. Along a pathway, some
distance away, is a dining *fare*. An activity core is located at the pier.
One element is the overwater bar. Another, at the end of the pier, is
a permanently moored schooner, *La Vaitere*. At one time it served as
the Kia Ora's disco but a hurricane broke its back and it is now
unsafe.

At the bar we met Mike Mooney who does public relations for Kia
Ora, a cherub of a man whose potbelly and British moustache look
incongruous in a Tahitian pareu. He knows he is a study of
contrasts.

"I am a racial Molotov cocktail," he declared. "My mother was a
North Ireland Catholic, my English father was Protestant.

"I am a Buddha baby," he said, patting his round tummy. "I am
for peace."

Kia Ora had seventy-five bungalows scattered around the gardens
and along the beachfront. Fifteen new bungalows were under construction, and a swimming pool was next on the expansion schedule.

Mike, who formerly worked for Club Med, was a good source of restaurant information. We put on our fine dining list the Coconut House, (French cuisine), Michel et Jackie (French and pizza), Le Hakka for seafood, Manava for Chinese food, Tipaniers for Italian food, Tiahura for steak.

After Kia Ora comes Temae, site of the airport. A new terminal was built where you check in for your seven-minute flight to Papeete.

There is no need for a reservation because the light planes are coming in and taking off constantly. Very casual.

Below your wing on take off is the Kia Ora Hotel and behind you is Lake Temae, the only lake on the island.

Then a string of restaurants, including several of the above, and then the Bali Hai.

The Bali House is a House of Legends.

And legendary people.

The Bali Hai Hotel was created by the "Happiness Boys" . . . or as they were more commonly called in international travel stories, the "Boys from Bali Hai."

Kelley, Jay and Muk had so much publicity that in the '70s you would have had to be cut off from the printed word not to have read feature stories in national magazines about them.

Little wonder. The trio furnished ideal material for easy-to-write, fun-to-read travel stores. To a travel writer who is often faced with the task of making the dead come alive by relying heavily on those ingredients a critic attributed to Melville: "fashion, fact, fancy, felony," the Bali Hai Boys provided a day off from hard work.

A short refresher history.

In 1961, three steady chums in the footloose area of Newport Beach chucked the civilized life of Southern California and ran away to Tahiti.

They looked and acted like a cast of leading characters from a musical comedy.

Their order of appearance in Tahiti is still the order in which their names are used when grouped: Kelley, Jay and Muk.

Hugh Kelley, a big brawling Irishman, had passed the bar examination in California in 1956, and three years later, crewed his way to Tahiti in a yacht race. He found, on Moorea, a 420-acre vanilla plantation for sale.

Back in Newport Beach, he propositioned his two cronies and the three decided they would take a flier on running a plantation in

French Polynesia.

Hugh came first. Jay second.

Jay Carlisle held a seat on the Pacific Coast Stock Exchange and looked like a stockbroker. Slight physique. Intense countenance. Short-cropped, no-nonsense hair. A dark "rep" tie under a Brooks Brothers buttoned-down shirt. Not your average run-away-to-the-South-Pacific type of fella.

Muk stayed behind to clean up, following a year later.

Donald "Muk" McCallum was a wholesale sporting goods salesman for a family-held firm. One look at him and you'd believe he would do anything. Tall, gangly arms and legs flapped loosely in the general direction of his progress. He looked like a Lloyd Bridges without hinges.

Running a vanilla plantation didn't turn out to be the envisioned life of sitting in the shade and waving off flies and pretty *vahines*. It was drudgery of the first order, it wasn't very successful, and the vanilla market was going to hell in a basket with the introduction of "imitation" vanilla.

Worse yet, the French authorities didn't quite recognize the potential economic contribution of the trio and constantly nipped at them to leave.

What Kelley, Jay and Muk didn't lose on the plantation, they lost in airfares flying out of the country periodically to renew short-term visas. It was the only way they were permitted to stay legally.

About this time, a small hotel—which wasn't making it either—came on the market.

It held a great attraction to the travel weary threesome because, while the French officialdom felt no economic need for agricultural expertise—or visa exemptions—they acknowledged a need for tourism expertise. Hotel ownership would provide the exhausted partners assured long-term status, they thought.

By this time, the boys had hocked everything they owned including the stock exchange seat, a small bar in Newport, an apartment, a house. Everything had gone into the plantation.

Undaunted, they sold stock to California friends to raise funds to buy the six-unit hotel. Eventually, their work visas became reality.

Their expertise in tourism, specifically innkeeping, was about as deep as their knowledge of vanilla production, but the boys learned quickly. And their instincts were sound.

First, the name "Bali Hai" was picked because it not only sounded romantic, the smash hit song from the Rogers and Hammerstein musical, "South Pacific," had made it romantic.

Taking turns as head chef, head bartender and head bellboy, they provided a riotous retreat for English-speaking Americans who wanted an experience, sure, but they also wanted the familiar in their accommodations.

The critical acclaim by charmed guests alerted the media who, also, were captivated by the spunky operators.

Unable to afford the high price of advertising in America, their publicity was their road to gold.

The Bali Hai complex grew to over sixty bungalows; the most popular being the over-the-water fares which, predictably, are the most expensive. But meals are included.

On the other end of the scale, you can have a garden room, single, for less money. Same size. Just landlocked.

Soon the "Boys from Bali Hai" had added thirty-six rooms on the island of Raiatea and then built a new complex on the island of Huahine siting forty-four bungalows alongside the beach and a manmade lake, and twelve garden rooms facing a swimming pool.

The trio moved out of the kitchen and from behind the bar and seldom had to carry luggage.

The macho-moustached Kelley was in charge of construction. He had an ingenious touch for designing bathrooms.

Jay became the organizational inside man, taking care of management and administration.

Muk was the farmer. The former vanilla plantation supplied first the hotels and, secondly, Moorea with fresh produce and eggs. The chicken farm housed 16,000 egg-laying hens, the source of Muk's pride and joy, and the cause for his weeping.

"A dead chicken is happiness," he told us.

It's changed now. Jay has gone back to Newport Beach to take care of family. Muk was forced to return for serious medical reasons. Kelley, the stone mountain, remains, indefatigable, leg shattered by a motorcycle accident, but freshly married and, moustache bristling, optimistic.

But we must go back to the time when everything was in full bloom. We were looking for a base camp, preferably in a quiet spot away from the traffic flow yet near enough to an airport for fast travel convenience.

Initially failing to find suitable quarters on Tahiti island, we called

Muk on Moorea. A mutual friend had told him of our desires.

"Pick a date and come on over. I'll find out what might be available and we'll see what kind of a deal we can make to get a car for you."

His get-it-done-and-get-it-done-quickly attitude was such a refreshing change from the struggle we had had in the Tahiti marketplace, we practically hopped the next plane over. We arranged to meet Muk in the lobby of the Bali Hai to begin our search-and-occupy mission.

The walls of the lobby were lined with plastic protected newspaper and magazine clippings extolling the paradisiac virtues of the Bali Hai . . . but, mostly, the stories were about the "Bali Hai Boys." *Esquire, Travel & Leisure,* USA weekend newspaper supplements, magazine articles from Canada, the US, Australia and New Zealand focused on photographs of Kelley asleep with a *vahine* curled around his shoulder . . . the trio of young men in a beachfront tree strumming ukulele and guitars (frankly faked) . . . carrying luggage . . . shoving wheelbarrows . . . pouring drinks.

You get the flavor of their hospitality by the chairs at the registration desk. You *must* sit down to register. The registration girls work behind a sunken counter, on an eye level with the seated guest who is being registered.

At the bar, hanging from posts, are stalks of bananas. You just walk up and help yourself. Baskets of fresh coconut pieces are also there for the taking at the bar and on the registration desk.

Muk entered in tattered shorts, mussed hair, a clean but ancient tee-shirt and barefooted.

His tombstone should be engraved with "How You Doing, Folks!"—just probably his first words on earth—following the date of his birth, and "Holy Moly" after the date of his demise.

As he moved through the lobby, the bars, and the restaurant, he would stop momentarily at every group and exclaim—it was never a question—"How You Doing, Folks!"

He took charge of us with easy authority and gave us the day. We bounced in and out of beach cottages, hotel-rooms-with-kitchens, shacky cottages and posh cottages priced from $350 to $1,400 a month, and drove from one end of the island to the other. None of the little bells that signal "this will do" went off . . . but Muk tried. Oh, how he tried.

Before we left the hotel, Jay passed us in a near run. Muk slowed him down for an introduction. Jay apologized for his preoccupation with, "It's Monday morning, and it's like Monday morning everywhere, I guess. Nothing but problems."

He lightened up and added cheerfully "But I'll be all through in an hour!"

We didn't quite believe him.

Throughout the day, Muk's litany of Bali Hai "firsts" in French Polynesia's resort industry gave us glimpses of what made Jay run . . . as well as Kelley and Muk, too.

The swimming pool was built as a complement to the beach which is excellent for sunbathing but poor for swimming.

"Then we heard there was a double canoe for sale and we bought it not knowing exactly what we were going to do with a double canoe. It just seemed like a good idea at the time.

"Well, we eventually built a deck across it, put a little canopy overhead, and a small motor on the back. It was an instant hit with the guests. *The Liki Tiki,* we called it, and used it for snorkeling parties, picnics, sunset cocktail parties.

"We had to build *The Liki Tiki II* to take care of the increased number of guests. Holy Moly! It just goes on and on."

At the Bali Hai there are all sorts of water sports—no charge—speed canoes for lagoon trip—no charge—a good tennis court—no charge. Bicycles can be rented across the street.

There is also a boutique which can underwrite all three.

Lady at next table at lunch: "Muk, where else can I shop? I've already spent a hundred dollars in that little hotel boutique."

Muk, roaring: "Bartender, bring champagne and a pair of handcuffs for that lady. Holy Moly, I don't want her to leave the hotel!"

At the time, we were talking about the vicissitudes of the hotel business.

"Oh, we've had everything happen," Muk said. "I remember one period when we were going through a wave of kooks. We don't know why it happens but they never come one at a time. Always in waves. The guy who jumps up on the bar and exposes himself. The lady drunk who wants to strip. The homosexual stutterer — 'Th-th-th-*thay,*' he says. We always make them sit with Jay, all together. He's just perfect with them.

"Well, during one of these periods a lady calls me from the doorway of her bungalow and yells, 'Muk, will you come and help me? My toilet is boiling over!'

" 'Oh sure,' I thought. 'And your cold water tap in the bathtub is serving banana milkshakes.' But I went over and went into her bathroom and Holy Moly, the place was full of more steam than a Chinese pants-presser and, sure enough, her toilet was boiling over! The master hot water thermostat had locked into an 'on' position and the resultant hot water backed up through the entire system.

"The damndest things happen.

"Once we had a wild dog running around the premises that made us all nervous. We didn't know whether it was going to carry off a guest or what and we couldn't catch it. There was no other choice and I put out a chunk of poisoned meat. Well, the next day here comes the dog over the bridge shaking like it had a seven day hangover. 'Oh, Muk,' says one of our little old lady guests, 'Look at that poor miserable little dog. What are you going to do for it?''

"'I know just what to do for it, Lady,' I said. And I got a hold of the damn hound and took it around in back and hit it over the head with a four-inch pipe and it let out a dying yell that echoed in Papeete.

"'I heard the little old lady running out at the sound of the noise and shoved the dead animal under the truck with my foot. 'What happened to the dear little dog?' she wanted to know.

"'I met her halfway and steered her back into the lobby and said, 'Lady, it is *cured*. It is *cured!*' "

Driving around with Muk was like driving around with the popular sheriff of a small country county. He waved. They waved. Shouts at each other were exchanged in Tahitian. Obviously there was a rapport based on common affection.

When Muk goes to Papeete, we heard from a friend, he goes to one of the back bars in the city and spends all of his time with Tahitians. He spends a couple hundred dollars buying drinks. They all know who he is.

During the drive, the Lady Navigator asked Muk, who in the course of years had had several "Tahitian wives," to tell us about Tahitian girls.

"The first thing you have to understand about Tahitian women is that they are shy. Oh, sure, some of them become bar girls. Some of them get into a jet set. Most of them however remain shy.

"Then there is another inexplicable part of her that takes you a while to learn. In Tahiti you have to learn to bat a woman. Sounds terrible, I know. But a Tahitian woman will push you and push you and push you until you prove you love her by batting her—preferably across the room. If you don't, you are going to end up with a real problem. Finally she'll run away with another man—one who will bat her!''

"Does a Tahitian man care?" the Lady Navigator asked. "Or does he run off and get another woman?"

"Care! A Tahitian man will cry if he loses his woman. *Cry.* And ninety percent of them get back together and when they finally form a union they usually stay together forever."

Later we visited the farm which is the next valley to Opunohu and it was an agricultural paradise. Lime trees, grapefruit trees, bananas, breadfruit. Bean crops, tomato crops. Year-round bearing avocado trees. Stakes of vines holding experimental table grapes.

In four long metal sheds, looking like a modern California poultry farm, were the golden-egg-laying hens. Sixteen thousands of them. Every sixteen weeks another five thousand chicks are flown in from San Francisco and five thousand exhausted hens are culled out.

"We sell them for practically nothing or give them away, making sure that they are beyong production, of course. We don't want any more competition than we have to have."

At the top of the valley, reached by a series of hand-laid concrete slabs grooved to provide tire traction on the frequent wet days (200''/year)—at the very top—was an enchanting house built for Muk. The story behind the house went like this:

Jay had a house on the beach next to the Bali Hai. Kelley had his house on the beach next to Jay's. For years, Muk's house in the valley, he said, was a cross between an army tent and a shepherd's shack.

One day Kelley said to Jay, "This is terrible. We have to build Muk a house. Muk, what kind of house would you like to have?"

"I would like a sprawling kind of ranch house with a shake roof. It has to have a shake roof. I want an open kitchen and bar that is part of the living room and a pantry that looks like a Chinese store with open shelves filled with tin goods . . . "

That's as far as he got.

Kelley, the construction project engineer-designer-supervisor, built Muk a sprawling ranch house with a shake roof and an open-to-the-living-room kitchen and bar, its shelves loaded with canned goods.

Then Kelley built, to satisfy himself, three exquisite bathrooms as part of three master bedroom wings that extended off each side of the living room and down a level in front.

Each bathroom made you think "Now, that's a sensational setting for a cocktail party."

The view from the living room with its round, open fireplace faced toward the twin bays, Opunohu and Cook's. Stunning.

In back of the house was an elaborately designed swimming pool with showers and a bar and a waterfall. Kelley was big on waterfalls. Beside the swimming pool, as if part of its decoration, reclined a sunbathing, jaybird-naked Polynesian girl, equally stunning.

Flying back to Papeete that afternoon, holding my arms around the typewriter for protection, I said to the Lady Navigator, "I don't know about the rest of Muk's experimental garden, but that crop out by the swimming pool . . ."

Before we left the house on the hill, the Lady Navigator asked one last question: "What do you call your home, Muk?"

He almost blushed.

"One time we had a hotel guest who was probably the bitchiest woman who ever, ever walked through our doors. She complained, sent dishes back to the kitchen, threw temper tantrums . . . you name it, she did it. We had experienced bitchy people before, but this one insulted and demeaned our staff and that shook us down to our roots.

"I told her to leave.

"She said she would report me to the management and she wanted to know my name."

"God! Lady. You are talking to God, you understand? That's me!' Before I threw her out, I gave her a dressing down beyond anything I had ever said to a woman. But the phrase that everyone within earshot remembered was "Before you open your mouth to anyone in this hotel again, you come and talk to God, do you understand? That's me. GOD!'"

"And . . . ?"

"And, so, that's what they call my house. Fare Atua. God's House."

And that is why travel writers headed for Moorea and why there were endless good stories about the Bali Hai Hotel and the "Bali Hai Boys" in publications around the world.

TETIAROA . . . The Toy of Marlon Brando

The island of Tetiaroa is actually a cluster of twelve islands which surround a lagoon without a pass. You can enter the lagoon by boat only by floating over the reef at high tide.

The island group was originally a royal property which came into the hands of an American dentist who married into the royal family. For some time it was operated as a copra plantation, but finally abandoned.

Marlon Brando, star of the film, "Mutiny on the Bounty," fell in love with Tahiti during the shooting, and also became enchanted with a local beauty, Tarita, who became his Tahitian wife and mother of their two children.

Brando bought Tetiaroa.

During the 'Seventies a great deal of work was put into Tetiaroa including the completion of informal guest *fares*. In 1973, the island was opened as a limited guest resort island.

When guests came to the island at the same time the motion picture star was in residence, he would hide out in his bungalow and surface only to run on the beach when the guests were at dinner.

In 1975, it abruptly closed. In 1977, it opened again.

In the 'Eighties, a heavy hurricane blew much of the development into the lagoon.

After the hurricane Brando moved into the school buildings he had erected for the education of his children. He occupied a large classroom where he played with radios and computers and did a lot of reading. He had an electric car, went night fishing and lobstering. Being isolated and very private suited him just fine.

The last time we checked with Richard Johnson, the Papeete general manager for the Brando properties, there were daytime excursions to the island by plane, providing there were six people.

The routine was to leave at nine in the morning, fly to the island where there was a bungalow with shower available for changing, make a trip to Bird Island, eat in the small dining room—with new kitchen and bar—lounge around for two hours and fly back at four in the afternoon. Expensive.

Tetiaroa is a primitive atoll. The attraction is its isolation, birds, fishing, private lagoon—and the stardust of its being owned by movie star Brando.

7. Downwind And Way Out Of Town

The Leeward Islands . . . Huahine, And Its Enviable Village . . . Raiatea, The Former Seat Of Power And Its Sister Island Of Tahaa . . . Bora Bora, The Beautiful . . . And The Non-Hotel Island Of Maupiti.

Were you to float on the southeast tradewinds from Tahiti you would drift into the islands under the wind...the leeward islands...*les îles sous de vent.*

When Captain Cook left Matavai Bay on the thirteenth of July, 1769 he took on board Tupaia, a priest, a son of famous sailing forefathers who had already drawn for Cook a long list of nearby islands.

Before heading south on his quest for the Great Southern Continent according to his orders, Cook, with Tupaia as his pilot, detoured a little more than a hundred miles downwind, northwest, and landed and mapped a series of uncharted islands.

His three week visit was peaceful and productive.

Because, as he wrote, "...they are contiguous to one another," he named them the Society Islands. He did not, as has been commonly written, name them after the Royal Society.

Today thousands of visitors to French Polynesia follow Cook's heading and explore the islands under the wind with the musical names...Huahine...Raiatea...Tahaa...Bora Bora...Maupiti.

HUAHINE

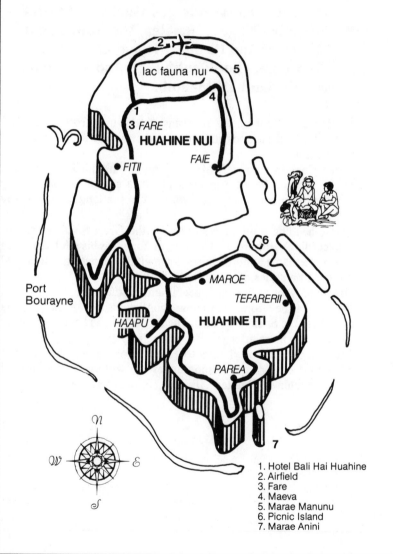

lac fauna nui

FARE
HUAHINE NUI

FAIE

FITII

Port
Bourayne

MAROE

TEFARERII

HAAPU

HUAHINE ITI

PAREA

1. Hotel Bali Hai Huahine
2. Airfield
3. Fare
4. Maeva
5. Marae Manunu
6. Picnic Island
7. Marae Anini

HUAHINE . . . Melon Heaven . . . The Pleasant Village Of Fare . . . The Bali Hai Touches . . . A Tiny-Island Picnic . . . A Rare Symbol Of Pre-European Togetherness.

Huahine is a growing favorite island of many travelers. Count us among them. Although it is only one hundred and ten miles from Papeete, Huahine is a thousand miles away from the crowded modern world of today.

To the gourmet the name Huahine is synonymous with watermelon and succulent cantaloupe. The flat off-shore *motus* are filled with cultivated fields where melons not only survive but prosper on brackish irrigation water.

To the anthropologist Huahine is famous for its unique remains of Polynesian *maraes* clustered around the former royal village of Maeva.

Our first smiles of delight were produced by the village of Fare, a five-minute stroll from the hotel Bali Hai Huahine along a native beachside path.

The village is a handful of shade protecting a waterfront dock. Wednesday morning early the boat comes in from Papeete to pick up melons and to leave off goods. Market Day takes place *then,* not later, not all day. Friday afternoon the boat comes in from Raiatea. Same thing. Take a camera. Take a picture for us.

Fare is two blocks long and has six stores. At the last store you can rent a car or buy a frozen steak or catch *le truck.*

If you went around in back, you could probably buy a spare DC-10 jet engine. They sell *everything* especially on boat day.

A timid American tourist peeked in a window and with raised eyebrows turned to his party and said, "I don't think we'd better go in *there.*" He missed a lot.

Fare is peaceful and the roaming in and out of the Chinese stores is an important part of the social scene. In French Polynesia the most joyous social is the *tamaaraa* held as often as funds will allow. The second get-together is for Sunday church...a short-lived time but a chance to dress and a chance to exchange greetings with friends seen only weekly.

But the Chinese store, for those within commuting reach, provides the opportunity for the daily social mix. Probably more important than goods and commerce is the psychological rubbing of shoulders, shaking of hands.

Fare is the Lahaina of Hawaii or the Russell of New Zealand, villages of the past.

Beyond the stores, including several new ones in a new block building, is the Gendarmerie, neatly laid out by the water, and on the other side of the street is the hospital, a small white building with the inevitable crowd of clients waiting to see the medic.

The Huahine Hotel, on the Bali Hai side of the village, has perhaps twelve rooms and a street-level restaurant. Across the street, a competitive restaurant advertises cold beer.

The nice part about the village of Fare is that it cannot be changed too much by tourism. The forty-four room Bali Hai Hotel cannot expand much beyond its present layout because of a limited water supply. To say you needn't rush to see Huahine now would be a disservice to you, but the truth is, Fare will remain the simple, lovely spot it is for a predictably long period of time.

We revisited Bali Hai and found new tennis and volleyball courts, another *Liki Tiki* addition to the Bali Hai fleet, and a ping pong table.

The ten poolside rooms had been completed as was the swimming pool which was under construction when we were last there.

We had a cold beer with Mike Gibbons of Honolulu who is now the general manager of the Bali Hai properties.

"I think that Huahine has the best beach and is the most Polynesian of any island. People still live off the land. Although we are only a forty-four room hotel, we are the island's largest employer."

We did a fast fox-trot around the premises which are extremely appealing to the eye. The restaurant, bar and some of the cottages front a white sand beach, but folks occupying back-of-the-beach cottages are also oriented to water. They look out over a manmade lake filled with lily pads and reflections of coconut trees. The lake provides privacy space between guest facilities—each with its private deck jutting into the water—as do sand and green lawns, walking paths, small bridges, and garden patches of flowers.

Water is a central theme to the Bali Hai design package. Kelley has always taken visual advantage of the ocean, lagoon, lakes, swimming pools and waterfalls.

The Kelley-designed swimming pool and submerged bar had the same characteristics as the pool he built for Muk on the Moorea mountainside, including the waterfall.

The beach in front of the hotel offers good swimming. Good sand and clear water. There are free canoes for your paddling around as well as snorkels, masks and fins.

Kelley was there during our first visit. He was down at the bottom of the dry swimming pool adding finishing touches. With a moustache somewhere between handlebar and noble, he looked and acted like a turn-of-the-century Irish construction foreman. When he was not involved in a building project, you could find him racing motorcycles in Baja California or racing to the top of Mauna Kea in Hawaii.

We never found a character so divergent. He had an angel's touch when designing and building bathrooms that captured a feeling of nature—he did it with twigs and rocks, fernery and bamboo. At the same time, he was a Hell's Angel on a bike.

At the time of our first visit, our room was not ready, but no matter. It was picnic day and we were told not to miss it. We obediently changed into gear, got on board *le truck* and away we went.

We were joined by three couples from California, an older French couple from Paris visiting a son in the military in Papeete and two Tahitian girls from the hotel to act as entertainers, information guides, waitresses and general factotums. Their English was halting, but their smiles were enchanting.

The picnic locale was on a leased island, Topati, and reaching it involved a half-hour leisurely, bumpy ride past the historical village of Maeva. One of the girls promised we could stop on the way back. At the tiny village of Faie, we transferred to an open boat, crossed the lagoon, and twenty minutes later, stepped onto the postage stamp atoll.

After such an *exhausting* travel experience, a rum punch or an ice cold beer or a soft drink was offered. Both would be offered repeatedly for the next four hours.

The half-acre island's only building was a large A-frame shelter with long tables and benches scattered around to provide shade for hiding from the noontime sun. People followed various pursuits: they slept, read, chatted, or played bridge. No football.

The lagoon was so inviting that, really, all we wanted to do was stay in the water. Underfoot was a soft white sandy bottom.

Although our guides said the best snorkeling was on the reef side of the island, we found the water much too shallow to be fun, about knee deep.

Before donning fins and masks, I asked a smoker from California for a cigarette butt. Wet tobacco rubbed inside the mask provides a fine film of oil which prevents fogging.

"No, no, no," said one of the girls and she went to a nearby tree and snipped a few leaves, crushed them in water and rubbed them inside our masks. It worked much better than tobacco.

In the lee of the islet, we found good swimming, a bit of live coral and a few fish but nothing particularly spectacular. Still it was a pleasant way to pass the time. Drinking cold beer. Playing around in the warm water. We always stayed in the green water, never venturing into the blue because the island faced a pass into the lagoon and passes are places where bigger fish like to catch smaller fish.

The picnic lunch was extensive. Salads, cold meat, hot meats, French bread, more beer and Huahine watermelon for dessert.

The French gentlemen who bordered on the corpulent was in winter trousers and silk shirt. Not dressed exactly for a South Sea island picnic. He was an agricultural specialist at home but he looked at the watermelon in horror. In French he said to his wife, "It has no taste, it has no authority and it has too many, many black seeds."

The wife was a pleasant, humorous-eyed French matron, who tut-tutted in agreement with everything her husband said, which is an excellent way to get along with any Frenchman.

Was it their first trip to French Polynesia?

"Yes," said the agriculturist, tapping the table for emphasis of one whose idea of going to the end of the earth is Deauville, "And the last!"

After lunch, the Polynesian boys who had driven the boat or were on the island when we arrived took up instruments and for an hour there was a casual, make-up music session. They all sang. Occasionally one of the girls would dance a bit. Nice music. Nice time.

The Lady Navigator turned to one of the girls after the last swim of the day and complained that she couldn't find any shells.

"Shells? No, Lady, too many tourists. You return next year. We put shells back." Eager to please.

The troupe bottled the remaining rum punch, probably for a private party that night, filled the boat with passengers, opened more beer and we started back to Faie, the girls singing, drinking beer and the Frenchman taking motion pictures of them. He liked that.

We glided along the neck of water which leads into Lake Fauna, a major body of brackish water, known for its eels. Farther along the neck are fish weir traps which are still being used.

At Faie there were little boys waiting to receive the leftover soft drinks and we were on the way back to the hotel by bus.

Maeva And Its Unique History

The hotel offers a daily excursion—or let's say, most days—to Maeva, a guided tour through the *maraes*. Included in the tour is a visit to a melon plantation, an important income producer for Huahine.

Maeva was unique. Instead of island ruling chiefs—eight in all—living on their separate pieces of turf and warring, back and forth, they lived side by side.

Side by side, they erected their different family temples. From the roadside you can see the restored slabs of family *maraes*. It is the most remarkable assemblage of *maraes* in the Leeward Islands, according to archaeological authorities, not only for the state of restoration but because it represents a facet of society not seen elsewhere . . . a centralized government.

Why and how did this happen here?

One theory is that because the village was built on an island lake, the society was not torn apart by the wild activities suffered at oceanside port towns, resulting in a heritage of unbroken occupancy.

Today, at Maeva, the families of former rulers still live on the same property.

In addition, the highly productive fish weirs made the village self-supporting and therefore self-contained.

Amid the remnants of the past society, Maeva built a replica of a century-old *fare potee*, a community meeting house. It was rebuilt in 1874 using only local materials.

The twin islands of Huahine are rich in history. Between Nui and Iti (big and little), over sixty-five *maraes* have been found. Most are ancestral temples but the communal *marae*, the Marae Manunu, can still be seen by crossing the lake to a footpath through the swamp.

The saying is "Huahine, where rises the eye of the North" because Northern Eye is the name of Manunu. In the same area you can see fish hatcheries constructed of stones in the lagoon, villages on stilts, drying coconut and pig pens.

Maeva is a rarity in Polynesia and should top "must do" lists.

When you are touring through the island you can convince the bus driver to stop, permitting you to take close ups of the historical sites. One symbol you will see carved into the stone slabs repetitively is the form of a turtle.

Why the turtle? The turtle was the favorite food of the gods.

Almost throughout the South Pacific the turtle was a food reserved to the chiefs and forbidden to the common people.

That night there was a dance show by a local troupe. Several striking beauties but the first sign of a dance show is a signal for me to hide behind the nearest post.

In Hawaii the dancers at one time or another go out into the audience and drag partners up on stage who go through a hysterical time trying to do the *hula*.

In French Polynesia when a dancer goes out into the crowd she invariably brings back a partner who is excellent in the *tamure*. They are often semi-professional.

All the more reason for hiding behind a post.

The Bali Hai Hotel at Huahine was for the great part created out of a swamp.

Once a permanent water supply for the hotel was found — and water is still a major problem for the next-door neighbors in Fare — work started on creating land on which to build the hotel out of an existing swamp.

The swamp was made into a pretty lake and the dredged earth became the base for the bungalows.

Almost the first dragging with a giant clamshell digger produced what was determined to be a treasury of artifacts. The Bishop Museum in Honolulu was notified and Dr. Sinoto, the man responsible for many important archeological digs and restoration projects in French Polynesia including the restoration at Maeva, went to Huahine to supervise the exploration in the swamp.

Three important finds came out of the dig.

Most dramatic were wooden hand-held *patus,* the same size and shape as those made out of greenstone by the Maoris in New Zealand. The *patu* provided a definite physical link between the two countries and because the wooden *patu* could be carbon-dated to a time prior to any New Zealand *patu* it established the fact that the natives from Huahine or its companion islands voyaged to New Zealand. (The Musée de Tahiti has one of the wooden *patus* found at Huahine...the only ones found in French Polynesia and the only ones found outside of New Zealand.)

Secondly, the construction method of store houses was a matter of debate among the archaeologists and the excavated evidence at Huahine pointed conclusively to the method used.

Thirdly, underwater, they found parts of an ancient 80-foot long, ocean-going canoe. For many years it was left in place for fear that exposure to air would deteriorate it. Parts of the canoe were dug out and can be seen in the museum at Point des Pecheurs on Tahiti.

In the lobby of the hotel are pictures of the *patus*, pictures of the excavation of the store house during the dig and sketches of the store house as it once looked. There are photos of the fallen floorboards in the original locations and the bases of wooden house posts and two stone supporting posts.

There is a picture of a broken canoe paddle which has been repaired with a piece of spliced wood and coconut cord or sennit. The binding has survived intact over one thousand years.

Part of the exhibit includes wooden adze handles, discarded shells, pearl shell coconut graters, pearl shell fishhooks, canoe anchors, shell chisels, pestles and grindstones.

A built-in museum!

Once Again Around The Island

You are not long in French Polynesia before you begin to think that without the Circle Island Tour the visitor industry would sink.

At Huahine the tour is not of the big island but of the little island, Huahine Iti. (Remember: the island was split by the spear that pierced the mountain top on Moorea.)

I have gone through my notes and through my stacks of material to find enthusiastic reasons for taking the four-hour Huahine Iti Circle Island Tour and I can't find any.

You'll see taro plantations, vanilla plantations, and banana plantations and even our young, limited English-speaking girl guide, before the end of the four hours, was saying with evident effort: "Another banana plantation. Taro plantation. Coffee plantation."

The tour stops on the bridge between Huahine Nui and Huahine Iti. Good photostop.

On the bridge we saw a large splashing in the lagoon.

"Look at the turtles," said our guide.

They were dogs.

She made one other contribution to the morning. Although there is very little tide, the water-empty marshes can have a distinctive unpleasant odor.

Our guide, seeing the reaction of her passengers, commented, "We have no good smell, no?"

The Dengue

It might be that our unenthusiastic reaction to the morning tour was influenced by my physical condition that was at best shaky.

At noon the shaking stopped and the lightning struck.

For the next thirty-six hours between the fever and the chills, between the bed and the bathroom, there is only a dark, unhappy curtain.

Pain can erase memory.

There is in French Polynesia an illness called the *dengue.* There were some amateur physicians who said I had it. Others, more experienced, said that, no, the true *dengue* was of hospital calibre and of weekly duration.

No matter.

The personal reaction was that of being thrown through a plate glass window and then laid across the stomach with a two-by-four piece of lumber.

And these were minor physical problems compared to the internal.

The hotel said it was a virus caused by a change in the wind.

I said it was the mayonnaise.

Because the average length of stay in French Polynesia is about seven days and the traffic pattern is from Tahiti to Moorea and the Leeward Islands, we found many fellow victims.

The management said it was a flash flu bug that happened at Raiatea and Bora Bora as well as Huahine.

I still think it was the mayonnaise.

Sunset at the Bali Hai on Huahine is the Holy Hour. The sun sets behind Raiatea in the distance and the peaks of Bora Bora can faintly be seen to the right.

Racing canoes in evening training paddle rhythmically across the slanting last lights of the day.

From the direction of the village comes a steady concert of native drums.

A visitor, mesmerized, stood ankle deep in the lagoon and shot up two rolls of film.

His wife said to anyone who would listen: "He's done this every night since we have been here."

"How long have you been here?"

"Two weeks," she said in despair.

RAIATEA ... A Reputation For Gossip ... The Second Largest Town in French Polynesia ... A Navigable River ... The Voice Of Authority, The Gentleman Barber ... Firewalking ... Castilian Maidens.

You land at the airport in Raiatea and are surprised at its evident affluence.

The airport terminal is large, modern, holds an excellent restaurant and bar...even a boutique.

Why is this? Easy. Raiatea is the largest island of the Leeward Group, the most populous, and more important, the government center. To the victors, armored or political, belong the spoils.

On Raiatea there are several things you can do.

For example you can take the only navigable river trip in French Polynesia. It may not be much but it beats going around the island in a bus. You *can't* go around the island in a bus but you can in an outrigger canoe. (Your outrigger canoe best have an outboard motor because the island is twenty-three miles by ten miles and that is a hell of a paddle.)

Only at Raiatea can you see firewalking. Local firewalking...not imported from Fiji.

Also on Raiatea are major *maraes* because it must be remembered that this was the power center of Polynesia when the axis shifted south from the Marquesas.

But start at the top of the things to do.

When we checked into the Bali Hai Hotel on Raiatea at midday, the manager said, "I have made an appointment for you with Charles Brotherson at two o'clock."

"Good," I thought still suffering from the dingaling *dengue* and went out to the dock and fell asleep in the sun. Two hours later, refusing the offer of a ride or a bicycle I walked the couple of kilometers into Uturoa, the largest town in French Polynesia after Papeete.

The walk wasn't disturbed by any traffic lights because the second largest city in French Polynesia doesn't have a traffic light.

Charles Brotherson, known as "the gentleman barber," I was told had a shop next to the only hotel and I couldn't miss it.

Missed it.

There are *two* barbershops and the one closest to the hotel belongs

121

to a Chinese who, when I asked for Monsieur Brotherson, pointed in the direction of the Gobi desert. I was at the Gendarmerie on the other side of town before I got turned around and finally found the object of my appointment.

In the middle of the narrow shop was an ancient swivel chair. A large Buddha-shaped Polynesian was half asleep on the hard bench by the doorway, his shirt open for coolness exposing a brown, round stomach. His head would slowly drop at the same rate as his eyes would close and then fall abruptly on his chest as he fell asleep. The jarring would snap him awake and he would jerk his head back into an upright position and then his eyes would start to close, the head droop and the process would be repeated.

On the wall was a sign:

Tarifs
Hommes: 700
Femmes: 600
Enfants: 400

Along the wall were magnificent ancient ceiling-high canoe paddles used for steering. They were two feet wide at the bottom and made of polished mara wood. Really pieces of sculpture. Not for sale.

In cases along both side walls were artifacts, pestles, shells, shell necklaces that had been taken in trade for haircuts. Fruit, eggs, vegetables were also legal tender.

Chez Brotherson.

The back of the shop widened out to house rental bicycles and velos and at a small desk sat Charles Brotherson.

What a delight. Little wonder that Charles Brotherson was on the first-to-visit list.

He is a small, neat gentleman with grey hair and a precise grey moustache. If you took him to Paris and put him in a striped suit with a silken cravat and placed him anywhere near the Bourse, you would say, :"Yes, another French banker."

He was wearing jogging shoes because he gets up at four ayem and runs three kilometers. He is probably edging a bit over sixty years of age.

Charles Brotherson is accustomed to talking to journalists because he is a known source of material. The author Robert Langdon had recently finished an interview about a Spanish ship wrecked on the neighboring island of Tahaa in the nineteenth century which, Charles claimed, resulted in a line of ladies with classic Castilian features.

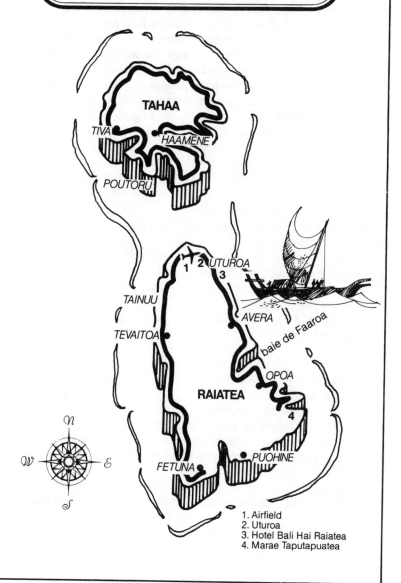

RAIATEA/TAHAA

TAHAA

TIVA
HAAMENE

POUTORU

TAINUU

TEVAITOA

1
2 UTUROA
3

AVERA

baie de Faaroa

OPOA

RAIATEA

4

FETUNA
PUOHINE

1. Airfield
2. Uturoa
3. Hotel Bali Hai Raiatea
4. Marae Taputapuatea

N
W E
S

The *Los Angeles Times* had done an extensive interview with him about the nuclear experiments. (Charles is against them and has written over fifty unanswered letters to the government expressing his strong views.)

I asked him where he had learned such excellent English and he replied without hesitation, "From talking to people like you."

Charles Brotherson was born in Raiatea in a family founded in French Polynesia by a Danish grandfather who had been shipwrecked in the Tuamotus. Seven Danish sailors made a small boat out of the remains of the ship and sailed to Papeete.

Grandfather Brotherson moved to Raiatea and raised livestock and harvested coconuts for copra. He married a local girl, part Polynesian, part English. Her father was an English sea captain. The Brotherson children became prominent throughout French Polynesia.

Father Brotherson worked on ships and on the phosphate island of Makatea until the phosphate was exhausted.

Charles married a girl who was part American and part Chilean and they had five children. Cutting the hair of his children was one way he learned to barber professionally.

When we returned to Uturoa, the first place we headed for was Brotherson's barbershop.

He looked exactly the same. Calm. Neat. Only he wasn't wearing jogging shoes. "Don't you run anymore?"

"Oh, yes. Four miles every day."

"You are how old now?"

"Sixty-eight. People have read your book and have come by to visit with me."

"Good."

"You made a mistake. You said my wife was a strict Catholic. She's a Seventh Day Adventist."

"I'll change it."

"I don't rent bicycles anymore either. Just mopeds and scooters."

"Do you still write anti-nuclear letters to the government?"

"No, the French just laugh at your nose. In 1984, I was chosen by the local government to represent all of the people of Oceania and the people of the third age—."

"Third age?"

"Senior citizens, you call them. And they sent me to Paris and to Limoge."

"Were they buying you off?"

"At first I thought so. But I am grateful. I spent a month in France.

"I am the first French Polynesian to visit Limoge where they purify uranium. The mayor took me to visit one of those big factories. Big, big buildings. We wore special uniforms.

"I have a collection of beautiful china that was given to me by the third-age people of Limoge.

"My attitude about nuclear testing is the same. It is dangerous to the people. Every Tahitian will tell you the same thing.

"In another ten of fifteen years, the island will be completely independent of France."

Charles was an independent and believed in Tahitian independence. He said that in the 1958 referendum the margin was very narrow. The separatists were concentrated in the Protestants communities. In the Catholic islands of the Marquesas and the Tuamotus the people, educated by the Catholic French priests, were more loyal to France.

A slender Raiatean came into the barber shop and Charles introduced him as the pastor of the Reformed Protestant Church, a remainder of the London Missionary Society. The pastor's wife accompanied him into the shop, saw that he was comfortably taken care of like a kind mother, and left.

His face was not handsome but tranquil. Thoughtful but at peace. When he became part of the interview, his brow would furrow and he would think carefully before slowly, carefully giving a response.

He didn't look like he needed a haircut but Charles gave him his two hundred and fifty francs worth of clippers. The pastor resembled a Marine chaplain when he left.

Charles said that we could go right on with our talk while he worked.

The pastor presented an opportunity not to be missed.

What were their attitudes on tourism?

Frown. Very slow answer. The pastor replied in Tahitian or French and Charles added his own opinion in English.

Before the arrival of tourists, the pastor said, his people without the outside contact were very pure in their way of life. Since then a great change has taken place.

The tourist too often set bad examples which his people, particularly the young people, were keen to imitate.

On Bora Bora, for example, the island people entertain only for money.

Deep frown.

They'll even sell their daughters.

The island of Tahiti is too commercialized and Papeete is only for foreigners.

The early missionaries set an example of discipline but it is disappearing. It all depends upon the education of the children. When the children leave the homes and go away to school and learn bad habits, they don't want to stay home and face parental discipline.

Shaking of head. It depends upon a good education.

When asked about the influence of the media — television, motion pictures, newspapers and magazines — the pastor nodded in agreement of their negative influence but thought them all one dimensional.

Tourism was three dimensional. There was a good side in that it provided jobs. But the living, moving examples of the visitors were not beneficial to his parish. He didn't want to see tourism grow.

He paid his money to Charles and left. A gentle, concerned pastor of the flock.

The gentleman barber said that if he could have his life over again, he would like to have been a doctor but he was satisfied that three of his children were doctors and another son was elected to the thirty-member Tahitian assembly.

A brother was mayor of Uturoa.

Everyone knew that Raiatea meant "blue clear sky" but did I know what Uturoa meant?

No.

Utu, he said, means mouth or lips. *Roa* is long. The town of "long lips" or the town of no secrets. A town known for gossip.

Charles Brotherson, the town crier, the fountainhead of knowledge, laughed at the significance.

"Write to me if you want to know anything," he said on parting.

Raiatea, being a volcanic island, has a 3,389-foot mountain, Mt. Temehani, and is prosperous in its own way with fertile lands and a lagoon rich with fish. The island exports five to ten tons of tuna weekly and five tons of bonita and *mahimahi.*

Good pig hunting in the interior.

There is an ice plant at Uturoa to pack down the fish and an electric power station.

There is a small hotel next to Charles Brotherson's shop called the Hotel Hinano. The latest information sheet published by the tourism office stated that there are seven rooms in the hotel and one of the rooms has a private shower. The prices at that time — three years earlier — started at $7.50 and zoomed up to $11 for two people wanting a private shower. It would not be everyone's cup of tea.

The Raiatea Bali Hai Hotel has about thirty-six rooms of which a dozen are built out over the water for the simple reason that there wasn't enough real estate to put them anywhere else.

The hotel doesn't have a beach but claims to have the world's biggest sandbox where you can build sand castles, bury each other or carve out a mermaid. There is also a drinking pool. (Here comes Kelley again.) The water comes out of the mountain, over a waterfall, into the pool, out to sea. Not deep enough to dive into. Deep enough to sit in and drink.

Next to the swimming pool is a pool hall with pool table and ping pong table.

From the hotel you can be guided through the attractions of Raiatea.

The Faaroa River trip takes off late in the afternoon in a speed canoe and goes south to Faaroa Bay and up the Faaroa River, the largest river in French Polynesia. The hotel urges you to take a camera. To history buffs the area is interesting because, according to oral history of the Polynesians, the river valley was the launch site for the Hawaii explorations.

One piece of hard evidence linking Raiatea with Hawaii was accidentally uncovered in 1962 when a gardener in Raiatea turned over a stone which was convex on one side and flat on the other. There was a notch on its edge. Anthropologists immediately identified it as a *quoit,* a game stone previously found only in Hawaii. Subsequent stones have since been found on Raiatea.

The Bali Hai Hotel sits in the middle of a road which goes twenty-five miles in each direction. One direction takes you to Tevaitoa, a view of Bora Bora and *marae* Tainuu which is in a good state of repair.

The other direction is to Opoa which will take you past many cultivated fields. ("On your left is a banana plantation.") Past Faaroa Bay and then to the *marae* of Taputapuatea. This is the most famous *marae* in traditional history and is a national monument.

Once a week at the Bali Hai there is an exhibition of the firewalking ceremony, the only remaining one to be seen in French Polynesia. It is not recommended for participants although one American did and was slightly singed but not burned. Before he stepped on the hot rocks he was touched on the shoulder by the high priest who gave him a blessing to cross unharmed.

He had a theory that the ability to walk on the hot stones lies somewhere in the fact that coral rock, being extremely porous, can be heated to a white hot temperature at one end and still be cool enough at the other end to be held by hand.

The hotel also offers mountain climbing, with and without guides, rental cars, water skiing, tennis on a private court in town, shuffleboard, bicycles and masks and snorkels and fins.

Wednesday and Fridays are market days in Uturoa, not to be missed, and the recommended visiting time is six-thirty ayem.

TAHAA

One lagoon encloses both Raiatea and the smaller sister island of Tahaa.

At one time the Bali Hai Hotel in Raiatea offered speed canoe trips to the island with a return stopover at a *motu* for swimming.

The newest thing on the island is the hideaway haven of Marina Iti, described in the chapter "Once Around Lightly—by Cruise Ship."

BORA BORA . . . The Isle of Cultural Shock
Beauty Above the Water . . . Hand-Fed Fish
Beauty Below the Water . . . Ballerina Manta Rays

Our plane from Raiatea to Bora Bora was late and the fading sunset meant that we arrived in darkness. A shame because one reason that Bora Bora is such a favorite among travelers is due to its dramatic appearance as you approach the island, either by air or sea.

The plane doesn't land on the island itself but on one of the reef *motus* where there is now a modern terminal. You step off the plane, into the terminal, onto a special ferry that takes you on a forty-five-minute ride across the lagoon. The boat ride is included in your airfare.

The approach over the lagoon enhances the visual satisfaction of Bora Bora because it is exactly what your mind wants a South Seas island to look like. The *motu* behind you, as you glide across the broad lagoon, is a circle of white sand surrounding an intensely blue lagoon. Before you, volcanic peaks thrust skyward as if they had been squirted out of the ground. A shoreline fringed with palm fronds that stir with the slightest breeze is necklaced with the luminescence froth of an ocean as it tumbles over the reef.

Because it is a small island, Bora Bora can be taken in with one all encompassing and most satisfying glance. "Mesmerizing" would be a better word. Oh, yes, it is a beautiful island.

From the airport you approach the principal village of Vaitape through the waters of the Teauanui Harbor, a tranquil, lovely anchorage for visiting yachtsmen.

Today, the *Liberte* might be riding at anchor, or the *Majestic Explorer* or the 350-passenger ferry could be at dockside.

A white steepled church marks the village and at the long pier where the airport ferry ties up, you are met by a hotel bus.

The principal hotels on the island, during our last visit, were the Hotel Bora Bora, the Club Med and the Marara. Hotel Sofitel, who operates Marara, announced plans to add another major hotel at Matira Beach.

Today you can rent bicycles or scooters or automobiles near the pier which allows more flexibility in transportation than in the olden days when the only transportation was by *le truck*. Or by foot.

Modern Bora Bora has experienced more than one cultural shock.

The major impact occurred during World War II when the American Navy landed in February, 1942 and built two major military bases to station 5,000 men.

As with most displaced nationalities, the Americans brought with them their cultural trappings: Hollywood movies, baseball and hot dogs, ice cream and apple pie.

When they departed, they left hangars, jeeps, several little blond haired coconuts and a first-class airfield.

Another shock came in 1978 when a famous film producer, Dino de Laurentis, who annually vacationed at the Hotel Bora Bora, saw in the Norman and Hall novel, *Hurricane,* the potential of a major motion picture and selected Bora Bora as its filming site.

He created four disposable sets: a Samoan waterfront town, a native village, a governor's mansion, and a mockup of a ship on the waterfront at the baie de Poofai.

The other construction Senor de Laurentis authorized was more enduring. The film crews' quarters built on the southeastern shore of the island, beyond Matira Point, remained to become the Hotel Sofitel Marara.

Bora Bora, during the heat of movie making, was Hollywood chaotic.

The producer selected an Italian film company to shoot a Samoan love story in French Polynesia which included a cast of English, Swedish, American and Hawaiian actors.

The film bombed. You can still see it on old TV reruns. Many of the scenes are embarrassingly bad, but I thought the hurricane was first class. A realistic big blow.

What the film left behind was a luxury hotel of sixty-four units, the only swimming pool on Bora Bora, and its own desalinization plant. Twenty-one of the units are over-the-water bungalows. Expensive. But they are the hardest to get.

Nice bar and restaurant. Large dock for nautique sports. Beautiful blue water.

Bora Bora survived the U.S. Navy and the film company and continued on its placid way.

Cultural shocks have a way of being absorbed, engulfed and/or smothered in the ample laps of French Polynesia.

The beauty remains.

BORA BORA

1

FAANUI Pt. Tuivahora

2
3
VAITAPE ANAU

Teauanui
Harbor

5

6

Pt. Paoaoa

4   5

Matira
Point

N
W   E
S

1. Airfield
2. Club Med Bora Bora
3. Yacht Harbor
4. Hotel Bora Bora &
   (on road) Moana Art Boutique
5. Martine's Boutique
6. Hotel Sofitel Marara

The Hotel Bora Bora, the first class hotel on the island, is very, very popular and very, very expensive. Always has been. It is sited on Point Raititi, its lobby and public areas on a knoll down which bungalows spill on either side. We recently returned after too long an absence to see how Hotel Bora Bora had changed . . . or *if* it had changed. The first difference is the cadre of guards at the entrance. Unless you are a guest, you need a very good reason for entering.

There are fifteen over-the-lagoon bungalows ($305 double), two suites, thirty-five garden bungalows and twenty-eight beach bungalows. (On every island, the water bungalows are the most expensive by far—and the most popular.)

All overwater bungalows now are equipped with refrigerators, hair dryers and coffee makers; you get a basket of fruit, a bottle of wine and a daily call from a hostess to check your health and welfare.

There are also two new tennis courts. "Concrete, I zink," said the assistant manager as we toured a new gameroom with billiard and ping pong tables, local and international newspapers. "Tea and coffee are served promptly at 4 o'clock daily."

Between the cottages are new giant ice-making machines, a great improvement over the often empty—nay, predictably empty—ice chests of our first visit. Back then, at $150 a day for overwater *fares,* we thought guests deserved better.

Our first morning dawned bright and clear and the *motu* across the lagoon looked to be on the step of our beach bungalow it was so clear.

There is an expansive feeling when you wake up on the beach in the South Pacific. Your eyes widen with the pleasure of the world: uncluttered sunshine...soft sand underfoot, soft breeze on the cheek... a sparkle of diamonds glinting on the surface of the lagoon waters. Sunrise and sunset are the best times of the day in the South Pacific.

Breakfast brings you back into the world and you find there are too many people cluttering it.

The Lady Navigator took the first assignment of the glass bottom boat leaving my stomach tranquil on shore.

She returned with an "A+" report.

Lots of interesting fish, big variety. Eric, the Bora Bora guide, was knowledgeable and sensitive about his job. They hand-feed the fish.

A four-foot shark passed by and Eric was asked if the local sharks were dangerous.

Gently: "No, Lady, here the sharks don't eat man. Man eats the sharks."

We found that the best place to eat lunch was at the Beach Shack. Good hamburgers and an excellent Bora Bora special with ham, tomato and cheese or a fruit salad. With a cold beer in the shade and next to the sand and the water it was always our favorite spot.

After lunch and a long nap we hit the water.

One of the best features of the Hotel Bora Bora is its location on a point of land where the lagoon narrows into Pofai Bay. The fast current of the pass keeps the water fresh and clear as a result and filled with fish.

A superb spot for snorkeling.

For example fifteen yards off the Point and another fifteen yards to the left, you will find a huge spread of coral, fan-shaped, akin to an immense Japanese garden. You can suspend yourself in the current of water, holding your position with the barest effort and enjoy it to the fullest.

Let yourself go in the current and you are pushed back abreast of the Point. Here the fish start to multiply. Fantastic. They seem to be the friendliest fish in the Pacific. A school of butterfly fish float closer and closer and closer until they are almost within your mask.

When you put out your hand, they aren't touchable but they don't spook away either. Are they just curious? Hungry?

Again you can let yourself be pushed along by the current and you tuck in your tummy to pass over a shelf of coral and you enter into a marvelous third world. The small fish give way to larger fish which are as calm and unperturbed as the butterfly fish. The water gets deeper but more intriguing. You swim through canyons of coral. White highways are created below in the channels by the Borax white sand.

We saw one butterfly fish as large as a dinner plate.

Farther out you might see an occasional shark. But nothing to fear. They are friendly. Eric said so.

And Now The Circle Island Tour!

The next day we reluctantly boarded the bus for the traditional circle island tour. The driver-owner of the bus and also the owner of the Bora Bora Rent-a-Car establishment was a jovial Alfred Doom.

He was a round man with a cheerful, cherubic countenance topped with a perky Tahitian hat.

Alfred had been signed to play the local judge in *Hurricane* and also had one speaking line. He'd already learned his entire part.

Also on board we had an unbelievable Texan...loud, crass, crude and constant.

Why in a vast State full of gallant people the law allows such misrepresentative types who have escaped from dry oil wells to get beyond the borders, we don't understand.

Ol' Tex dominated every comment by the driver with a loud remark of his own. If there wasn't an observation from Alfred, Ol' Tex would supply it.

Our tour around the island was counter-clockwise. Why? Because when Alfred got bored with the tour that went from left to right, he went from right to left. Easy.

We passed a good swimming beach, Matira Point, and several hotel sites. (Climat de France, a moderated priced facility, now occupies one; Hotel Sofitel Marara, the hotel that "Hurricane" built, operates sixty-four bungalows. Its sister hotel is being built within canoe range and the two will share many of the same recreational facilities.)

At that time, the Marara was bogged down in mud and not very attractive, a far departure from the little Polynesian paradise which Sofitel has created today.

In the tour we would occasionally pass a roadside shed with a meager collection of local crafts...they appeared to be part of Alfred's operation. Nobody ever bought anything. The stock was really meager.

We passed breadfruit trees and Alfred said that the new crop was just coming in. It is a twice-a-year crop — once in winter and once in summer. The French and Tahitian word for breadfruit is *maiore,* although many Tahitians say *uru,* and the Marquesan word, *mei.*

The east side of the island had practically no population. Tex: "Wha-y?"

Because, Alfred explained: 1. there was no water and 2. there was no Chinese store.

We passed lush double hibiscus trees and remains of many *maraes* but didn't stop to pick or inspect.

Alfred explained why the coconuts don't fall on anybody because they have two eyes.

Tex, in amazement: "Durn!"

There were signs of coconut gathering and signs of coconuts not being gathered. "People making too much money." Dried copra at the time was bringing 15¢ a pound and it took one and one-half coconuts to make a pound.

In other words if you gathered three thousand coconuts, husked them, split them, dug out the meat, dried it in the sun, bagged and took the copra to market you would earn $300. Better to work in motion pictures.

Tex loudly: "Hey, *Alfred-o*, do you know the bus driver on Moorea, Albert?"

"Oh, yes," said Alfred.

Twice as loud: "He's got plenty of money, huh? Properties. Houses. Cars?"

Silence from the front of the bus. We were sitting in the first seats and heard a near-whispered *"nouveau riche"* response.

We passed the Club Med which now has grown to an attractive establishment of forty cottages on or over the water, accommodating eighty people at $100 a day, but that includes all meals and activities.

Their center of action is a private *motu*—called Motu Tapu—where there is an organized picnic twice a week. The rest of the week the *motu* is served by a shuttle boat. It has a white sand beach, good snorkeling, and idyllic spots that lend themselves to tearing off your clothes and playing native.

On the outskirts of the village of Vaitape, we stopped at Chin Lee's store where all good things happen. On the front porch were new mattresses for sale. Bright red. Bright pink. Bright blue.

Inside you could buy jeans, Malibu T-shirts, ice cream, groceries, booze, cold drinks and cold beer.

The village communication center is Chin Lee's.

The village of Vaitape is the headquarters of Bora Bora. Here centered around the wharf is the mairie, the post office, police station, bank, the infirmary and the Air Polynésie office, in back of which is a local handicrafts sales room. Most of the crafts are made out of shells.

Back in the bus we passed the village churches and then between Vaitape and the Hotel Bora Bora the location sets of the film.

Ol' Tex: "Durn! Will you jes' look at *that*! Uh-*uh*."

Returning to the hotel we quickly changed into swimming gear and headed for the soundless, Tex-less lagoon.

Still curious about the curious butterfly fish...the butterfly fish is the pretty vertically black and yellow striped fish you see in all aquariums...we took a few of our travel biscuits into the water.

Oh, yes!

The spoiled little monsters were literally looking for handouts.

The Lady Navigator fed a bouquet of them. An odd thing: although the water was shallow enough to stand on the bottom, the feeding fish were more at ease if we floated in the current. Perhaps we then seemed to be one of them.

Friends of the butterflies joined the feasting and a great time was had by all.

The hotel's water activities are extensive.

The aquatic affairs are supervised by Erwin Christian, one of the better photographers in French Polynesia. He and his wife also operate a posh and popular boutique next to the hotel.

From the solid wooden wharf, you can take a glass bottom boat excursion. You can also go exploring the reef for an hour, or go to a remote island for a day which doesn't included lunch. You make up your own picnic basket from Chin Lee's store or order a lunch from the hotel.

You can water ski or go for a sail in the new 46-foot racing catamaran, *Vehia,* operated by Captain Richard Postma whom we first met on the island of Rangiroa.

The Lady Navigator took the Barrier Reef Trip but gave it a minus rating. No help at all from the guide, she said.

Snorkeling gear and scuba gear can be rented and guides can be hired to go inside or outside the reef.

Scuba diving is regulated. Divers must go in pairs.

The wharf is a swimming, snorkeling and sailing take-off terminal. It is also a great place to people, fish or yacht-watch.

The wharf was our favorite destination during the first hour of the morning and the last hour of light in the evening. We threw bits of left-over bread pirated from the evening dinner table to the fish. From the wharf we took our own mock-Christian photos and held hands and told stories.

On our last night at twilight we were going down to the wharf for a last swim with fins and masks in hand when there was a flurry from the over-the-lagoon bungalows.

"What's the action?"

"Manta rays!"

There were already people in the water and we hurriedly joined them.

The only reason I was the last one in the water was due to the difficulty I had getting into my fins. My hands were shaking.

A neighbor swimmer at the wharf ladder removed his snorkel tube and cautioned in a Slavic accent, "Be quiet. They are bashful."

Bashful! I hid behind the wharf pier. More than one can play the bashful game.

The Lady Navigator, true to type however, was out in the middle of everything.

Edging away from the pier I heard shouts from those on the wharf: "Here one comes. Here one comes."

Oh, Lord, Lord. Out of the turquoise wall of water came the biggest damn flapping monster I ever saw, grey and ominously silent, sliding through the water with graceful ease. Flap, slide, flap, slide. An immense cavern of a mouth extended, it seemed, from wingtip to wingtip, inhaling plankton. Or stray swimmers?

It slipped past and I slipped again into the mother-womb protection of my wharf pier position.

Meanwhile the Lady Navigator was clear of the wharf with the ray. The ray passed under in one direction; she swam over in the other. The ray flapped up near the surface of the water, she was almost alongside of it.

Her story will claim she was swimming with the manta ray for an hour and a half with two curtain calls. I will say, at the risk of endangering pilot-navigator relations, that she wasn't in the water ten minutes.

In the meantime I had bravely abandoned my pier post and had taken a position on top of the dock for better viewing. At last the Lady Navigator joined me bubbling over with excitement, "I swam with a manta ray."

"Yes, Dear."

"I danced with a manta."

"Yes, you did, Dear."

"We did a ballet together."

"Especially good at the *entre-chat*. Yes, Dear."

The story was already growing.

Back on the watery stage the manta had not finished its performance. It was a beautifully marked fish with white streaks extending down its vast surface in a striking aerodynamic pattern.

In one pass right in front of the dock, from twenty feet down, it rose in a graceful arc and completed a loop as if to say, "How about that one!"

To prove that wasn't a rarity, the ray came back and did it again.

Our Slavic friend said that he had seen six manta rays at the same place do the same thing simultaneously, a la the ballet. That almost silenced the Lady Navigator, but not quite.

Guess what we talked about at dinner that night!

The Hotel Bora Bora has very smart management. Being isolated at the the end of the point, they offer a complete range of make-your-vacation-happy equipment, everything from ping pong balls and paddles to sailing canoes. One of the most attractive offers is of bicycles. Besides being free, bicycles promise exercise and mobility.

We took a pair the last morning and headed off for Vaitape, six kilometers away.

Except for a small rise near the hotel, the road is absolutely flat and makes a half-day outing very pleasant.

About half way to Vaitape, we reached the set of "Hurricane." It was an uncommon sight on the lagoon. A large Samoan interliner schooner has been created out of plywood—that is, half of a schooner had been built. The half that faced the waterfront trading village was nothing more than a network of frames and braces to hold the flat upright. The ship looked as if it had sailed up a log-cutting track at a lumber mill.

Behind the stores and warehouses of the Samoan township, it looked the same. Just fake painted fronts existed.

Behind it all, focused out to sea, were the string of huge four-prop airplane engines.

When the film crew had finished filming everything except the hurricane scenes, the engines would be turned on to blow the whole million-dollar-plus set into the lagoon.

Shortly before trekking to Bora Bora, I had been in Los Angeles writing a magazine article on Southern California, and part of the research included a morning tour of Universal City Studios. What was most impressive was the amount of effort, time, talent and money that goes into creating the sets of a make-believe world . . . cities of any size or country or era . . . houses, castles, highrises . . . underwater monsters or celestial aliens. What a way to make a living, I thought. Now, I reconsidered. It's better than picking coconuts.

It was Sunday morning and, as we pedaled closer to town, the young and old in their Sunday dress and Sunday hats were walking the road to Vaitape. Destination: church.

Our destination was Chin Lee's store which, on Sunday morning, was a center of bustling activity.

People going to and from church stopped off at Chin Lee's for the last items for the Sunday feast or just to have a cold drink out of an aluminum can while standing on the porch saying good morning to all their friends and then, when finished with the drink casually tossing the can into the street.

A golden girl in church dress of white knit with white, broad-brimmed hat, sipped from a can of Libby's Peach Nectar. Her hair was half blond and straight and waist length down her back. Her Polynesian mouth was accented by full, sensuous lips and her eyes were a soft brown. She gazed emptily into the street, absent-mindedly sucking on the straw.

We pedaled back to the pier where there is a tomb of Alain Gerbault, a famous French yachtsman who sailed solo around the world and lived to write about it. He was famous in France, loved Bora Bora, and when he died, he was buried in 1948 in Vaitape, his second home. He is credited for popularizing soccer in French Polynesia.

On the pier two Italian men were swiftly painting a number of *pirogues* — obviously built for the film — the proper shade of brown...or whatever color the Italian designer thought would be proper for Samoa.

On the way back to the hotel we passed a parking lot for the film company which besides having a lot full of utility jeeps had a magnificent 1926 Chrysler roadster wrapped in clear plastic.

We passed a clutch of small children making — we thought — a typical gracious Polynesian gesture. They held out to us singular blossoms of the luscious double hibiscus. One couldn't refuse. No sooner was the bicycle stopped and the flowers accepted with humble thanks than the tiny hands came shooting out flat and peremptory with a familiar sound: "Money. Money."

Ah, well. The world changes.

Note: there are two concrete tennis courts also on the outskirts of Vaitape which appeared to be public.

There is a public restaurant called Restaurant Recif which we didn't try but it looked decent and we heard knowledgeable guests asking for reservations.

That afternoon we left Bora Bora. On the boat trip to the *motu* airport and to Papeete one hundred and forty-three miles away, we had the view we missed coming in. The dramatic peaks of Pahia and Temanu — photographers' delight — the calm green lagoon waters, the touches of white beach.

We left Bora Bora with mixed emotions. Loved the fish, the clear water lagoon, the lovely passages through the coral and the white-sand highways twenty feet below.

We felt sorry for the people being run over with too much action and too much money.

Didn't miss Ol' Tex.

It will all recover. Peace will come again to Bora Bora. The calmness of the lagoon will resettle over everybody and the world will swing back into its proper Polynesian orbit. Scenic. Serene. Where only the pretty fish ask for a handout.

MAUPITI . . . Isolated And Lovely . . . Long Swims And Long Walks...The Art Of Weaving And Making Fishhooks...

A hotel man told us that he ached to build a resort on Maupiti because he thought it the prettiest island in French Polynesia. A lack of water is the island's problem.

At one time there were nine villages on Maupiti. Today there are two, Vaiea and Farauru.

The people have left for Papeete, for water, for jobs, for schools.

Maupiti offers visitors the luxury of solitude and long walks... around the island is only six miles...and swims on beautiful beaches of white sand along the way.

The island is twenty-three miles west of Bora Bora. Air Polynésie's three weekly flights include a six-hour layover, which gives you a chance to visit the island without staying overnight. However, private home accommodations are available. The tourist office in Papeete has a current list of private homes you can write to make reservations direct. There isn't that much tourist traffic and it is possible to make your arrangements after you arrive.

The income for the people who remain comes from copra, watermelon which is grown on the surrounding *motus* and the

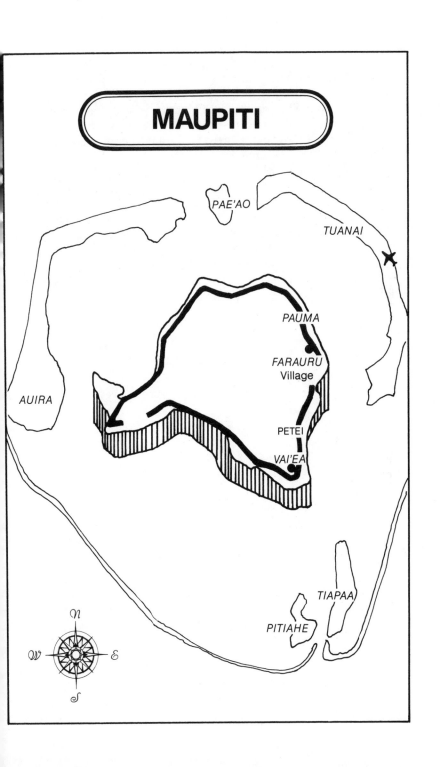

weaving of exceptionally fine hats and baskets out of pandanus leaves.

At one time Maupiti, then known as Maurua, was known for wood and stone carving. Today the inhabitants still are known for making seven kinds of fish hooks out of seven kinds of mother of pearl, each hook being used for a separate kind of fish.

In your walk around the island, which you can do in about three leisurely hours, you will find remains of old housing, an ancient mill where a fine-powdered flour was made out of *manioc* root (tapioca) and fresh-water springs, the only fresh water on the island.

The highest elevation is 1220 feet. There is no mountain climbing.

Like Bora Bora the airplane lands on a *motu* called Tuanai and you have to boat over to Farauru.

Oh, yes, the hotel man also said that the people didn't have much money but they were the nicest people in Polynesia.

8. The Treacherous Archipelago

The Most Dangerous Diving Waters In The World . . . The Most Exhilarating Waters In The World . . . The Largest Lagoon In The World . . . Rangiroa . . . Manihi . . . And Ninety Hotel-less Atolls.

"The Rangiroa pass is about three hundred yards wide, eighty feet deep and courses about a mile into the lagoon inside. With each change of tide, an avalanche of water surges through the narrow slot. The ebb tide carries with it an abundance of sea organisms from the lagoon providing an endless food supply for an unbelievable assortment of sea life. It is thus small wonder that fish of every size and specie have taken up permanent residence here, finding no need to forage in the open sea.

"And nowhere else in the world have I seen such a concentration of sharks.

"The Tuamotus (Treacherous Islands) are aptly named and the Rangiroa pass is the most dangerous diving in French Polynesia if not the world. The current often reaches ten knots against which a swimmer is helpless; small boats are hazarded by eddies and whirlpools."

We read that quote in an article on underwater experiences in French Polynesia by Dewey Bergman, well-known, respected underwater specialist and writer, and founder of a travel agency in San Francisco, See and Sea Underwater Travel Service.

Our eyes widened simply from reading the description. Heady stuff.

Our eyes widened a lot further when the director of activities said shortly after trucking us from the Rangiroa airport to the Kia Ora Hotel, "Our afternoon activity is going to be to shoot the pass at Tiputa. You have a choice. You can go in the glass bottom boat or you

143

can go in a separate boat and drift-snorkel through the pass."

(This couldn't be the pass that Bergman wrote about, we asked each other. No, of course not. It couldn't be. Or could it?)

There are about three direct one-hour fights into Rangiroa a week.

Rangiroa is the principal island of the Tuamotu archipelago which stretches across the face of French Polynesia in a northwest to southeast line and includes the Tuamotu islands and the Gambier islands. (Sometimes the Gambiers are considered a fifth archipelago, depending upon the book you read.)

There are about one hundred islands in the two island groups.

Only two of the islands have accommodations, Rangiroa and, a fifty-minute flight beyond, the atoll of Manihi.

When you fly from Papeete to Los Angeles at 35,000 feet, the captain of Air New Zealand announces, "Below is Rangiroa with the largest lagoon of its type in the world."

From such an altitude Rangiroa looked like an emerald and pearl necklace, each atoll in the green circle baguetted with a fringe of reef-and-sand white.

The lagoon looked like a swimming pool...*not a four hundred square mile lagoon*!

We were more than pleased with the prospect of playing in the Tuamotus because they would be our first coral atolls as opposed to the volcanic islands in the rest of French Polynesia.

Atolls offer a visitor poster scenery. Coral sand beaches, white and appealing. Interior lagoons promising excellent snorkeling. A backdrop of palm trees and frothy waves coming out of the deep blue of the ocean. We looked forward to Rangiroa with keen pleasure.

We were not disappointed.

At the airport we were met by a strikingly handsome couple, Richard Postma, a California blond, tall and lithe, and his helper, Martine, a toothsome, willowy French-Polynesian.

They decorated us with flower leis.

At the hotel the first thing they did was put a rum punch in our hands.

It looked like all promises were going to be kept. Little did we know.

The Kia Ora Hotel on Rangiroa is composed of twenty-five individual bungalows, thatched-roofed, bordering the lagoon. The dining room and bar split the row of bungalows.

You are taken into the bar, seated at a cocktail table to register and

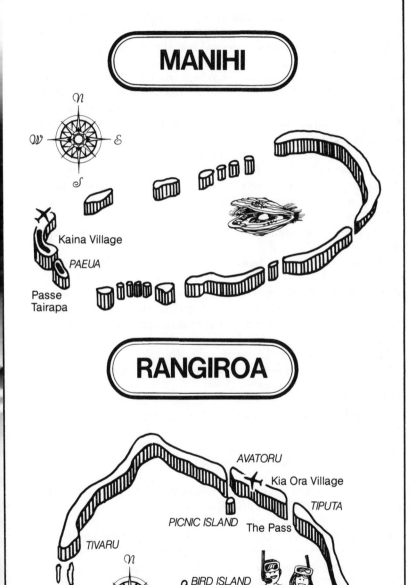

MANIHI

N
W *E*
S

Kaina Village

PAEUA

Passe
Tairapa

RANGIROA

AVATORU

Kia Ora Village

TIPUTA

PICNIC ISLAND The Pass

TIVARU

N
W *E*
S

BIRD ISLAND

given the rum punch...not a church social rum punch but a drink with whacking authority.

That handsome bar, decorated with shells, is built out over the water and on the lagoon side has a broad open deck terrace. Beneath the deck terrace is a pen holding three kinds of sharks. (In my hotel, I said I would give you the strong rum drink but not the shark pen. The Lady Navigator disagreed and said it added interest.) Richard interrupted our whispering by announcing the afternoon's activities and said lunch was ready.

Lunch was excellent...*poisson cru* followed by baked pork with raisin sauce, saffron rice, fruit and an outstanding cheese tray. The cheese tray showed admirable taste...a hotel far away from Papeete and the best cheese tray we encountered. We had lucked into a talented chef.

However, the best thing at lunch was not the chef. Close, but not the chef.

The best thing at lunch was André...an outlandish character, out of Papillon.

His trousers of pink and yellow circus stripes wasn't your normal *maitre d'* uniform. His head was covered with a small turned-up-brim straw hat that was crowned with a shell lei and decorated with fresh red hibiscus flowers on one side.

He stood an erect, dignified five-foot-five.

The face was pure pixie with a twinkle of humor and mischief always playing in his eyes.

When he found out we would laugh at anything he said or did, he played to us like a vaudeville character. During our three-day stay, André was a constant source of joy.

What did we talk about at lunch?

The pass of course.

Would we take the glass bottom boat or would we go into the water with fins and snorkels and drift through?

Was this the Bergman pass?

(If they just hadn't put that shark pen in front of the bar!)

In a voice vote, one enthusiastic, one quavering, it was unanimously agreed that we would take the snorkel boat.

After a small siesta without sleeping ("It can't be the same pass. *Or can it?*"), we picked up our snorkeling gear and took off for the end of the hotel pier to join the assembling guests.

Richard, the director of activities, motioned those who wanted to snorkel in one boat and Martine, pencil-thin and looking even more glamorous in a bikini, claimed the others for the glass bottom boat. Most of the guests quickly went in Martine's boat and I was about to join them but I found myself being shoved into the snorkel boat with two other couples.

We clutched hands on the ten-minute ride to the pass which lies between a point of land nearest the hotel and Tiputa, the principal village of the Tuamotus.

Breathing heavily now.

Richard: "A couple of things to remember. Everybody in the water at the same time. Try to stay together and close to the boat — it will drift with you. Don't try to swim against the current. When you get to deeper water the current will slow down and the water will become murky. Swim to the boat. Hand up your flippers and mask. It will make getting into the boat much easier.

He handed out native leaves to crush and wet and rub inside the mask to prevent the glass from fogging.

Swallowing now with a little difficulty.

The boat approached the middle of the current which was sweeping by with evident power.

I had trouble putting down that Mother-of-God-what-am-I-doing-here feeling.

"Okay, everybody in the swimming pool!"

The Lady Navigator was the first in. (Why does she always do that?) "Everybody in the water at the same time," he had said.

There was no solution but to jump out of the boat quickly holding the mask close to the face to keep out the water, put the snorkeling tube in the mouth, roll over and put the head down in the water and go for a ride.

What a ride!

It was like being put in the middle of a large rushing river. The speed of the water could be judged by the objects flying by beneath the surface.

What a sight!

The different formations of coral passed underneath like a giant roll of film on rewind. A mountain of coral would replace clusters of coral. Cliffs of coral would form, then quickly dissolve. Occasionally a pass through the coral formations would be marked by white sand beneath.

From the surface to the ocean bottom was an incredible aquarium of fish of every size and shape, big, little, light, dark; some swimming into the current individually but mostly in schools.

You've seen pictures of sky divers spread-eagled in their fall floating endlessly in the air.

Fellow snorkelers, seen out of the corner of our masks, looked like that. (*"Try to stay together."*)

A couple from Phoenix, Arizona (experienced divers) had an underwater camera and he was posing his wife in different attitudes as we were swept through the pass and another experienced diver with a band of weights around his belt to facilitate descent made long, graceful sweeping dives to the bottom.

We just held hands sky-diver fashion and floated through.

Suspended over the giant three-dimensional screen — it seemed as though it were speeding by at much more rapid speed that we had read about — we seemed to go for miles.

Then the water slowed around us and became darker and darker.

At the boat we dutifully handed in our fins and masks and climbed up the small ladder.

It was like a kindergarten. Everyone was bubbling over with things to say and bubbling with the excitement of it all.

The Lady Navigator and I looked at each other and laughed and pounded each other's knees in delight.

Sensational.

The next ride, with most of our nervousness gone, was even more enjoyable. We began to look closer at the fish and try to remember their names (impossible), their size and shape and color.

That night at the bar with Richard's help we ticked off what we had seen.

There were silver jacks, horse-eyed jacks, pompano, mullet, surgeon fish with razor sharp fins, zebra surgeons, convict surgeons, red-eyed surgeons.

Unicorn, parrot fish, wrasse, grouper, six-barrel wrasse, yellow and black butterfly fish, picasso, trigger fish, puffer fish, striped toby, angel fish, moorish idols and damsel fish of every color...black and white, electric turquoise and deep blue.

There were schools of long, transparent, skinny trumpet fish and warty nosed mullet.

"This time," Richard said before we went into the mainstream for a third ride, "you'll see a shark."

I stayed very close to the boat.

As the fantasy swim began again, the eye became increasingly aware of more details of the — what — coralscape, bottomscape?

More aware of the fish.

And then down at the bottom swimming quite leisurely were two sharks. Small sharks. Black-tipped, non-dangerous sharks. Friendly sharks.

They were at least thirty feet below, nonchalant, obviously well-fed. What shark would want a tenderloin of hard rubber when it was surrounded by such a fresh fish market?

Before the next dive we asked Richard how he knew we would see a shark

He said, "The glass bottom boat had worked its way near us and one thing they do is to cut a fresh fish in two and hold it out over the end of the boat from a spear and a shark will come along and come out of the water and snatch the bait off the spear. The guests think it is quite exciting. The sharks seem to like it too."

Uh-huh.

More exciting for the swimmers too. From then on I saw sharks.

But this couldn't have been the most dangerous water in the world that Dewey Bergman had written about.

"Yes, it is the same," said Richard later. "But the really dangerous sharks have gone. In all of my time here I have only seen two. And the shark is a coward. He won't attack unless he gives lots of warning, circling with others like a pack of wild dogs, coming closer and closer. That's the time when you get out of the water.

"The theory here is that the outboard motor of the villagers has driven the man-eaters out of the pass."

"How fast were we drifting...how far did we go?" The questions came from every swimmer. All in the boat agreed that it was at least ten knots and over a mile.

"Oh, five knots at the fastest...and about four or five hundred yards." Dangerous? "Naw. I have taken eighty-year-old grand-mothers and three-year-old children out. Usually about sixty percent of the guests go snorkeling. Today was exceptional."

Grandmothers and infants notwithstanding, to us it was one of our most exhilarating experiences of any kind, in any country. A swing-on-a-cloud thrill.

There are a couple of problems in the Tuamotus for a hotel operator. A high wind or a large wave can blow away or wash away his entire investment. That's one problem.

The second problem is water.

By contrast, in Fiji, the isolated island resorts are close enough to

the main island of Viti Levu to barge in water. Kia Ora, however, is
two hundred and eighteen miles northeast of Papeete.

Water was drilled for and found — brackish but usable.

Rainwater is used in ice cubes and for table water. You can buy
bottled water which we always did, taking half-filled bottles back to
the *fare*.

In the bathroom was an ecology sign which pleaded:

> "Save water.
> Shower with a friend.
> Thank you."

It is also written in French and Japanese.

Another ecology sign pasted on the wall read:

> "It takes ten years for a thirty kilogram Napoleon
> fish to grow...it only takes one second to kill it with
> a spear-gun. Don't be trigger happy!"

André, the waiter, is also André, the painter. The small but
surprisingly excellent hotel boutique includes a few of his pastel
watercolors of the Tuamotu atolls. We bought a small painting.

He later told us of an experience of showing one of his works and
saying, "And in this painting I have used all the warm colors."

To which an American lady replied, "That's all right. I'll take it.
My house is air-conditioned."

That night at dinner we met a couple from Loomis, California who
were going off by themselves for a two-day Robinson Crusoe
experience, on a remote *motu*. The idea had been suggested by a
travel agency in Sacramento, California and the details had been
worked out by Tahiti Nui Travel in Papeete. The details were rather
hazy. All they knew was that a boat was to pick them up at the hotel
the next day and the boat would have all the supplies and information
and take them to their unknown destination.

The cost was nominal.

The idea was adventurous.

Only the boat never showed up. That is not too unusual in Tahiti.
The couple who had paid in advance were confident that since they

had worked through leading agencies they would get their money back.

We talked to Richard about such a project because it sounded attractive for many of the people we know.

He said that the hotel had made a considerable investment in this same direction and had leased three spots around the atoll where guests could go and live and move on or, better, could go to a simple camp which the hotel had set up on a remote island with open-aired thatch-covered platforms for sleeping and a cook shed.

A castaway, deserted island experience with a few rudimentary comforts thrown in. Like a cook and a guide.

He couldn't quote a price or a program but to make it feasible would require a minimum group of six compatible people and probably about three nights. Interested parties could work out their own program and schedule and arrive at a price by writing directly to Kia Ora in Papeete, he said.

The next day was picnic day. Picnic day is a standard part of the French Polynesian hotel routine which also includes the *tamaaraa,* the photographers lunch, the barbecue and the cocktail sunset sail.

However, the Rangiroa picnic had a couple of added attractions which were appealing.

One, they were going to catch fresh fish and broil them on heated coral stones.

Secondly, for those who desired to do so, we would shoot two other passes which sweep around the picnic island of Motu Fara.

There are only three passes into the huge lagoon which is two hundred and twenty-five kilometers in circumference, eighty kilometers long and thirty kilometers wide. When you stand on one shore, you can't see the opposite shore.

The first pass is at Tiputa. A second pass is only big enough for a canoe. The third pass is at the other end of the atoll on which Kia Ora is located. Like the village it is called Avatoru...*ava,* pass, and *toru,* third.

We took off about an hour after breakfast...breakfast consisted of fruit juices, cereals and urns of tea and coffee to which you helped yourself. Also you could help yourself to a stack of chafing dish *crêpes,* not pancakes, which were feather light. Just the little dab you needed before ordering eggs and bacon.

Sparkling morning. Bounced over the small waves to the other end of the atoll, passing the airfield, passing the little *hoa* where the boats were stored in time of storms and eventually arriving at our little island.

Martine and two of the waitresses set about cutting off palm branches from which they wove mats for the wooden picnic tables. Ideal throw-away table cloths.

The older privileged boys from the hotel went out into the lagoon with their spear guns to get lunch. The younger boys stayed behind and with the help of the guests gathered wood for a fire.

With the preliminary tasks done, the party split into groups doing different things. Swimming, shelling, sunning, sleeping, wading. The girls from the hotel took a remote corner and removed most of their clothes — surely so they wouldn't get soiled — and swam and sunned. Martine in a black G-string. Incredible. (I heard this only by rumor. I was busy playing backgammon at the time.)

The happy hunters came back with about thirty-five pounds of fresh fish: parrot fish, jack, surgeon, goat fish, grouper.

When the fire had heated the coral rocks to a white hot stage, the ashes were swept away and the cleaned fish were placed on a screen atop the stones.

While the fish was cooking, a mixed salad of greens, cheese, ham, potato and cucumbers was served with hunks of fresh French bread and then a whole fish was put on a banana leaf and presented to each guest. The fish was first lightly patted with butter and then fresh limes were squeezed over the whole thing, salt and pepper and...heaven. The best of fish.

Pitchers of sangria were spotted down the long table and melting camembert, fresh pineapple slices and quarters of fresh oranges with coffee finished the menu.

Despite the French cooking in Papeete and the Chinese cuisine in competition, the Rangiroa picnic was one of the more memorable meals in French Polynesia.

Richard: "You have a choice. Visit the village directly across from the island or shoot the Avatoru Pass."

We were the first to hold up our hands for the pass.

We were joined in the snorkel boat by the photographer from Phoenix whose wife wasn't feeling too well and was probably tired of being photographed under water, a young man from Zurich and the couple from Loomis who had joined the group when their boat to far away places failed to arrive.

Richard took the village group and our driver-lifesaver-guide was

Matahi. *Matahi* means "fish eye" or one who can spot fish and in the first part of the float through the pass, his hulking figure could be seen standing on the prow of the boat keeping a watch over his charges.

The boat went into the swift current of the pass away from the village side of the island. Once we dropped into the water it was immediately apparent that we were in for a faster ride because the gap between the island and the other shore was much narrower. We were shot through an aperture with sheer walls on either side and even the fish couldn't swim in place.

After a couple of hundred yards the pass widened. The current slowed somewhat but continued to push us along among a more abundant number of fish.

The ride lasted far into the lagoon before the waves made snorkeling too rough and the waters started to deepen and darken.

But what a glorious float through!

We must have been ten minutes in the water.

In the chop we swam back to the boat. No ladder.

We passed up our gear to Matahi on his instructions and then turned our backs to the boat and one by one he reached down, this huge man, and taking hold under the armpits, pulled us into the boat. Strong!

He then drove the boat back into the pass but this time on the close side to the village and instead of flying through the pass on the right side of the island, the current took us to the left of the island and down the length of the village.

It was a piece of cake.

The second pass was gentle, slower, the bottom often of white sand...but it was a long, lazy, leisurely ride for well over a mile before Matahi came alongside and did his weight lifting act again.

We rode back to the hotel in a moderate chop — the waves in the lagoon can get to seven feet — but happy in the afternoon sunshine with the whole day.

The *pièce de résistance* from the chef that night was a huge ham, sparkling with glaze and dotted with chunks of pineapple.

André carried the masterpiece by each table for admiration.

When he came abreast of us, he leaned aside and stage whispered, "Frog leg."

The activity on the third day was a choice between a speedboat to Bird Island, a nesting place for a variety of birds almost in the middle of the lagoon, or a trip to the village of Tiputa.

The original list of people who optioned for the boat trip dwindled to one other person and myself.

The Lady Navigator took the village tour.

She won.

Bird Island

The Bird Island tour was a bust.

The other passenger, a handsome German executive for an international company based in London, saved the trip by a long discussion of the life, economics and politics of his current post, Buenos Aires.

Dimly I later recalled the voice of Martine explaining before the Bird Island trip, "The more of you who go, the cheaper the trip." I didn't realize that the boat cost $100 which the German and I halved.

After a half an hour ride through a fairly heavy sea, we swung into the lee of the tiny island which was covered with coconut trees and brush and landed on a soft sand beach. Mack, our boat driver and guide, led the way into the bush.

Midway into the island a white bird flew off a tree and on a bare branch was a single white egg.

Mack explained with gestures and his four-word English vocabulary that the island's white birds laid their eggs on the branches of trees. The black bird inhabitants laid their eggs in nests.

That was the end of the guided tour.

Mack was soon in the water spear-fishing for his family's table and we were left to do our own thing. Fortunately I had brought mask and fins and went into the shallows of the island on the lee side only because the windward side was too rough.

For a while I was able to shadow Mack and watch him dive when he spotted a fish, go to the bottom and stay and stay and stay. Never pulled a trigger. Later he came back with two fish and for him the trip was a moderate success.

I'd rather have given $50 to a children's charity...or perhaps to a medical fund for those who don't listen closely enough.

Tiputa, Town Of Another Time

The five-minute launch shuttle across the pass to Tiputa deposits you at a long pier under big shade trees.

You sense something different about this village without being able to identify what.

Richard, now-turned-historian, put it into perspective. Trees. That's what was different. Besides the coconut trees that grow on most coral atolls, Tiputa had flowering and fruit trees — and grass!

Tiputa's greenery dated back to a more affluent time before plastics destroyed its mother-of-pearl industry. In those turn-of-the-century days, soil was imported from Tahiti. When there was enough soil, trees were brought in: plumeria from Singapore, banana from Samoa, citrus and breadfruit from Tahiti, even Ceylon palms.

The village was further beautified by communal white-washed coral walls running the length of "main" street behind which were neat lawns, floored with grass, bordered with flowers. There was obvious pride in Tiputa.

Tiputa was a municipal commune. Water catchments and several electric generators were operated for the entire village.

As the administrative center for nine northern islands of the Tuamotus, Tiputa provided the district's high school. Most of the enrollment of about three hundred were boarders from the eight other islands. Each island had its own primary school.

The Gendarmerie had a staff of five: a French station commandant, two Tahitians and two Tuamotuans. Their primary job was monitoring the incoming yachts and copra boats. The chiefs (now called "mayors") of each village still controlled law enforcement. It was a rare occasion when the national force had to step in, Richard said.

"The biggest problem comes from the young people who get a supply of yeast and sugar and make their own home brew and get swacko-ed."

Richard who received an "A" for his conduct of the tour stopped in front of a gracious concrete building behind a gate-arched stone fence. The mansion, formerly the residence of a Tuamotuan governor, now serves the community as an infirmary. Its gatepost crest, a centipede biting a hand, had been whitewashed over.

Next door was an abandoned house, the date 1885 above the door.

There were a lot of abandoned houses in Tiputa.

Some of these were victims of a declining population. Others, according to Richard, had just been walked away from temporarily.

"Tiputa, with its five hundred population, is too crowded, too busy, for some Tuamotuans. They fill a sack with a mixture of flour and grated coconut (*ipo*), shut the doors of their house, close the windows, get in their little *pirogues* and leave.

"It is the equivalent of the Australian 'walkabout.'

"They go to an isolated atoll and set up a lean-to and perhaps gather, split and dry coconuts and bring back copra to Tiputa — or perhaps they don't. If they do not own the *motu*, they split the proceeds of the copra with the owner.

"They live on fish from the lagoon, the *ipo* for starch and coconut water for drink. When they get tired of the country life they sail back to Tiputa and resume the city life."

Not bad when you think about it.

(Of course it all depends on your mental attitude. I'm typing this copy on a wicker table in a back bedroom of a small wooden house in the village of Hane, population eighty, on the island of Ua Huka, total population three hundred and sixty, in the lost Marquesas. It has rained for ten straight days. Yesterday I was tramping back over the steep coast road from the next valley where I had gone to buy canned corned beef and my attitude then was that civilization starts with dinner in the Monarch Room at the Royal Hawaiian in Waikiki on Saturday night. But I feel better this morning.)

One of the features of Tiputa village was a school of dolphins which surf with regularity in the pass directly in front of the village.

The Lady Navigator reported that she wanted to swim with them and test their ballet.

One of the characters of Rangiroa is Serge Arnoux, the manager and co-owner of Kia Ora. He has a reputation as a raconteur and a diver.

He was ten years with the Club Med developing properties in the Pacific. He thinks that twenty-five units is perfect for Rangiroa and doesn't plan more.

Another important person at Rangiroa is the chef.

We are reluctant to say too much about a good or bad table at any hotel because cooking, it seems, is a nomadic business. The excellent chef of today is replaced by a plumber tomorrow. We picked up a couple in the Society Islands who said they couldn't wait to get back to a certain hotel because of the cuisine in general and the pastries in particular. Of course when they came back with mouths watering, the hotel was featuring greasy omelettes and lumpy sauces and the chef was an escaped convict from a glue factory where he had flunked the quality control test.

But the chef at Rangiroa, during our time was André Vallerre. His *mahimahi en croûte* was superb.

Here is his recipe:

MAHIMAHI EN CROÛTE

WHAT YOU NEED

4   filets of mahimahi (about 1 pound)
    paper thin pastry
¼ pound of chopped shallots
½ pound of minced mushrooms
½ bouquet of chopped parsley
    salt, pepper
1½ lemons
1   egg, beaten
¼ pound fresh butter

WHAT YOU DO

Stretch half of the pastry (*pâte feuilletèe*) on a fireproof plate. Place the filets on the pastry and cover with a mixture of chopped shallots, minced mushrooms, chopped parsley and two tablespoons butter cut in thin slices. Cover with the remaining pastry, brush with beaten egg, cook in a hot oven for around an hour.

Sauce

Squeeze the lemons. Heat the juice with salt and pepper, pull off the fire and add the rest of the butter mixing it together quickly.

Andre, who lightened every meal, came bouncing to the table. His family, we understood from others, was wealthy from New Caledonia mining and Andre said he was one-quarter Japanese, which might have given his face its interesting countenance.

We asked him one night why in his Rangiroa landscapes he didn't include more of the ocean or lagoon.

"Becauth," he said in his slight lisp lifting his head in comic hauteur, "I can't thwim."

The bill for room and meals and wine with most meals but a small bar bill was quite reasonable. Plus Bird Island. Plus tax.

We didn't want to leave. Great place and shooting the pass in "the most dangerous waters in the world" was a lifetime thrill.

At a travel conference in Papeete we were delighted to read on the list of attendees the name of Dewey Bergman and we asked to be introduced at the first function.

Dewey Bergman, sans beard unlike his photos, is an amiable, low-key, bear of a man who looks more like an economics professor than a famous underwater explorer and guide.

We couldn't wait to tell him that we had swum "the most dangerous waters in the world" and that the sharks had heard we were coming and had swum away in fear.

"The people tell you the sharks are gone, eh?" rumbled Dewey without any great animation.

"Ten months ago I was back there.

"You know the little house on the edge of the pass opposite Tiputa?

"You go around the corner of coral nearest the house and there they are. Oh, they are still there."

"Dewey," asked the Lady Navigator, "Did you ever surf with the dolphins at Tiputa?"

"Oh, sure," said Dewey to the Lady Navigator, "Many times."

I thought she was going to cry.

PEARL ISLAND...The Atoll Of Manihi...The New Village Of Kaina ...The Old Village Of Turipaoa...The Pearl Farm...Millionaire's Salad And Other Food Items.

Our first eye-catching sight on the remote island of Manihi in the Tuamotus was an oh-wow Polynesian-Oriental girl barely dressed in wisps of yellow shirting sitting in the shade of the just-arrived Air Polynésie plane making out the passenger and baggage manifest.

Three couples bound for Kaina Village deplaned and were directed to a large open boat on a sliver of a channel for transporting to the newest resort in French Polynesia.

Last person to jump in the boat was the yellow-shirted employee of Air Polynesie who had now become the resort's hostess. We didn't know it at the time but she was also the principal chef, housekeeper, bookkeeper, dining room hostess and activities director. Her name was Mareva Coquille, wife of the manager, and she was excellent in all jobs. And beautiful.

Manihi is three hundred and sixty miles from Papeete or about another one hundred and ten miles beyond Rangiroa.

Kaina Village built next to the airstrip was still under construction when we arrived. Six of the individual *fares* built on pilings over the lagoon had been completed as had a "youth bungalow" with twelve beds in a half a dozen rooms where parents could stash their children while they enjoyed a honeymoon cottage. (Princess Caroline on her honeymoon was supposed to arrive during the same week. She didn't.)

Each cottage consists of a bedroom, with a small deck over the water and a bathroom with spring attachments to the wash-basin and shower spouts which limit the user to thirty seconds of water at one time.

The roofs of the cottages, instead of being Polynesian thatch are of blue plastic, designed and manufactured in France. They are constructed as rain catchments and the top of the structure is designed for solar heating.

I thought the brochure copy delicately handled an item of curiosity: "...and not one drop of waste water will sully the sparkling waters of the lagoon — a special biological cleansing cycle leaves all that is less than pure with the flowers."

The boat ride to the village takes five minutes. Coming to your destination over water makes a more romantic, South Pacifica arrival. You could walk or ride around by the road but the single jeep doesn't have enough room for passengers and besides it hauls the trailer with the luggage. At Kaina Village you come down the dock past a *fare* with a pool table and a library of paperbacks...then a *fare* for the office and a boutique.

A large open-aired, peaked-roof pavilion serves as restaurant and in the middle of the dance floor is a handsome but incongruous New Guinea war canoe.

You should know if you take the two-hour noon flight from Papeete that you shouldn't have a quick lunch at the airport bar...and you shouldn't get off the airplane at Rangiroa and buy a hot fruit tart from the lady with the big basket.

You will be fed a sizeable lunch on arrival at the Kaina Village.

The wine list consisted of one white, one red, and one rose, price by the bottle or the carafe. Bar drinks were cheaper than in Papeete.

Breakfasts are continental with tea and coffee and hot toast, butter and marmalade. There was no fruit juice during our stay because the twice-a-month boat from Papeete hadn't brought any.

Although the chef was leaving after an unsuccessful thirty-day tryout, it didn't make any difference because Mareva fortunately dominated the kitchen. Luncheons and dinners were generally quite good, sometimes outstanding.

At one lunch we had feather-light potato puffs about which we raved but Mareva indicated we weren't eating potato. The French word just didn't translate. She went into the kitchen and came back with an eggplant. (*Aubergine.*)

I followed her back into the kitchen to see the cooking in process.

The eggplant — and a zucchini works just as well — is peeled and thinly sliced but not paper thin. A batter is prepared of flour and salt and enough beer to set it up slightly thicker than water. Mareva said the secret is to let the batter rest for about four hours outside of the refrigerator. If you use the batter immediately after it is made, "zay-row," said Mareva.

The slices of eggplant are then dipped in the batter and dropped into a large kettle of very hot peanut oil and taken out when puffed and brown. Scrumptious. Try it.

Our last dinner was one of the best we had in French Polynesia and it began with *fresh* hearts of palm salad. It was our first experience of tasting the heart of a palm tree. This one had come from a tree growing too tall at the end of the runway that had to be cut down. You have to have permission to cut down any tree in French Polynesia and the heart of palm is rare even in these islands. The narrow watermelon-shaped heart is peeled and cut into wafers. It is crunchy and crisp with just a delicate whisper of coconut flavoring. Very different from the preserved product.

Next came piglette that had been baked in beer with a crackling that was crisp but very tender and meat that was as succulent as anything we had ever tasted. (I have to mop up the droolings from the typewriter just thinking about it.) The sauce for the baked pig was a thickened coconut cream. An assortment of starch vegetables were offered: red wild bananas found only in Tahiti (*fei*) which can be eaten only when cooked; baked breadfruit; and pureed pumpkin.

Two other quick items and then we'll leave the kitchen. Mareva also made an outstanding *poisson cru* and, at our last lunch, we had French-fried breadfruit. If you go to Tahiti during the winter or summer, take a tip and try French-fried breadfruit.

There was more to do at Manihi than just eat.

The first afternoon after lunch we swam off the dock. There is no white sand beach going into swimable waters and there are no outstanding coral gardens either — both prominently featured in tourist brochures.

There are pearl farms in the Tuamotus. The first pearl farm was established at Manihi and this was our activity highlight the second day.

First we boated across the Tairapa Pass, deep and serious looking, not made for drift snorkeling according to Guy Coquille, our leader to Turipaoa Village.

Tying up to the dock of Turipaoa, the only village in the atoll of islands ringing the lagoon, we first visited the village shark pen at dockside with a half dozen sleeping nurse sharks. Big nurse sharks.

"Why a shark pen?"

It is an amusement for the inhabitants who lasso the monsters in the pass, Guy said. One of the village sports.

Turipaoa consists of ninety inhabitants who live in neat houses bordered with low-lying concrete walls built with municipal funds. There is one municipal building which serves as a post office, city hall, school, and cinema. ("Queen Sheba and the Children of Salome" was playing that week.)

There is a small village store. The unusual item at the store was a pile of cases of Hinano beer. The store doesn't usually sell beer but the Fête was only two weeks off and for the Fête many exceptions are made to the rules.

Almost all the villagers are Mormon. Only two families are Tahitian Protestant and one family is Catholic.

"Why aren't they also Mormon?" Guy was asked.

"So they can go on drinking," he said.

In a corner of the village is a separate building marked with the letters SPM (*Société Perlière de Manihi*). This is the operating room for the "surgeons" who go to Manihi during the season of harvesting of mature pearls and replanting of new pearls.

The vast lagoon of Manihi is divided into three parts and every year the divers from the village work one third of the lagoon bringing fresh oysters to be implanted with small plastic balls. Their shells are drilled through on the edge and a small wire hanger is passed through the hole. The shells are then taken to a grid-farm in the lagoon where they are suspended for three years. At that time they are brought back to the shed and passed individually before a scanning machine to see if the plastic ball has been covered with enough layers of mother of pearl to form a harvestable individual pearl. "Yes" and it is opened. The oyster is dead but the shell is saved for decorations, etc. "No" and the oyster goes back to the grid.

Visiting the "pearl farm" is only to look down twenty to thirty feet in the lagoon at a mass of oysters each the size of your hand suspended on wire grids.

The black pearl comes from a black-mouth oyster found only in French Polynesia. The Tuamotu lagoons offer ideal farming conditions: constant water temperature, little turbulence and the correct amount of salinity.

After ten years of development, Manihi had sixty thousand oysters on the "farm" and harvested five thousand pearls annually.

By the 'Eighties, the yield had climbed to thirty thousand, an amazing figure when you know that only twenty-five percent of the imprisoned oysters produce marketable pearls, and that the industry suffered a devastating hurricane in the early 'Eighties.

Today, there are dozens of small pearl farms, but two major companies produce the bulk of the annual crop.

The industry of pearl farming is now worth millions of dollars to French Polynesia and has become a major income producer.

In our expedition a diver went over the side and brought up an oyster. It was pried barely open and then handed to Guy Coquille who opened it all the way and extracted a pearl. It was pronounced a bad pearl as it was handed around the boat. (I kept it thinking it was worthless but later had to give it back. It was evidently worth something.)

From the pearl farm the expedition went to a nearby quiet cove with a white sand bottom and the Lady Navigator and I went exploring with borrowed masks in the coral heads.

The coral heads grew like crooked mushrooms up from the bottom bordering the blue waters of the lagoon. Pretty sight. The fish were few but of enough variety and size and color to satisfy.

The borrowed mask of my swimming partner kept leaking and she gave up and swam back to the boat but I continued to laze around the coral heads, sometimes peeking over the edge of the coral where the white sand bottom dived down into deeper, bluer water.

I don't know what made me think shark.

Once I saw a film on New Caledonia's shallow waters such as these and there was a scene of sharks passing near the cameraman and that scene flashed in my mind for some reason and I turned — and there it was!

My first all-alone-you-and-me shark.

There was no pier to hide behind. No wharf to stand on. The boat was fifty yards away.

I wasn't frightened or nervous or scared. I was simply shocked with terror. My face froze in disbelief and there was a huge hunk of ice in my stomach.

It couldn't be. But it was.

The fish was probably three feet long and three blocks away but in the repeated telling of the incident the only eye-witness account says that the shark was three blocks long and three feet away. Under a truth test it had to be about twenty feet away and about six feet long.

The shark was almost white and without a friendly black tip on its dorsal fin. It turned and swam back and down the second I saw it.

I never turned my back on the spot but cautiously started back-paddling toward the boat. I wanted to get on top of the water and run. A couple of times I splashed with my back-stroking arms but immediately slowed down. *Don't panic. Don't splash.*

Never saw it again.

Going back to Kaina Village, Guy just laughed.

"The shark was as afraid of you as you were of him," he said.

"I've read that," I replied. "But has the shark read it?"

The next day was picnic day.

Before you go on a picnic at Kaina Village ask if the wind means there are going to be flies or no flies.

If the wind in the far-off atoll is behind the picnic spot it brings flies in numbers to cover you, cover your plate, cover your food. Unless you are like one of our party, an Indochina "Old Hand" who had eaten in every condition imaginable, don't go.

If the wind is right however and you haven't eaten freshly caught fish grilled on coral stones, go. Besides you'll have Mareva's *poisson cru*, lots of red wine, rosé wine and cold beer.

Also you'll have the sight of Mareva who supervises the cooking and the table and the serving dressed only in a strip of bikini bottom and a straw hat.

A beautiful figure and worth the day.

While on that subject I must also tell you about being alone on the end of the dock late one afternoon reading and getting the last of the sun when the three teen-age waitresses came out for a swim and, after extracting a half-promise from me not to turn around, they stripped to bikini bottoms and splashed around in the water like playful puppies. When I'd turn from my book and scowl down into the playpen, they would shriek and laugh and then climb the ladder in front of me and dive quickly back in again. We added to each other's afternoon enjoyment.

It seems in retrospect that several times in this book the subject of either sharks or bare-bosomed ladies has come up. The intention is not to lay undue emphasis on either subject but perhaps because of a Rocky Mountain youthful period of upbringing, they capture the attention faster than other subjects. You know, in Colorado Springs during my childhood, you didn't see many sharks or topless women.

The last night at Kaina Village a three-piece band played while guests and waitresses shook and wiggled and waved their arms. Like Navajos war dancing.

Post Script: Richard Postma and Martine have moved to Bora Bora to raise a family. He skippers the new catamaran, *Vehia,* at the Hotel Bora Bora and she operates a little roadside boutique near the hotel called Martine's. Stop by. She is still a rare, toothsome, willowy beauty.

9. The Mysterious Marquesas

**The First To Be Discovered By Polynesians...
The First To Be Discovered By Europeans...A
Tragic History Of Slavers, Whalers And
Missionaries.**

The Marquesas are haunting islands.

Not a place to go. Not a place to miss.

The geography is savage, islands shooting out of the sea, ungraced by a lacy collar of reefs or made peaceful by calm lagoons. The ocean beats incessantly against the steep cliffs with furious, white-crashing waves, pounding like battering rams trying to smash down the castle walls.

Steep valleys are separated from each other by tall ridges which cast constant shadows onto their lonely floors.

If people are shaped by their environment, little wonder that the Marquesans were known for their rugged ferocity.

Wild cattle, wild pigs and wild horses roam many of the upper plateaus keeping as company giant stone *tikis* whose massive cousins are found on the Easter Islands two thousand miles away.

Curious islands with a history of discovery, adventure, art and cannibalism. And a people who in the end were defeated by the spectre of diseases and a loss of culture and wanted to curl up and die.

The history of the Marquesas is dated back to a time before the birth of Christ when the earliest known discoverers sailed, according to one school of archaeologists, from Savaii in Samoa where they had been enough time to evolve into a new race of "Polynesians." They established in the Marquesas the first home of the eastern Polynesians.

From a base in these forbidding isles the ancient mariners fanned out in all directions and found other islands. Small miracle.

Then they evidently sailed back again. No miracle. Skill.

The first European known to land on any part of today's French Polynesia was Alvaro Mendana who sailed from Peru intending to set up a gold colony in the Pacific.

Mendana saw the islands of the southern group of the Marquesas in July of 1595. He named them "Islas Marquesas de Mendoza" after his patron, the Viceroy of Peru.

Not being able to find anchorage on "La Dominica" (Hiva Oa) he found a small harbor on "Santa Christina" (Tahu Ata).

He stayed ten days provisioning his ships but his men were responsible for frightful carnage among the natives. Some two hundred were wantonly slain.

Mendana called the little harbor "Madre de Dios." Three crosses were raised to commemorate the coming of Christianity. Mother of God.

Almost two hundred years later the same islands were "rediscovered" by Captain Cook and he landed at the same little port, which he called "Resolution Bay," on April 8, 1774.

Even with Cook the coming of the white man was marred by bloodshed when a native, caught in pilfering, was shot dead.

In the next century the islands were visited and scarred by slavers who took away natives as laborers and by whalers whose recreational visits left behind ravaging diseases.

What the slavers and sailors didn't destroy physically the missionaries completed with the morale destruction of the people.

Christianity meant a removal of the Marquesan religion...their gods and temples, the rituals and customs...songs, dances, prayers, statues, carvings, tattooing, cannibalism. The cultural shock was so great that they no longer had a will to live and wasted away to the point that, when touched with the slightest illness they died in vast numbers.

The Marquesans serve as prime examples of dedicated missionaries on thankless, difficult, often dangerous tasks, unconsciously rendering total devastation to the souls they strived to save.

"Follow the righteous path we will show you," said the missionaries, "and we will show you the way from the ancient world of horrible paganism to the shining new world of Christianity."

Few of the natives ever arrived.

In the nineteenth century they died in such numbers to border total annihilation.

HIVA OA...Melville, Stevenson And Gauguin...The First Landfall For American Yachts...A Sky-High Airport...The Belgian Television Crew...

"Sit down," said the Lady Navigator, fresh from her morning trip into Papeete.

"I don't want to sit down."

"Sit down," said the Lady Navigator. In addition to her morning errands of mail, food, research, that morning included confirming our reservations for the once-a-week flight to the Marquesas leaving at six-thirty the next morning. The difficult-to-get seats had been reserved for almost two months.

"The plane?"

"The airplane for the Marquesas doesn't leave at six-thirty. It leaves at five ayem."

"That's okay."

"It doesn't leave on Tuesdays. It leaves on Mondays."

"This morning!"

"This morning."

"We missed it!"

"We missed it."

I sat down.

There is no emptiness which quite matches the irretrievable, dropped-egg finality of missing an airplane.

The result was very straining.

In June and July air traffic is heavy with school children going to and from the islands and French *fonctionnaires* who take precedent over everybody including those with confirmed reservations and military going home to vacation on their *annuel* and school teachers, heavy in purse, and those already heading for Papeete and the Fête.

Only through the graciousness of Air Polynésie were we able to get a *single* seat on the next Monday flight and a confirmed seat on a return flight two weeks later.

The Lady Navigator could get a standby ticket for Monday but there wasn't any guarantee when she could get out of the Marquesas. None.

In the airline office I heard a man shouting into the telephone trying to get on a return boat *in September.*

That did it.

The next Monday morning in the pre-dawn darkness I left a thunder-browed, mirthless companion at the gate.

"Don't forget to take your dramamine," she said with the same loving warmth that Rasputin heard when he was told to be sure and finish the last crumb of poisoned cake.

The flight to Hiva Oa from Papeete takes seven hours in an eighteen-place DeHavilland Otter.

After my trip a new airfield was completed at Nuku Hiva, the administrative headquarters of the Marquesas. The field will be continually enlarged until it can take a forty-passenger plane which will relieve part of the traffic load. Smaller aircraft will then service the other islands within the Marquesas.

Time in the Marquesas is a half hour earlier than the rest of French Polynesia, and it was past noon Marquesan time when, through a heavy, dark rain, we first saw the forbidding cliffs of Tahu Ata and then Hiva Oa.

They said that the airfield was on top of a plateau.

They should have said on the edge of a plateau.

"*Eh, voilà, la piste!*" said my seat neighbor peering through the cockpit and between the two pilots' shoulders.

Following his example I saw a flat finger of a mountain pointing in our direction. We passed by the valley of Atuona black in a bowl of rain and descended to meet the oncoming airstrip shrouded with clouds and wet with the storm.

The squeak of the wheels and the retarding of engines were very sweet sounds. To create the runway the engineers had simply sliced off the top of a mountain ridge. The resulting turbulent air currents and the mountain fog were two parts of the location.

The open shed terminal, cold, swept with wind, was a third.

If you stand around dumb enough in a Polynesian airport, someone will eventually take care of you and after ten minutes of freezing (incredible at a latitude of less than ten degrees below the equator!), I was shoved into the back of a jeep for the trip down the mountain.

Frightening ride.

The steep downhill dirt road was awash with rain and slippery with mud and the jeep would start a slide and the nonchalant driver would turn his wheels into the slide swinging the jeep back into position until the next slide. There was cliff on one side of the road and on the other — emptiness. No guard-rail of course.

HIVA OA

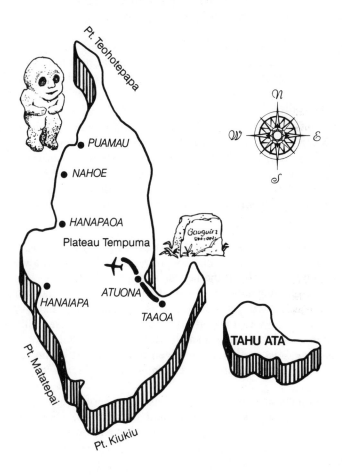

Pt. Teohotepapa

PUAMAU

NAHOE

HANAPAOA

Plateau Tempuma

Gauguin

ATUONA

HANAIAPA

TAAOA

Pt. Matatepai

Pt. Kiukiu

TAHU ATA

It was the ideal location for one of those, "my-god-look-at-that-over-the-side-tumbling-crashing-tinkling-glass-bursting-into-flame-oh-those-poor-children" accidents. I kept my eyes on the cliff side.

Fifteen kilometers and ten fingernails later we came around a giant turn to face the ocean and, just below, the bay of Tahauku, a narrow, surging anchorage where a cluster of yachts and the inter-island steamer were moored. Behind the black sand and black stone beach lay a lush valley of coconuts. In the distance an abandoned copra shed.

Robert Louis Stevenson, in a chartered yacht, the *Casco,* anchored in this same bay in 1888, and climbed the next hill as we did and made the last turn and looked down on the next valley of Atuona.

In his book "In the South Seas" under a chapter headed "In a Cannibal Valley," he describes what he saw:

> *"At the turn of the land, Atuona came in view: a long beach, a heavy and loud surf, a shore-side village scattered among the trees, and the guttered mountains drawing near on both sides above a narrow and rich ravine. Its infamous repute perhaps affected me; but I thought it the loveliest, and by far the most ominous spot on earth."*

The shore-side houses are now gone, probably washed away in a tidal wave and the village has now retreated safely into the valley. The coconut trees shield the houses and stores from view.

The surrounding half-cup of mountains condenses the moisture of the tradewinds and torrents of fresh water pour into the valley. After a heavy rain, twenty-two waterfalls cascade down the steep cliffs.

On the outskirts there is a small white war memorial surrounded with a heavy, decorative chain. Even in this remote corner of the French empire, the tradition of remembering the village war dead is carried on.

Behind the memorial is the Gendarmerie where incoming yachts must register their ships' papers and their crews. (The yachts' skippers are responsible for the crews' bills and behavior. A crew member cannot switch ships without signing off one yacht and onto another at the Gendarmerie.)

At the split of the road at the memorial, you go to the right and up the hill to the cemetery and the tomb of Gauguin.

To the left you go to the village.

On the right of the village road is a two-story yellow building which is called the "Number One" store by the yacht crews not because it is the best — just the nearest.

They understand English and stock most items you want, including frozen New Zealand lamb chops, canned Australian milk, cold beer, and most unusual, a liter of rum decanted from a barrel into a former plastic water bottle. About $5.50. Not bad rum.

A hundred yards beyond is a new sports complex for the youth of the village, "Maison des Jeunes," which includes a basketball court, volleyball court, covered play shed, a new night-lighted tennis court and an open space for outdoor motion pictures.

Nearby, behind a wire fence, is a convent secondary school for about three hundred students, and "Number Two" store, also Chinese, then one house farther, the twenty-five yard driveway to the Rauzy Realm. A local entrepreneur, Rauzv — who also is the mayor and the elected representative to the Territorial Assembly — builds, organizes, sells. Whatever. He is French Marquesan and aggressive.

The "Number Three" store belongs to Rauzy. It is dark and dusty and there is not a great variety on the shelves but it draws a sizeable trade.

Next door is the village bakery, also belonging to Rauzy. Behind the bakery is the tourist complex where I was taken.

Two thatched bungalows and an open-air restaurant.

They put my bags in one bungalow and told me lunch was being served.

I was prepared for the worst but having been up since three in the morning, without breakfast, I was ready to eat the worst.

There were about ten tables, four of which were prepared for service with clean linen and linen napkins confirming the fact that the farther you get away from civilization the farther you get away from paper napkins. There are advantages.

No menu.

A pitcher of wine soon was joined with a bottle of water and a small bucket of ice with escargot pinchers for ice tongs and a basket of fresh baked French bread. Things were looking up.

The first course was cold white fish and fresh sliced tomatoes on a bed of lettuce accompanied with home-made mayonnaise. Hey!

Baked pork in tomato sauce with the small French bean, *haricot vert,* followed. Hey! Hey!

Dessert was half of a sweet juicy grapefruit.

Roughing it in the Marquesas was not going to be too bad. I was to eat at Chez Rauzy for a week. Breakfast, lunch and dinner. I ate too much and too well. The round, cheerful Marquesan *cuisinière* became a good friend.

That afternoon it rained solidly.

During the entire week in Atuona it rained daily.

I don't believe in witchcraft but the memory of my left-behind partner together with the constant rain, the ants found later in bed and the *gheko* (lizard) that fell off the ceiling onto my left eyebrow scaring me out of ten pages of Melville did bring to mind a niggle that someone, somewhere was not wishing me well.

My *fare* consisted of a bedroom with iron cots with sheets and a thin blanket. There was a running water toilet with a broken cover and no seat, a wash bowl, and a shower. (When I told them that the hot water was broken, they hooted. "Take a cold water shower like we do.")

There was an outdoor covered *lanai* as part of the *fare* with two chairs, a table and another bed.

When you go to Chez Rauzy you really get a bed and not a *fare*. Whatever the visitor traffic is on Hiva Oa gets accommodated. There is nowhere else to go.

Except for one night I had the *fare* to myself.

Finally at the end of the first afternoon there was a let up in the rain which seemed to be a pattern. Rain in the morning. Semi-clear in the afternoon. In four different reference books I had read four different reports about the Marquesas' rainy season. A tourist board publication came closest to the truth: "the seasons are not well stressed."

One blessing was the coolness at night.

Venturing out on a preliminary walk-through of the village of Atuona, population perhaps six hundred plus neighbor island school children, I was hailed by a trio in yellow sailing slickers. They were off an Auckland yacht and had spotted my Air New Zealand flight bag.

The skipper had sailed across to Cape Horn and up the South American coast and then across to Easter Island. During the six months voyage he had never anchored with another foreign yacht. When he sailed into Hiva Oa, his first landfall since the Easter Islands, there were six yachts!

"Number One" store turned out to be the international yacht club.

Crew T-shirts read: "Echo Bay Curling Club Port Radium N.W.T." (Canadian Northwest Territories) worn by a giant bearded

Canadian.

"Escapade, Port Vila, New Hebrides" worn by another bearded chap.

"Yacht Club Italiano, Genoa."

Still another carried a kiwi bird symbol and read: "Arapawa."

We were joined by a California foursome, two couples, who had been dismasted a day out and had come in under power.

A fourth crew joined us, owners of a large converted fishing boat bought in Norway seven years earlier. St. Thomas was its home port. They had come from Acapulco in thirty-three days, not good time, hampered by freakish winds.

The co-owner had on board her husband, daughter, son-in-law and two young boys whose international traveling provided an economic education. Like getting a $5-a-week allowance and finding that one chocolate bar and one large bottle of orange drink cost $2.50 in Atuona. The boys were still recovering from the inflationary shock.

The yachtslady said they had encountered northeast wind coming into the Marquesas from Acapulco.

"Can you imagine! Northeast winds *here*?"

"Yes," inserted a bystander. "There is a local name for those winds."

"Sure," said the lady of the seventy-one-foot yacht, "*Screwed!*"

Hiva Oa is a favorite landfall of yachts leaving Californian, Mexican, South American ports.

The Gendarmerie said two hundred yachts pass through Atuona during the year. Although the rolling waters of the harbor didn't appear to be ideal compared to the romantic lagoons of the Tuamotus, still it is understandable that after being at sea for a month, crews were not anxious to push off again but lingered to enjoy the feel of earth underfoot, fresh fruit and unlimited fresh water.

One attractive young English adventurer sailed alone from the Island of Wight which he had left two and a half years before in his twenty-four-foot sloop.

In his last leg he had come directly to Hiva Oa from the Galápagos. Did he end up talking to himself?

No.

Didn't the lonesomeness get to him?

No. He found it quite pleasant in fact. The worst part was coming into a new port and learning to socialize again.

Walking around the cliff above the yacht harbor, I met a couple on the road who bounced to my side to talk. Most yachtsmen in Atuona, just finishing a month-long sail, were anxious to hear a new voice, see a new face, hear a new story.

What was I doing here? How long? Where was I from? What was my favorite island?

My questions followed just as rapidly.

Where were they from?

France.

What was their last port?

Panama.

How long were they staying in Hiva Oa?

No idea.

Where were they going from here?

No idea.

What a life! I said in admiration.

They laughed with the joy of it and we parted.

My *fare* during the pre-dawn hours was a living purgatory.

The Rauzy bakery started operating at four ayem with a collection of machinery noises and forced fires.

Sleep from then on was fitful at best.

The wakeful moments however were blessed by heavenly smells. Fresh bread odors filled every corner.

The subconscious rejection of the clanking noises was wedded to the acceptance of the vision of new French bread, crunchy, brown-crusted, melting with butter, floating in dreams.

I went to breakfast sleepy but ravenous.

With the constant morning rain and without an outdoor future, I set up an office in the corner of the restaurant — putting a couple of tables together, padding a chair with a bed pillow — and set to work at the first morning light. Typed roughs, collated notes, read reference materials.

I was never alone.

The concrete floor was populated with pecking chickens, hungry cats, wagging dogs and wet-nosed children.

Immediately behind the restaurant was a small pig-sty and the grunting and squealing added fresh sounds to the pecking, clawing, lapping, sniffling noises of the audience.

The clickety-clack of the typewriter however brought out the kitchen help. They nudged each other and exclaimed over the speed of the words appearing on paper and would come to stare over my shoulder at the operation.

And when I looked up at them and held their gaze while continuing to type...! They almost broke out in applause.

Every afternoon I ventured out as far as I could go on the wet roads and still return before dinner.

I found the craftmanship of precisely laid black stone floored *paepaes* of former Hiva Oa homes. A house site is only occupied once in the Marquesas because of the belief that the ground is forever taken by the spirits of the former tenants.

I walked to the upper part of the Atuona Valley, past the public school, past private homes, a lady taking a bath in the river — no pictures — past the municipal generator.

It wasn't until the third day that I could negotiate the slippery muddy road up the flank of the hill to the Catholic cemetery.

There are probably one hundred graves in the cemetery, many decorated with real or plastic flowers, some boasting both a cross and a *tiki*.

Near the front of the cemetery, overlooking the valley and the bay and the ocean, is a low tomb built in three layers of black volcanic stone and on the front in white letters is printed *Paul Gauguin, 1903*.

On the left rear corner of the tomb there's a carved statue of a woman, beneath which is printed *Oviri*, meaning savage. The carving is a cast of an original he wanted placed on his grave.

Gauguin lived in Atuona in a house he had built across from the present location of the "Number One" Chinese store. Nothing remains of the house today. Only the well where he kept a water bottle cooling on a string.

He called his home *Maison du Jouir*, House of Pleasure, which immediately offended the clerics.

In a place where he should have found peace and time to create, he found neither. He created his own problems with the authorities and was even brought to trial...he preferred war to peace. And time was running out.

A certain social disease he had picked up from a cabaret girl in Paris was ending his life in Atuona at the other end of the earth.

One morning he didn't answer the calls upstairs to his bedroom and they found him dead, two bottles of painkiller by his side.

They auctioned off his possessions. The carvings he was learning to do from the talented Marquesans, his remaining paintings and his rifle with a Gauguin-carved woodstock. One painting, his last it is said, recalled the earlier times in Brittany: *Paysage breton sous la neige*. It sold for ten francs and now hangs in the Louvre. Priceless. Only the cast of his original carving on his gravesite is a reminder of his work in Hiva Oa.

Behind the "Number One" store and next to the convent is the Church of the Immaculate Mary.

The art of Marquesan wood carving is now lost in Hiva Oa but on the front of the church are double doors on which are carved six scenes from the life of Christ.

The wood, *temanu*, was carefully selected on Hiva Oa and sent to a master carver on Nuku Hiva. The beautiful doors are excellent examples of ancient Marquesan artistry.

Inside are two hand-carved statues, one of Mary after whom the church is named, and over the altar, Jesus Christ on the cross.

To the side is a carved coconut tree trunk holding the tabernacle, done in Hiva Oa by Eric Kimitete.

Attending church service is a part of Polynesia and the Sunday Mass at eight-thirty shouldn't be missed. The singing is so sweet and genuine. Easy harmony unaccompanied by instrument. Lovely to hear.

The most desirable place to visit on Hiva Oa is the village of Puamau on the northwest corner of the island because here are the giant *tikis*, ten feet tall, which are considered a direct link to the giant stone statues of the Easter Islands.

Heavy rains had made the roads impassable during my visit but pictures show the statues to be more animated than the rigid forms of the Easter Island curiosities.

When they were carved and why is not known. It is interesting to note the similarity in the giant round eyes and the slit-smile of the Marquesan statues to those found on Easter Island two thousand miles to the southeast and the same characteristics of stone statues found on Necker Island in the Hawaiian archipelago two thousand miles to the northwest!

There was a time when the Marquesans were a vibrant, adventuresome, talented race but as Peter Buck said in his book *Vikings of the Sunrise:*

> *"It was something we Polynesians have lost and cannot find, something we yearn for and cannot re-create. The background in which that spirit was engendered has changed beyond recovery."*

My stay at Chez Rauzy was enlarged by a trio of television gentlemen who took their meals at the restaurant while staying in a rented house. They came all the way from Brussels to produce an hour and a half documentary as part of a series called *Visa for the World*.

Why were they in the Marquesas?

"It is the end of the earth," said Maurice Vermeersch, the producer.

For me they served as extra eyes and ears.

For example, they hired guides to lead them into a nearby river to find a giant, round twenty-foot high stone covered with petroglyphs. They climed the stone like alpinists and filled the carvings with white chalk to get their shots.

The team brought back pictures to show me. A huge thing. One day there will be marked paths to the *tiki* in the river and it will be one of the wonders of Atuona.

They charted a boat to the nearby island of Tahu Ata to witness the first telephone going into operation and to film the first customer talking to his sister in Papeete. He was so trembly with emotion he could barely hold the telephone.

Another time the team went to Fatu Hiva where *tapa*, bark cloth, is still made. "About twenty families are involved in creating the ancient *tapa* but you have to know which families to go to for the best cloth." Prices, they said, ranged from $12.50 to $25 for a large piece.

At breakfast together before parting we exchanged impressions.

Their overall impression after two weeks of filming in the Marquesas was the lassitude of the people.

"In the Orient," said Maurice, "the people will work twenty hours a day without stopping. Here the people are perfectly content to sit on a rock twenty hours a day."

Big discussion. The missionaries were responsible. The earliest French government was responsible.

Today the Marquesan takes the French underwritten copra, the family allotment, the free freight transportation, the free medicine as part of his due. He sits on a rock and watches the world go by.

The television team had a great advantage in having in Atuona an international *chanteur* who had found in Hiva Oa his hiding place. He wouldn't talk to an American journalist but welcomed the Belgium countrymen with open hospitality including piloting them about in his twin-engine Piper.

Baudouin Saeremans, the cameraman, nominated as his most memorable impression the aerial tour of the islands, often only three or four yards above the waves, looking up never-visited valleys and sweeping at the best camera angle along the rugged coasts.

The sound man, Vincent Verhaeren, thought the giant *tiki* in the river most outstanding as it symbolized the past power of the Marquesan people.

Hiva Oa is part of the southern group of islands which also includes Tahu Ata and Fatu Hiva.

The north group of islands includes the island of Nuku Hiva where the new airfield is, Ua-Pou and Ua Huka with a serviceable airfield. Ua Huka was my next destination.

I left my little run-down bungalow with new-found appreciation for homely comforts.

I had spent the evenings reading Melville and Stevenson under a single, bare light bulb.

I had battled mosquitos and bakery noises.

But the *fare* took on a new substance when one day a couple from a yacht lunched with me at Chez Rauzy and the lady, accustomed to a minute bunk and a tiny stateroom and a sponge bath, looked at my bungalow and asked, "Do you live in that building all by yourself?"

Stevenson concluded his visit to Atuona with a vignette which is memorable.

A former chief who boasted of his cannibalism came on board to say goodbye. Stevenson never liked the man. The chief had stated in his bragging that his favorite human morsels were the fingers.

When it came to the final farewells, Stevenson couldn't erase the picture of the former cannibal bending tenderly — lovingly — over Mrs. Stevenson's hand.

UA HUKA…The End Of The Northern Line …Where Wild Horses Run And Stone Gods Wait On A Hill…The Village Of Hane…The World's Quaintest Post Office.

On a small scale map, the island of Ua Huka looks like it is a five-minute flight away from Hiva Oa but the two-engined Otter of Air Polynésie kept going and going through the cloudy, dismal sky.

A half an hour later an island appeared in view and the plane made its descent, flying over a small bay, through a pass of low hills.

Wild goats were spotted by experienced passengers on a cliff face. The inexperienced passengers had no trouble spotting the wild horses which dotted the landscape.

The surprise at Ua Huka airport was the lack of transportation. There wasn't any.

The theory of waiting around with a dumb expression until somebody took charge of you didn't work at all at Ua Huka.

I looked dumb for four hours at the open-air airport shed until a ride was finally organized.

A young French couple, Gérard Tompa and his attractive blond wife, Françoise, along with a sub-teen age daughter, Carole, were obviously in the same predicament although they had such a large amount of luggage that I assumed that they were surely an official family of the state or the church.

But no, they were from a town near Paris and on a long vacation and going to visit a boyhood friend of Gérard's, a character who had gone back to nature and started a banana plantation back in the bush, a three-hour hike from the nearest village.

Finally the manager of the airfield pulled up in a jeep, motioned us to put our baggage in and we began another cliff-hugging, one-way muddy road descent for about ten breathless kilometers to the tiny village of Hane.

He pulled up in front of a small wooden cottage and the French family unloaded their gear and the manager asked me where I wanted to go. I gave him the name of a person who supposedly rented bungalows. He told me the person was off the island. It was almost dark.

There was no choice but to move in with the French family into the house of Mme. Vii Fournier.

Our hostess was dark of skin and black of hair which was tinged with grey. The hair was pulled back into a bun and at night she let it down and carefully brushed it in the light of the kerosene lantern. She had an ageless face although she had to be over fifty. She had a thirty-two-year-old daughter living in France married to a musician and another daughter living in Hane with ten children married to a local wood carver. With a good make-up artist, Mme. Fournier could have played a voodoo sorceress or, properly draped, the elegant lady with a past clientele of rich friends.

There were two bedrooms. The French family took the room with one double and one single bed and I took the other. Big double bed. No sheets. (Mme. Fournier made it clear that we were to sleep on top of the beds...not in them.)

For a week the beach towel I had fortunately packed served as coverlet, bath towel and security blanket.

Off a small living room, a concrete walk led to the kitchen. We were to learn that Mme. Fournier, during the time of my stay, slept on a mat on the kitchen floor.

Between the living room and the kitchen were two small rooms for a washbowl and toilet and a shower, cold water of course.

Mme. Fournier said there was nothing to eat but we could go down to the "store" and buy food for dinner.

How many times now when I go into an air-conditioned, brightly lighted, thoroughly stocked supermarket do I think of the "store" at Hane.

It was a room of a house. About six feet by twelve feet. No lights. Dusty. A wooden counter ran its length and three wooden shelves held a pitiful assortment of canned and bottled goods.

The only protein item was canned mackerel. No other fish. No meat. No bread.

We bought two tins of mackerel, two packages of biscuits, a can of Australian canned milk, some rice and sugar.

Not what you'd call gourmet dining.

After dinner, being as there was no electricity, there was little to do but go to bed. Or go onto bed. And lie there. And put your hands behind your head and think: "What am I doing here?"

Outside the rain of the witch continued.

The next morning Gérard took off in the rain up the mountain to find their friend. He was prepared to spend the night in the bush if necessary.

UA HUKA

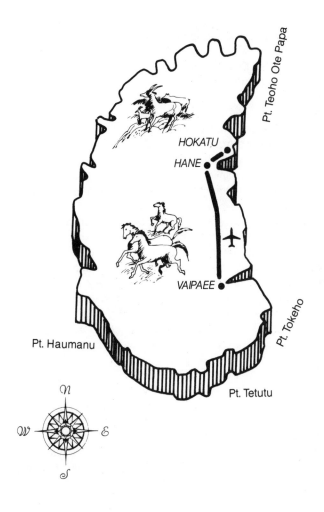

Pt. Teoho Ote Papa

HOKATU

HANE

VAIPAEE

Pt. Tokeho

Pt. Haumanu

Pt. Tetutu

In my back bedroom I set up a wicker table for my typewriter and while it rained, assembled and reviewed notes and wrote first impressions:

Hane is one of three villages on Ua Huka. It has an infirmary and a post office. There are fourteen houses.

Hokatu, a village in the next valley, about two kilometers east, has only a half dozen houses but the store there bakes bread several times a week. It is the only bakery on the island.

Vaipaee is the largest village on Ua Huka with about twenty houses. It is also the port town. A wharf was under construction so that inter-island boats could tie up to a dock.

The coconut trees are not banded with metal to keep the rats from the nuts because there are no rats on Ua Huka. When the boats begin to tie up alongside the shore, infestation of rats is anticipated.

Gérard returned after lunch with his friend, Paul, who led a fat horse, formerly wild and thin, now fat and sleek from eating coconuts and bananas and leaves of palm.

Paul was around fifty, bespectacled, unshaven. He had been in the bush for twelve years and came to Hane about once a month for his mail, mostly magazines from France.

Once he took back a teen-age girl from the village but she left him.

While Paul was at the house, Mme. Fournier would continually chase his two dogs off the concrete runway between the kitchen and the cottage and I heard Paul speak to them softly while massaging their ears, "Ah, visiting is hard."

Paul took us down to one of the local woodcarvers in his outdoor *atelier.* The workroom was formerly a *chefferie,* the official office of the village chief. When the system of chiefs was replaced with elected mayors, a new office, *la mairie,* was built for the mayor, *le maire.*

Mme. Fournier's son-in-law, Moe Puhetini, forty, had been carving all of his life. Currently he was working on a spear and also finishing a carved bowl. The spear was of redwood, easy to carve but the bowl was of *toa,* a handsome but tough hardwood, difficult to work.

The price of the spear, about a yard and a half long, was $36. A similar spear, one yard long, would be $24. Moe evidently priced his carvings by the foot.

The handsome bowl would cost the same as the spear, $36. I asked him if it would be finished by Saturday morning and would he take a check on the Bank of Tahiti. The response was enthusiastically affirmative. It being my birthday, I bought myself a birthday present.

Moe was using as a carving tool half an umbrella stave stuck into a wooden handle and for paring wood, a blade from a pair of scissors honed down to razor sharpness.

He estimated there were about ten active sculptors on Ua Huka and they sold their carvings to the weekly boats, the airline pilots and the few tourists who find their way to the Marquesas.

Later we went up to the end of the village to the home of John Fournier, Moe's *patron* or boss, and looked at a carved two-foot table top for a little over $200 and an axe with a carved handle and original adze for its cutting tool for $85.

We then crossed the dirt road to Joseph Fournier's house — half of the valley is made up of Fourniers — and looked at a *tanoa,* a traditional wooden bowl which in olden times would hold the head of the chief who was decapitated at death.

Can't you picture a Western host passing cocktail peanuts in a *tanoa*?

Joseph also had for sale sweetly scented wooden hair pins carved into Marquesan figures made out of precious sandalwood. Each, $3.60.

That night made me appreciate birthdays of the past. One recent birthday had been spent at Gleneagles in Scotland and we had much wine and a sparkling birthday cake and tuxedoed waiters surrounding the table singing in Italian and German accents and we danced until the orchestra quit and we laughed until the last light went out.

That night in Hane the entire birthday dinner was a limeade beverage, a first course of fresh grapefruit segments, a second course of fresh coconut and a fresh banana for dessert.

Lantern out at seven-thirty.

Miracle of miracles, the next day the sun came out!

In two weeks in the Marquesas that was the single dry day. Unseasonal. Unless you factored in the lost-companion witchery.

Hane is cradled between two long arms of land reaching into the sea and with the sunshine beckoning I went for a three hour walk along the coast road, first reaching the tip of the eastern arm in an easy thirty minute stroll. Off the end of the land a huge rock juts out of the sea and is known as *Pain du sucre* or in English "Sugar

Loaf." On top of the rock there appeared to be the remains of a *meae* (Marquesan for temple) but I was later told it is only what is left of a geographical base marker used in former surveying.

From the Point I could see down into the next valley of Hokatu with its green floor and the white steepled church. Pretty.

Mme. Fournier had said the village store in Hokatu had a few more things to offer than the Hane store...it was also operated by a Fournier.

Making the descent I finally found in the almost empty village a person to point out the house which doubled as the store. The owners — uncharacteristically not Chinese —were having lunch but the lady, much amused by my French, opened the store for my convenience. No bread. That would be the next day. She did have *firifiri,* the doughnut type cake I had bought at the Sunday market in Papeete. Took one *firifiri,* two cans of corned beef, a large can of sardines, a can of beets, a can of *petit pois.* $5.65.

That afternoon I went by Moe's *atelier* again and talked to the village school teacher. Renée and his wife who is also a school teacher each make about $1,100 a month, tax free. They are the wealthiest couple on the island.

He explained that for the coming Fête they were starting to revive the old Marquesan chants and dances.

If I were to be at Hane where the three villages were going to gather to celebrate the fourteenth of July, I would hear the *tarava* which is similar to that of Tahiti and also the *ruu,* the chants of the northern group. (The same chanting is called *rari* in the southern group.)

The local Marquesan dances are called *mahua* and *putu.*

He invited us to come to his house that night to hear the local music.

Gérard had harpooned an eel in the river that morning which was the *pièce de résistance* for dinner that night. I resisted.

My main course was fried bananas with a peanut butter biscuit.

On the way down to Renée's house the stars were out. Magnificent night.

To Mme. Fournier: "It will be a beautiful day tomorrow."

Mme. Fournier: *"Peut-être."* (Perhaps)

"It wouldn't rain, surely?"

"Peut-être."

"In any case it will be good for fishing."

"Peut-être."

From then on she was known as *Madame Peut-être.*

In Renée's concrete triplex there was a side table completely covered with stereo equipment. Obviously a place of honor and a source of pride.

In the middle of the room stood a double bed. A couch was along one wall, chairs along another.

Renée played *tarava* songs with the familiar Tahitian beat and then *ruu* chants, religious, antique songs which had their own rhythm and discreet syncopation.

When our group of five entered the house, it was the signal for gathering and the room soon swelled with people. There were twenty-four adults, teen-agers and infants in the room.

Moe was there and his wife, Sophie, pregnant. A few of their ten children were there.

For each child in French Polynesia there is a subsistence allowance and a visitor begins to wonder if the largest industry isn't the begetting of children.

"How many children do you have?" asked Moe.

"Two daughters," I answered.

He shouted with laughter. "You don't work!" he said.

Françoise made a dish for lunch of grapefruit segments and sliced bananas covered with lime juice. Heavenly.

Gérard came back from ocean fishing, pale from seasickness but with a pailful of fish including a mess of squid.

That afternoon we went down to the infirmary which also serves as the post office.

The infirmary is operated by a male nurse...*infirmier*...who is a paramedic.

The *infirmier* is also the postmaster.

The hospital was closed but the post office was open. The post office consisted of the *infirmier's* office desk.

Amidst the odors of disinfectant he took my two letters to the next room and weighed them on baby scales! One letter was to the United States and the other letter was to England.

It cost less to mail the letters from Hane than it would have from Papeete.

I drew this fact to the attention of the jolly *infirmier* and he just gave a what-the-hell shrug and said, "I never mailed letters to the United States or England before."

Living with Mme. Peut-être was one of Moe's and Sophie's ten children, Oscar, a bright boy of about ten years who lived to fish.

After school and despite the morning rain, he promised to guide us into the hills to see the *tikis*.

The path was slushy, frequently ankle deep in mud up slopes so steep and so slippery we could only go ahead by pulling ourselves along with pathside trees and brush.

Mosquitoes were thick.

We walked over a *paepae*, a former house site, and skirted the remains of what must have been a large *meae*.

Perspiration was heavy when we took a minute break in a clearing of large trees. The hike had been promoted as a quarter of an hour walk and we had already been climbing thirty minutes.

"We are close to it now, aren't we, Oscar?"

I couldn't believe my ears.

"*Peut-être*," said Oscar.

A dense grove of wild bananas at the foot of a last knoll watchguarded three *tikis* hidden in tall grass.

Gérard macheted the surrounding grass so we could photograph them.

The *tikis* were about three feet high and shaped in oval columns on which faces of the gods had been carved. Solemn. Big-eyed. The slit-mouth smile. Watching. Waiting. Waiting for someone or something. When the person comes or the event comes, the *tikis* will be ready on top of the hill at the head of Hane Valley.

Coming back down took fifteen minutes, sometimes sliding on foot, sometimes sliding on the *derriére*.

I returned to Madame Peut-être, who had washed my clothes so meticulously the day before, with pants muddy up to the knees and a seat caked with mud, a shirt soiled and soaked with sweat. Like a good mother she shook her head and laughed and pointed to the tub in the washhouse.

For dinner, thanks to Gérard the fisherman, we had *poisson cru* and grilled fish.

The kerosene lamp was turned out at eight that night.

We stayed up late.

On Ua Huka you make up your own entertainment.

Hike up to the ancient *tikis*, climb higher to the plateaus where there are exhilarating views.

You can chase wild horses or shoot wild goats.

It was difficult to believe considering the continual rain during my stay but only a couple of years before there had been a dreadful drought — not an uncommon occurrence in the Marquesas — and much of the animal life had died.

The famous wild horses of Ua Huka are now comparatively few in number.

You can go fishing in the ocean where there are many lobsters and many sharks. Big lobsters. Big sharks.

You can go diving.

You can rent a horse to ride and even hire a car from Eduard Kavee and make the round trip to Vaipaee for one thousand francs, $12.50.

In Vaipaee you can eat at the restaurant Tantie Laura where your meal will cost about three hundred francs ($3.50), including wine. Also rent a room.

You can do your own archaeological exploring in the *meaes* and *paepaes*. Dr. Sinoto supervised a dig on the beach in front of Hane but with disappointing results, I was told.

You can catch freshwater shrimp in the streams and pick your own dinner.

Ua Huka offers a different experience.

The last afternoon, the sun found a hole through the overhead clouds and lighted a distant peak of sheer rock with gold. Framed by black clouds, it looked like a portal of the golden gates of heaven.

I went back to Moe the carver to pick up my bowl. He had finished two and gave me a choice. Difficult. I picked the larger one and couldn't get it into my suitcase and went back to Papeete with cabin baggage of one Marquesan bowl, one flight bag, a typewriter and tennis racquet. Fortunately Air Polynésie is accustomed to that kind of traveler.

I examined Moe's carving carefully and asked questions about the design work and the superb finish. "The oil of an exotic nut," I thought, "found only in hidden, remote valleys."

Moe showed me his magic finishing ingredient. A can of Johnson's floor wax.

The manager of the airfield came by to pick me up. Ten o'clock pick-up for a one o'clock airplane. No matter. You learn to go when there is a ride available.

I said good-bye to the brave French family who promised to write me about the conclusion of their adventure. They didn't and I have remained forever curious. To Mme. Fournier I gave a check on a Tahiti bank which she has yet to cash.

The day of departure also brought stronger winds and clear skies.

At the airport a loitering Marquesan looked at my carved bowl and asked, "How much?"

"How much do you think?"

"One thousand."

Crunch. I had paid three.

When the airplane took off I was able at last to see the valley of Hane. Filled with sunshine it looked idyllic nesting in its protecting arms of land...the large bayfront a playground for small white waves to frolic with black sand beach...its neat white houses and the steeple of the village church peeking from beneath a coconut tree camouflage. The thick cover of green extended a quarter of the way up the mountains until the slopes became sheer cliffs rising to God where white terns played tag in the thermal drafts.

Write it down. The village of Hane on the island of Ua Huka in the northern group of the Marquesan Archipelago.

About as far away as you can get...and want to go back.

10. Les Jours De Fête

The Biggest, Longest Party In The South Pacific...Bastille Day, The Fourteenth Of July...Independence Day For The French... Party Month For The Tahitians.

On the fourteenth of July, 1789 the insurgents in Paris stormed the fort-prison, the *Bastille*, and released the political inmates and destroyed the hated symbol of oppression.

There followed a large street party.

In Tahiti on the fourteenth of July, 1789 there were no French, no streets and no party. The Tahitians have been making up for it ever since.

The Jours de Fêtes is a season unto itself in Tahiti.

Four times bigger than Christmas. Twenty times as big as New Year's.

The Tahitians love to dance, sing and play...the Fête rolls them all together...and the people gather on each island in their population center and really get it on.

It is a *local* celebration. It is not designed as a tourist come-on. It is done by and for the local people and highlighted by friendly competition with their neighbors.

On the island of Tahiti, the first event in importance is the canoe (*pirogue*) races. Secondly in importance...no, there is no "first" and "second"...everything has its place and is part of the montage of the Fête.

There is a week-long song and dance contest.

In addition there are water-ski exhibitions, sailing, canoe races, a huge parade, javelin throwing, a golf tournament, motorboat racing, contests in palm weaving and coconut husking, a major dance party that goes all night — I mean, *all night* — two races of fruit porters, one in the day and one in the evening with torches.

A huge waterfront carnival scene is created for those who want to buy spun candy and ride a merry-go-round or take a chance on a spinning wheel and maybe win a blanket. (Win a blanket in Tahiti?)

The last night is the biggest emotional sky-rocket night when the awards are made for all the winners, especially for the best singers and dancers.

189

Did I forget horse racing?
The bicycle and motorcycle races?
The children's contests?
Roughly that is the content of the Papeete Fête.
It lasts from the thirteenth of July to the twenty-second of July.
Officially. Ten days.
Other islands have similar events but tailored to their own customs.
On each island the Mayor determines the end of the Fête and we have heard, on Bora Bora for example, everybody has so much fun the party keeps going on and on. The shattered population sometimes doesn't come back together until November.

On the Marquesan island of Ua Huka the Fête rotates among the three villages and the Mayor usually holds the celebration to three days depending upon the number of *bagarres,* the fights that break out.

Mind you, they aren't *serious* fights. Once upon a time I was at a Tahitian party and a local gentleman standing in a doorway turned around and slugged another local gentleman, knocking him down a flight of stairs.

"What did you do that for?" asked the second gentleman, picking himself up against the side of an automobile fender which had suddenly arrested his tumbling.

"You insulted me," said the first local gentleman.

"When," asked the second local gentleman looking around for a club.

"Last week," responded the first gentleman picking up a chair.

Ten minutes later they went home together arm in arm.

Throughout French Polynesia where the local population finds little creative inspiration in twentieth century activities, the return to the old customs focuses their talents on to what they like to do best. The whole place *pops.*

Know in advance that Les Fêtes de juillet de Tahiti avoid any mention of the fourteenth. It is assumed that the celebration is not one day. Good heavens. You'd barely get the party started. It is *July* that is important. Also the Tahitian word for July is *Tiurai* and you'll see the word on many posters and in many newspaper stories... *Tiurai*...July. All month long.

The first evidence of les Fêtes is at the waterfront when the booths of the fair start to go into place with much pounding and confusion.

There will be booths for minor games of chance. Booths for beer and wine. Booths for crepes and hot dogs and barbecued meats. Electric car circuits, miniature bikes and miniature racing cars. The scene blares with canned music and smells of food cooking. It is loud and messy and very much part of les Fêtes. The waterfront scene goes on for three weeks.

In 1978, for the first time, officials banned the sale of hard booze and gambling. The consensus of the operators themselves, except those with gambling and booze, was that the move made a happier fair.

If you went to the Marae Arahurahu at P.K. 21.5 during your round-the-island trip, you will remember its impressive setting in the valley. The temple is a lovely backdrop for the first event of les Fêtes on the thirteenth of July, when a royal scene from pre-European times is re-created.

The event takes place at dusk. Light enough to see where to park and where to sit and then in the dark, black enough for the torches and fires to set the mood of mysterious temple rituals.

Go early and get a parking place next to the temple. Don't be tempted to pull into a side-of-the-road parking place. Go all the way to the end. There will be enough room.

Three bleacher stands surround the open temple. Go to the right-hand bleacher stand and you'll see more action.

As the bleachers fill, pre-ceremony entertainment is the singing of traditional forms of Tahitian music...the swinging church hymns ...the ancient chanting songs (and when you hear that off-key falsetto it will first sound discordant but you learn to appreciate it)...and the familiar drum songs with their rat-a-tat-tatting.

The entertainment is particularly welcome because you'll find that Fête events tend to lag about a half an hour behind published starting times.

The first words you usually hear before any event are: *"Mesdames et messieurs, nous regrettons..."* or "sorry, folks, we're running a little late."

At dark the event starts with a torch-bearing runner touching off flickering torches around the perimeter and in the middle of the temple.

Behind the temple a bonfire is set ablaze, back-lighting the towering altar and casting white billows of smoke into the sky. A nice theatrical touch.

The re-created scene the night we went was the coronation of a new chief.

A high priest surrounded with attendant warriors entered slowly. He walked with Shakespearean majesty, each step in careful measure. (Because he was an important chief his "role" was a comfortable one, requiring little "acting.")

Following came the warriors with sacrifices: the stalks of bananas...the bundles of coconuts...and...g-a-s-p...a palm-wrapped object with an arm sticking out...a human body!

A witch doctor followed the procession at a distance...beating stones together in a particular rhythm to frighten the evil spirits away.

The young chief was brought on in the same careful, measured fashion and taken to the middle of the open temple where with many incantations and speeches to the gods he was wrapped in *tapa* and feathers and cloaks and crowned with a splendid headdress.

A string of lovely torch-bearing male and female dancers lined the side of the temple in the ceremony. (In the olden days the women wouldn't have been allowed to take any part in such a ceremony but in order to give the tableau more color and *whumph* there were women.)

As a finale, a living, pulsating, undulating *vahine* danced her way to the temple tempting the new chief and, still hip-swinging, slowly led him off the altar and around the temple and — *blackout!*

The entire performance took less than an hour and we thought it a fine way to start the Fête.

The day of days starts with a salvo of cannon.

Then a parade.

The crowd begins assembling early in the morning and as the sidewalks overflow you find that your "early bird" spot on the curb is difficult to maintain.

The parade comes down rue de Charles Gaulle from the direction of the Cathedral, passes the reviewing stand built in front of the Territorial Assembly building and the High Commissioner's Residence, then turns left at Avenue Bruat, goes to the Gendarmerie and disbands.

In the reviewing stand are the government *fonctionnaires,* the military brass and the elected politicos.

One of the delicious scenes of the Fête is to watch the tardy arriving *militaire.*

He is starched, neatly creased, unwrinkled, immaculately gloved...and furious. Why are they late? *She* is the reason they are late! Isn't she always!

She trails three steps behind him dressed in flowery matron style, her little high-heeled pumps going tickity-tickity on the pavement as she tries to catch up. Her cheeks are puffed both with the physical exertion and the effrontery. The hell it was her fault! I promise you a half a dozen such family scenes.

Then for another little giggle go down to the reviewing stand before the parade starts and watch the gathering of the Important Men Smoking Cigarettes. It is a scene out of a Peter Sellers *Pink Panther* motion picture. All of the characters are there.

The parade itself is very satisfactory.

Lots of uniforms pass in review. Um-pah-pah bands and the rattle of drums fill the air. Floats and firemen and dance groups. Fête queens smile and wave at the crowd.

A huge mob of youth pass wearing T-shirts of the YMCA and then a smaller mob of archers, their brown Tahitian faces looking slightly incongruous under little green William Tell hats.

A Polynesian group from Campbell, California is followed by a troupe of high-stepping, white-booted, baton-twirling majorettes complete with black net stockings, shimmering blue satin shorty uniforms and high cadet hats, white plumed!

Where were they from? New Caledonia!

Wait a minute, you say to yourself. Somebody must have switched the signs. The Polynesians must be from New Caledonia and the baton twirlers must be from Campbell, California.

But, no. That represents the modern people of the Pacific. Going everywhere. Doing everything. Borrowing from each other.

Not one but two separate groups of motorcyclists pass in review filling the air with numbing noises and horrid blue smoke. Each group features a stunting cyclist who hangs back and then roars forward on a rear wheel. They could be replaced. Or let them walk beside their bikes. The exercise would probably kill them. We voted them out.

Before the parade is finished hustle over to the residence of the High Commissioner.

After the parade, the folklorique dancers are officially presented to the officials who are seated, rajah fashion, on the front steps of the residence.

It is one of the best scenes of the Fête...and it is free.

Go early to get a place near the front of the building and on the left-hand side so that sun will be at your back. Cooler. Better visibility. Much better for pictures.

The dance groups in turn give short performances and some offer gifts — flowers, fruit, wooden bowls — to the High Commissioner and to his guest, in this instance the Prince of Tonga. You are close enough to touch them and to appreciate the cultural subtleties.

For example the visiting Samoan dance group gave a superb miniature performance, full of nuances, life and humor which were almost entirely missed when they performed on the large stage a week later during the dance contest.

Also, if you are a camera bug, it is an excellent place to get off-stage pictures of the dancers.

Mark it down on your Programme Officiel which is printed only in French: *Visite au haut commissaire par les groupes folkloriques en sa résidence de Tarahoi.*

Rated excellent.

The program listed a parade of canoes in the harbor for later the same day and we expected to see a colorful flotilla of clubs passing in review. Nothing of the kind. An occasional canoe would paddle to the starting line and rehearse a start. Individually. Haphazardly. Forget it.

Horse racing was another event scheduled at the Hippodrome that afternoon.

Surprisingly the stakes for the six "country races" were not so small. Purses per race averaged about $1,000.

If you drive to the Hippodrome, go early and take the right hand road which leads to an elevated parking place above the track and you can use your car as a grandstand seat.

You'll find a tiny spectators' stand, a parimutuel betting stand (one-hundred and one-thousand franc bets) and also a bar selling cold beer and iced champagne.

We went early. Found a perfect parking place in our high-seated Land Rover. We had picked our "winners" from the mimeographed list of races...had money at the ready...and it started to rain...and it rained...and it rained.

The famous sight of the jockeys riding bareback, dressed in *pareus* and wearing flowered *couronnes* was not to be ours.

Obviously the dirt track, probably clay, was too dangerous and they called off the meet for the day. Being a weekend, there were no newspapers and we never learned that the races were rescheduled for Sunday. We missed the event.

Shocking sequence when the races were held. A favorite horse was slipped a tranquillizer! "The cordial world of horse racing has been broken," said the *Le Journal de Tahiti* the next day reporting the doping.

Country horse racing, indeed!

The night of the fourteenth is the night of the Grand Bal.

At one time the Grand Bal was the season's social grand moment with the best dresses being brought from Paris or hand-made many months before the event and the dearest family jewelry being pulled out of dusty jewel boxes. Many of the men even stuffed themselves into formal attire. It was a glittering time.

But the inaugural dance became popularized and its location was moved to the waterfront and the facade slipped. The Grand Bal became less grand.

A movement was then begun to restore the Grand Bal to its former glorious station and in 1978 the location was moved to the lawn of the High Commissioner's residence.

The best tables for four cost $40 a table. Farther back they were $25. A sign at the ticket sales counter at the Fare Manihini informed you that the wearing of slippers, shorts, jeans or T-shirts was forbidden and also that you shouldn't bring your own liquor. (Standard drinks were $4 each. Champagne *started* at $35 a bottle.)

The poster advertising the evening said that the orchestra would be enlivened by the oldtimers from Quinn's Bar and the dancing would last from nine p.m. until *l'aube*...the dawn.

We had a ball at the Grand Bal.

When was the last time you danced to a tenor sax playing *Ramona?* Or a slide trombone leading the number *I Wonder Who's Kissing Her Now.* If you wanted to dance to something newer, there was a banjo swinging on *Ma, He's Making Eyes At Me.*

When was the last time you danced next to the Prince of Tonga who was dancing with the Fête queen dressed in a black gown slit to the thigh where it was clasped with a pink rose?

The fifty-foot square wooden plank floor thumped with the bouncing of the dancers. The overhead string of multi-colored lights swayed with the motion.

The sixteen-member band played almost constantly. They would do two numbers, take a short break and then launch into two more. Never took a longer break. If they were "oldtimers" from Quinn's, they had something in their Geritol besides ice cubes.

The whole evening was a big laugh.

There were two immense bars and even at $4 a drink the waitresses couldn't serve the dance-thirsty crowd fast enough and you went to the bar and ordered your own. Also you could buy a *quiche* or a pizza. Oh, yes, a local dance habit. It is considered very proper to ask any girl to dance. You go to her table, tap her on the shoulder and then go out to the dance floor and wait for her. You dance. At the end of the music...you walk away from her, letting her find her own way back to her own table. *Thunk*. You asked her to dance, not to chat.

We danced almost every number — memory tunes, rumbas, rock, Tahitian — from nine-thirty to two-thirty in the morning. The place was still jammed when we left. How many would last until dawn? About half, said a friend experienced from many past Fêtes. Then they would go downtown to a Chinese restaurant and eat noodles.

Our intention to stay until the end started to give out at the knees.

At eight ayem the next morning would begin the first of the two days of canoe racing and we didn't want to miss the opener.

In front of us was a drive out to the house in the country. At best three hours of sleep. Up. Shower. Back to Papeete for the races.

We tossed it in and slowly danced our way across the floor to the exit and reluctantly went home. Like aging ball players, the once record-breaking party-goers give out first in the legs.

Mark it down "Must." Grand Bal. Great evening.

The first day of canoe races is reserved for crews of three and six paddlers. There are four categories of competition: men, women, young men, young women. Eight races in all.

The second day, and more exciting, are the races for single rowers and crews of sixteen in double-hulled canoes. Another eight races.

Starting line for the contest is at the Charles de Gaulle Monument where a floating judges' stand is anchored in the harbor.

The race course is two miles long, to the harbor entrance, a short lateral leg left and then return to the mid-harbor starting point. About two miles.

If a major vessel were to come to Papeete during the canoe races, I have no doubt the captain would be told to stand off until the races were completed.

You have to remind yourself that this is the most important day of the year for the men and the women involved. They have slaved, trained, sweated, prayed for this day...and victory.

About thirty-five racing clubs are involved with a total membership of six thousand rowers!

The crowd is huge.No wonder. In addition to the mob of rowers add the girl friends, boy friends, relatives...all of the tourists...all the people from other islands. Boulevard Pomare is jammed with cars. Parked on sidewalks. Parked on the medial strip. Everywhere. People are crunch-to-crunch along the harbor front. Alongside the sidewalk are the brochette vans barbecuing meat, selling soft drinks, sandwiches, beer. Cold coconuts are being peddled by vendors from large ice chests and you find that it is not the tourists but the locals who buy them at 60¢, for the thirst-quenching water.

Under the trees where the rowing clubs are assembling around their canoes — they extend at least a half a mile — there is another mob scene. People sitting on pandanus mats, transistor radios hanging from tree branches playing music and news of the races, children crawling over grandmothers' laps, neighbors laughing and joking with neighbors, everyone — men, women, children — dressed in *pareus* and wearing flowered *couronnes*. It is a happy festival scene.

But not everywhere.

On a raft at water's edge sat a rumpled vahine in her peek-a-boo party dress...the faded couronne drooping over her brow. She dangled one leg over the edge of the raft, shoulders slumped forward, eyes vacant to the excitement of the day. It had obviously been a long night. My slightly sagging spirits coupled with hers in sympathy. Somehow, Little Lady, we would get through this day.

The starting line was clogged with three-man canoes ready for the first race.

Each club had entered at least three teams. The total number of canoes was well over one hundred.

Looking down the starting line from the shore to the buoy in mid-harbor, you could see the canoes jockeying for the farthest inch forward.

"*Haere muri! Haere muri!*" the judge kept pleading. "Get back. Get back."

A rower stood up at the far end of the line and yelled something back at the judge. Tempers were tender. No beer, no smokes for three months. No women for two weeks.

Then, almost as one body, the fleet of *pirogues* started to move forward like a huge animal, one body of sleek, muscular brown backs. The spectators on shore became enveloped with the pent-up emotions, the physical power. It was tight, tense.

The crack of the starting gun and the simultaneous starting command of the judge made everyone jump with released nervousness.

Hundreds of paddles slashed the water. The race was on.

The get-away in the packed throng of race canoes is critical.

The *pirogues* with only inches of freeboard are delicately trimmed and the slightest imbalance or a bumping from another canoe spells disaster.

Also the rear paddler has the non-enviable task of maintaining a straight line of direction without the help of a rudder using only his paddle which is also an important part of the forward driving force. A delicate job.

A paddle could break. An outrigger strut could collapse under the strain. A slight steering error could be made.

Suddenly it happened!

Fifty yards from the starting line a canoe capsized and collided with another. The accident created a domino effect of wrecks...two, three, four, five canoes went down.

The leaders wanted to get clear of the mob of boats as quickly as possible and, in a surprisingly short time, the first canoes were approaching the first buoy while the last canoes had barely cleared the starting line.

The leaders rounded the first buoy, headed laterally towards the shore to the second buoy and making the turn, headed back for the finish line.

If you stayed close to the judges' stand, you could hear which club was ahead.

On shore there were some shouts of encouragement but not a great deal.

The canoes carried no identification except for color trims known only to the local crowd.

Tautira, the favorite, was in the lead. Tautira. The loud-speaker blared the name repeatedly.

At the finish line, leading by two lengths, Tautira spurted forward just to show that the team had plenty left.

Tautira won.

The races present an intriguing lesson in Polynesian mannerisms. Down the beach where the teams started, calmness prevailed. The returning victors, at best, were casually applauded.

We had noted this custom earlier at the Maeva races.

Departing rowers for the following race were not sent off with any great volley of cheers from fellow rowers and families and friends. Maybe a good-natured jesting call followed by hoots of laughter.

The rah-rah football psychology of the coach-cheer-leader-rooting-section-team-spirit was absent.

Was today the most important day in their racing? We were surprised by the lack of emotion but reassured that this is the Polynesian manner. Even when they care most deeply, it is considered bad form to display undue enthusiasm.

Another lesson in Polynesian manners! No matter how late a crew left the beach, no matter how many canoes were already on the starting line, patience was practiced.

You'd think, well, now they are about to start when — woops — off in the distance you saw a flash of paddles...another contestant. And the rowers on the line sat patiently. And waited.

Each race took close to an hour...and by noon the Grand Bal fatigue began to win.

That night was the race of the fruit porters carrying thirty kilograms of fruit in a torchlit contest down Boulevard Pomare.

That night was a smashing party in honor of a Tahitian dancer who had done much to re-establish Tahitian dancing during the last forty years.

That night we had an early dinner and went to bed.

The next morning the second match of the canoe races featured single-crew canoes and the sixteen-man teams which are considered the ulimate test in team rowing.

Accordingly, we bought reserved "tribune" seats in a bleacher section near the judges' stand...$6 each. The ticket guarantees you a seat but not a specific seat. Go early and sit as high and as far to the left as possible so that you can see down the course. Also take binoculars and, if possible, a small transistor radio to follow the race.

The single-man canoe races had at least one hundred entries. Marvelous sight on a bright Sunday morning.

In such a pack it was surprising that they got away without the loss of a canoe.

Who won in the mile and a half race? Tautira, of course.
The women and juniors followed in single races and then the major
race began to form...the sixteen-man canoe race.

First prize, $2,500!

Directly behind the bleachers was the assembling point for the
Papara Club whose white canoes carried a blue trim. We watched
their preparations as they put three canoes into the race.

The double canoes are separate canoes bound together with two
yokes, one in front and one in the rear. No outrigger.

At the starting line the water was choked again with the boats and
the judge was going hoarse trying to get them in line.

"Haere muri...haere muri...!"

When the starting gun was sounded the water boiled as each
double canoe tried to gain a trouble-free front position.

It looked like a clean start. Then three hundred yards from the
starting line there was a collision. Three boats sunk. Half a mile later
a second mix-up occurred and three more canoes went down to the
gunwales.

Behind the bleachers there was no visible emotion. Just gloom.
Two of their three canoes had gone down.

Around the first buoy it was Tautira. Around the second buoy it
was Tautira.

The club was never headed.

Tautira came home a clean winner with another Tautira canoe
taking third place.

As the boats approached the finish line each tried to gain a place.
They used their last efforts and it was easy to see how a speeding
sixteen-man canoe could swamp a following canoe in its high wake. It
happened. A third canoe went down in front of the bleachers. The
canoe belonged to Papara. Three entered. Three sunk.

By the second day we had begun to distinguish the green-trimmed
white canoes of Tautira and the red and black canoes of Teva. From
the bleachers we could hear the judge call the race in progress...in
French and Polynesian.

Tautira dominated both days. The club won nine out of sixteen
races...Teva won six...leaving a single victory for one of the other
thirty-three clubs.

A new *pirogue* race was added in 1978, an open sea race, under the
sponsorship of Air New Zealand. A splendid canoe-trophy and a
$2,000 check.

Who won?

Tautira.
In the canoe racing events the little village at the end of the road won over $13,000.
Why Tautira?
Because they were closer to the sea?
Because they were farther removed from the bright lights and temptations of Papeete?
Because they had nothing better to do?
An official of the racing club association said one important reason was that due to the popularity of racing many new clubs had been formed around Tahiti, splitting up the best talent. He cited one area that formerly had one club and now they had four!
Tautira, isolated, remained single and strong. My, they were *strong*.

The following day was comparatively a day off from activity. Motorboat racing was held in the harbor. If you want to see fast boats go around and around, go and park at the overpass of the Route de l'Ouest just beyond the Olympic Swimming Pool and you can look down on the harbor and watch the action.

The next day was full of events.
First thing in the morning was a contest of palm-weaving which sounded dull but was delightful thanks to the great good humor of the Polynesian matrons who race against time to weave hats, baskets, table covers and placemats in a fun-filled contest. As a matter of fact the newspaper reported that the most enjoyable ingredient in the weaving contest is *la bonne humeur*...a sense of humor.
It took place at the Maison des Jeunes next to the Olympic pool and you should go. Especially camera freaks.
Immediately following the weaving was the coconut husking contest on the other side of the same buildings. My toes curl up at the memory of it.
Fourteen three-man teams took part in a speed contest to halve, husk, de-meat and sack ninety-three coconuts each.
Mothers were advised to keep children carefully back and under control because they could get hurt. (Hurt? They could get *split*.)
The contestants wore *pareus* and head *leis* called *heis* as uniforms. No helmets. No padded gloves. No safety shoes. A factory safety officer would have turned pale at the sight.
Two men sat on boxes with a ground-cover sheet in front of them.

They were armed with scoop-shaped knives.

The third man, barefooted mind you, would split the coconuts at his feet with an axe, break them in half manually and dump the halves at the stools of the "de-meaters" who would scoop out the meat with two or three deft strokes and toss the empty shells over their shoulders.

At the signal the contest started with the sound of the slashing axes. Chunk. Chunk. Chunk. Coconut water sprayed the air. The axe-men would stop occasionally and complete the halving job. Dump the pile before the scoopers. Take up the axes again and go through the next batch.

The ninety-three coconuts couldn't have taken more than ten minutes. Fast.

One team seemed to have victory in its hands only when they went to pour the coconut meat from their ground-cover into a sack, they missed the sack and dumped all the copra onto the ground! They came in second.

All teams finished with all toes intact.

That afternoon the javelin throwers convened at the Musée de Tahiti.

In a high wind the Tahitian throwers toss a spindly seven-foot dart at a coconut fixed on a pole thirty feet above the ground and one hundred feet away.

During the first round, they hit the coconut four times! But they were just getting their windage.

Before the afternoon was over, during a ten-minute round, the teams made a pin cushion out of the high-riding coconut, hitting it as many as twenty times!

Fun to watch.

Incredible to believe that such a small target could be hit that often.

That night was the opening of the five-night spectacle of the Tahitian song and dance contests including the participation of both amateur and professional groups.

Like the canoe racers, this would be the culmination of a year-long effort.

Three words of advice. Get a good afternoon nap. Take a sweater. Take binoculars or opera glasses. (You have to see those girls up closer!)

The scene for the dance and chant contest is at the waterfront between the Tourist Office and the Moorea boat dock. It is called Place Vaiete in the Fête program.

An immense square stage, almost at ground level, is built and surrounded on four sides by bleachers.

"Tribune A" with its back to the waterfront, is where the judges sit and to which the dancers and singers direct their performances. Seats cost $25 each. *Per night.*

The bleachers on each side are also reserved and they cost $12.50 each. The fourth side, on Boulevard Pomare, is where the singers and dancers enter and if you get an unreserved seat there you will see only the backsides of the dancers...which isn't all that bad.

We were advised that the two best nights of the five nights are opening night with all of its attendant excitement and the last night when the awards are made. I was further advised to buy the best seats for the opening night because it had more spirit, more movement and more singing and dancing...and to save money by buying the side bleachers for closing night.

Solid advice. Also we learned it was a good idea to buy tickets early and when buying side bleacher seats to get as close to "Tribune A" as possible in order to see the front of the dancers.

Tickets go on sale at the Fare Manihini tourist office about a week before the Fête. Pick up a free set of posters at the same time. They make fine give-away souvenirs when you get home.

The opening night of the "Soiree des Spectacles de Chants et Danses Folkloriques" is quite twittery with the electricity of any opening night. You win or lose a *pirogue* race cleanly but at a dance and song contest the judgement is very subjective...a matter of individual interpretation. The decisions reached over the five nights would be debated for an entire year in Papeete.

"Backstage" for the singers and dancers is half of Pomare Boulevard and the adjacent space in the park. You walk through this highly-charged scene in the half-light to get to your seat. A drum breaks out in a fast Tahitian rhythm and a nearby dancer automatically starts hip swinging as though a hidden button marked "Dance" has been pushed.

Entrances are crowded with ticket holders and those who don't have tickets...hoping for what? An extra free ticket? Or just watching the excitement?

At "Tribune A" a quarter of the way up is a solid line of desks with shaded hoods where the judges sit, their faces ghost-lighted from the bottom by their reading lamps.

At the stage apron is another solid length of press and sound consoles.

The stage bristles with microphones and the hopping in and out of soundmen adjusting mikes is a constant part of the "Soirees."

Every seat in the outdoor arena was packed when the master of ceremonies, apologizing for being tardy, announced the first contenders, a professional group.

The stage suddenly swarmed with an army of male and female dancers crossing the stage in fast rhythmic choreographed steps towards the judges' stand.

The number of participants gave a quick idea of the elaborateness of the presentations. The costumes were equally impressive and made only with indigenous Tahitian materials.

Later I was told by the manager of the professional group which won the "best costume" category that they spent $5,000 on materials alone. No estimating the labor costs for the costumes which took two months of handicraft effort.

The professional group presented five numbers including traditional dances and a chant dance *(ute)* and their "created" dance which was a dramatized legend.

Following the professional group a singing group, *himene*, presented traditional hymns and chants. They sat in a tight circle, bending to and fro rhythmically, unaccompanied by any musical instrument, a leader standing over them exhorting them with his body motions and waving hands like a conductor of a grand symphony.

Next a non-professional dance group followed the same general outline as the professional — five routines — and, like the professionals, took sample costumes after their performance to the judges for evaluation of their genuineness of Tahitian materials and the craftsmanship of work.

Each group nominated a boy and girl as their best dancer. While they performed together they were judged individually.

The groups numbered between fifty and one hundred.

No wonder the street was so crowded.

On opening night eleven groups participated . . . and the weather got colder . . . and the acts seemed to get longer.

We left at midnight. The opening night show finally finished at two ayem.

A Papeete newspaper reported the next day: "What a marvelous spectacle . . . but how long . . . and how cold!"

For four nights different groups appeared. Youngsters and grand-mothers alike sang and danced alongside all of the beautiful young people.

Church groups, organizations from other islands, district groups from around Tahiti, groups from other Pacific nations — Samoa, Hawaii, New Caledonia *and* Campbell, California! — all took part in the week-long event.

The morning of the fifth and final night the groups appeared at the Musée de Tahiti in Punaauia for film fanatics and camera bugs. The coconut trees and the lagoon and the peaks of Moorea in the background make it an ideal picture-taking location. It was crowded with people. Very popular. A great time to mingle with the per-formers, take photos of them, with them, watch the dancers go through part of their routines. A fine show and relatively inexpensive.

For a free show, the day before, at the invitation of the Mayor of Papeete, many of the dance groups appeared on the grounds of the Mairie. The groups were slipped a contribution by the Mayor who also hosted a gigantic buffet after the dancing. A solid, vote-getting gesture.

The fifth night was reserved for the people who had already won prizes and for the last review of the leading singing and dancing groups. Several would be asked to repeat segments of their routines.

Contrary to the canoe races there was to be much cheering and parochial applause. The great sporting event was taken stoically. The art form events were contrarily greeted with partisan cheering and yelling and whistling and clapping. High excitement.

Each group of singers and dancers were encouraged loudly by their backers when they mounted the stage. Their performances were loudly applauded when they finished.

A number of individual dancers in addition to the groups were asked by the judges to dance again.

More partisan cheering.

The presentation of prizes then started and it was a show unto itself.

The first place winners of the rowing, bicycle, motorcycle racing, the fruit carrying . . . all made appearances. The routine was for them to give a flower lei from their neck to the person making the presentation, a kiss on each cheek...and then perform a fast bit of *tamure!* A victory dance. The *tamure* routines were often more heartily applauded than the announcement of the prize.

Emotions began building towards the awards to the singers and the dancers.

Can you imagine the surrounding stage when a *himene* group of a hundred singers received the first prize!

But it was nothing compared to the emotional eruption that was to come.

The professional group which had performed last was still seated around the perimeter of the stage. When one of their dancers won the best male dance prize, they jumped with happiness for their colleague. But when they won the "best costume" category their applause seemed strangely subdued. Traditionally, we later learned, a group never wins the "best costume" prize and also the "best dance group" category.

Anticipation rose in the audience.

This was to be the last prize, the most coveted prize. Besides the grandiose cup and a check for $2,500, it meant a morale victory for two months of hard work. It meant more recognition and potentially more work in hotels.

The moment arrived.

The judges awarded the same group the "best dance group" prize! They leaped to their feet like wild animals, crazy with delight, breaking into spontaneous dances of joy, scrambling around each other to get in the front row for photographs, hugging and kissing each other, shouting out at friends. Hilarious.

It was a perfect note to end the Fête.

How big is the Fête?
How much does it cost?
The budget is around $500,000.
Just a little neighborhood street party.

11. Things To Know Before Going

What To Take...Laws And Customs... Do's & Don'ts...A Modicum Of Statistics

French Polynesia holds no great surprises for the average traveler but there are a few experiences to share and a few nuances we learned the hard way.

For example the food stores carry a surprisingly large inventory of American-International brands. On the other hand the pharmacies carry almost all French products. It is therefore a good idea to bring your own favorite brand medicine chest . . . lomotil, paregoric, aspirin, laxative, insect repellent, sun tan lotion, sun burn relievers, etc. Being that most medicines are mental placebos anyway, it is more effective to have those in which you have faith. "My mother always used it" syndrome.

Entry Requirements

Your passport with no visa required will permit you to stay one month if you reside in the United States, New Zealand or Australia. A three-month renewable visa is not difficult to obtain.

If you come from a Common Market country including the United Kingdom, your passport is good for a stay of three months.

Persons holding French national identity cards or passports have no visa requirement and no limit on length of stay.

A smallpox vaccination requirement has been eliminated. Yellow fever vaccinations are required for passengers coming from infected areas.

Work permits are difficult to get.

Customs clearance is easy at Faaa where you land. Respect the fact that the local agriculture is terribly important and fragile. A new bug can be devastating. The Lady Navigator had to throw away a pear from the airplane which she shouldn't have tried to bring in anyway.

To Those Arriving From Samoa Or Fiji:

Your luggage will be retained at the airport for a minimum two-hour fumigation process. Pack your overnight requirements as hand luggage and reclaim your luggage the next day.

Special Notes

Professional photographers must have written permission to import their equipment.

Pets are strictly forbidden. If you want a stray cat or dog just whistle. Tahiti is full of them.

No firearms. No drugs. And don't be foolish. The French are *tough.*

Camping equipment? Leave it home. There are no camping facilities in French Polynesia and before a camp is set up permission has to be gained from the land owner. In four months in French Polynesia, we saw only two tents.

Tipping

A sign at Faaa Airport in four languages says please don't tip.

The newspapers explain that tipping is contrary to Polynesian custom. It is considered an insult.

All brochures tell you not to tip.

Don't tip. (You'll be grateful when you see your restaurant check.)

Taxis

Taxis are expensive but regulated.

From your hotel you will pay a double fare — the cost of coming to get you from the taxi station and the cost of taking you where you want to go.

After 11 p.m. and before 5 a.m. the fares double.

The most desired taxi driver-chauffer-guide in Papeete is named Acajou. He is in constant demand by experienced Tahitian visitors. Acajou will take a party of four on a circle island tour of Tahiti in his air-conditioned Mercedes Benz. Whatever he charges will be reasonable. Remember, no tipping.

Language

The preponderance of visitors to Tahiti are English speaking and most hotel personnel, waiters, drivers and tour conductors will speak English to some degree.

An immersion course or a refresher course in French will make your stay more enjoyable but isn't necessary. Store signs are of course in French but the store personnel will speak English. Enough. A smile is international.

Notice how the Tahitians say hello with a little upward jerk of the head.

The Tahitian language is very much alive. It is part of the Austronesian family of languages which extends almost halfway around the world, from Madagascar to Easter Island.

Surprisingly there are very few French words adopted into the Tahitian language probably because the English missionaries were there by themselves for the first forty years. There are many English adopted words.

The most common Tahitian words the visitor will encounter are:

> **ia ora na**...good day
>
> **māururu**...thank you
>
> **maeva**...welcome
>
> **maitai**...good!
>
> **nana, nana**...goodbye

If you'd like a quick introduction to the language, buy a little booklet: *Say It in Tahitian* by D.T. Tryon.

Weather And Things To Wear

The average temperature is 75°...22 celsius. However the average humidity is 78 percent. That's why you'll see cars vying to park in the shade. People too.

The rainy months are from November to April and then usually the heaviest rains come at night. You might get a lot of rain or you might have a month of fantastic weather.

In any case it is cool in the evening when the *hupe* or mountain breeze makes good sleeping weather.

Your wearing apparel should be edited accordingly.

Wear breeze-through washable cottons during the day. The humidity makes the polyesters hot and sticky.

The simplest, most compact rain pancho is a good investment, one with a hood. Also an umbrella.

In June, July and August the evening air can have a nip in it particularly after a day in the sun. Take a light wrap.

A man can get by with walking shorts, cotton pants, tennis shoes and/or sandals and one pair of dress shoes. Loose shirts. No coats. No ties. No need.

Ladies, according to my travel friend, should pack loose-fitting voiles, gauzes, cottons. Washable loose shirts and skirts. Open slippers and sandals, high and low heel. For evenings, a long skirt or two for air-conditioned restaurants. For a "dressy" evening, a Hawaiian muumuu kind of dress is perfect. No hosiery. No pumps. No need.

Ladies more than men will find Tahitian clothing to buy. See the chapter on "Found and Treasured."

Two pair of swimming things each and your own beach towels.

One pair of plastic sandals for swimming. It is recommended to have covered soles when walking in the shallows.

You Want To Drive?

There are international and local cars for hire by the day, week or month. All companies take credit cards, preferably American Express. You will also need your driver's license.

It would be a good idea to have a St. Christopher's medal. The French drive like every road, day or night, wet or dry, is Le Mans.

The Tahitians, a Polynesian friend told us, do two things fast: dance and drive.

The result, on the narrow two-lane roads, is a disproportionate number of head-on collisions. Could ruin your whole week-end.

Drive carefully and give yourself enough road room to duck out of trouble. There is, frankly, a lot of drunk driving and it only takes one drunk to make a two-car accident.

You Don't Want To Drive?

Take *le truck*!

Les trucks are frequent, filled with music from either a passenger with a guitar or the truck cassette. The passengers are amiable and the prices are cheap.

All *trucks* are independent. They run on their own schedule. Few of them run on Sunday afternoons or evenings. Take the idea of going around the island in a *truck* with this word of caution: none of them go *around* the island. If you go to the end of the line, halfway around, it might be the last run that *le truck* will take that day and you will have no way back. Make sure of your return trip before leaving. (Now you have to speak French.)

There are also minitour buses and larger air-conditioned buses available through hotels. An around-the-island tour is not expensive. Remember you can't circle the island by *le truck*.

Another Word About Eating And Drinking

Between the restaurants of Papeete, neighbor island hotel dining rooms, and the marketplace, the pleasures of the table have been fairly well reported.

About drinking: the Polynesian custom of *ava* has been abandoned. The drink is beer supplied by two breweries. Most popular brands are Hinano and Vahine. The most popular imported beer is Heineken.

Bar prices are high but liquor store prices are, comparatively, reasonable.

You'll find a wide selection of French wines and you'll notice a great deal of rose wines from the Loire being drunk. Practically all restaurants have a decent house wine served in a full, half or quarter carafe.

Money, Money, Money

The currency in French Polynesia is the CPF, Centre Pacifique Franc. The rate fluctuates but not greatly.

Always trade money at the bank.

The coins are in one, two, five, ten, twenty, fifty and one hundred franc denominations.

The notes are five hundred, one thousand, and five thousand francs.

Banking hours are from 8:00 a.m. until 3:30 p.m. and banks are open during lunch hours. The Bank of Tahiti is open Saturday mornings from 8:00 to 11:30. Credit cards are accepted in many shops and boutiques, but not all. And never in the Chinese stores.

People And Races And Religions

The population of French Polynesia is now approaching 170,000. Almost three-quarters of that number live on Tahiti.

Of the entire population the Tahitians represent seventy-five percent, Europeans fifteen percent and the Asiatics ten percent.

The Protestant religion has more than twice the number of Catholics probably because the Protestant missionaries landed well in advance of the Catholic missionaries in the Society Islands where denser populations existed. The Catholics however were the first to settle in the Tuamotus, Marquesas and Gambier Islands and there the Catholic religion predominates.

The pastors of the Protestant churches are Tahitian but Catholic priests are predominately French. There is also a strong representation of Mormons, Adventists and Jehovah's Witnesses.

The ancient religion of the Tahitians has long been forgotten. Only the restored remains or forgotten *maraes* or temples remain.

Economic

The most important foreign exchange product in French Polynesia is the meat of the coconut, copra, and the coconut oil which is refined on Fare Utu.

Other sources of income are mother of pearl — once a prosperous industry but almost destroyed by plastics — cultured pearls, vanilla, coffee.

Under a five-year plan the strongest efforts are being made to further develop agricultural resources and above all exploit the potential of the vast ocean.

The interest in the other islands can be seen in the expansion of airports, essential for communication.

Tourism

The richest source of foreign exchange for French Polynesia is tourism.

Today there are approximately 120,000 visitors to the islands of which almost half come from the U.S.A., mostly the West Coast. Europe contributes about eighteen percent, including a strong number of French families visiting relatives. Australia and Canada constitute about ten percent each of the market; South America and Japan supply the remainder.

The most popular months are the winter months of North America, January through March, July for the days of the Fête and, unaccountably, October and November.

The growth of tourism is going to depend on airline seats, their cost and the number of hotel rooms available. The local government is determined to double the guest rooms now available and is funding, through tax benefits, a new wave of construction. The future promises that tourism in Tahiti will be more profitable than it is today.

From an international evaluation, Tahiti's tourist industry is still small and to the visitor that is one of its greatest attractions.

To put it in perspective: the entire hotel room inventory in French Polynesia—in all hotels, on all islands, even if doubled—is less than two of Sheraton's hotels on Waikiki Beach in Hawaii.

Sick?

Excellent French doctors and dentists are available in Papeete. Every island has a "hospital." A major hospital and two clinics are located in Papeete. The pharmacies sell French equivalents of most English (American or British) prescriptions. If communication is a problem, your hotel can arrange for bilingual assistance.

Hair Curlers?

Modern electrical plants generate 220-volt alternating current. Older plants will produce 110-volt. Before using electrical appliances, check with the hotel to determine which is in use. If your appliances are not dual voltage and you did not bring your own converter, the hotel can supply one.

What Is Going On In The World

There are local French daily newspapers in Papeete. *Le Journal* was our preference.

There is also a weekly paper in English, the *Tahiti Sun Press.* Most of the pages are standing tourist ads which can be helpful. After a time in a foreign country, you'll read anything in your mother tongue.

The editorial content covers information like international airline schedules, money rates of exchange, news within the tourist industry.

Tahiti Magazine, a slick four-color format, includes feature articles on Tahiti's cultures and pleasures available to visitors such as her songs and dances, black pearls, her individual islands. Copies are on most incoming international flights.

214 *How To Get Lost And Found In Tahiti*

Newsstands have English magazines and old copies of New Zealand and Australian newspapers. Even the *International Herald Tribune*. Just check the date first.

There is one radio station which broadcasts in French and Tahitian from 6 a.m. until 10 p.m.

The single television channel also offers only French and Tahitian programs.

Letters, Telegrams, Telephone Calls

One-stop communications center: you can post your letters, cable home or place a telephone call at the Central Post Office in downtown Papeete and at branches throughout French Polynesia.

Three-minute conversations to New Zealand or Australia are surprisingly efficient and not too expensive.

Odds And Ends

It is possible to have your color film developed but we were advised to have it done at home.

Hotels provide a one-day laundry and dry-cleaning service or you can have it done in downtown Papeete for half the price. (There's a Laundromat at Vaima Centre, remember.)

In time zones, French Polynesia is the same as Honolulu . . . two hours later than Los Angeles . . . five hours later than New York . . . ten hours later than London . . . twenty hours later than Sydney . . . twenty-one hours later than Auckland.

International organizations such as the Lions Club and Rotary meet weekly in Papeete, just as they do at home. Most likely at the Beachcomber Hotel, but check for current location.

Last words: *Don't Tip!*

12. Found And Treasured

. . . By The Lady Navigator

"Vanilla beans and pareus," flashed the hotel executive in a practiced reaction about Tahiti's 'best' buys.

"After that, everything is expensive." He, like most residents, did not hide from the high cost of shopping in an over-heated economy.

"Black pearls, too, if you can afford them. Prices rise from fifteen to twenty percent at the auction for commercial buyers conducted every October. The Japanese—strong bidders—keep pushing the prices higher.

"But," Bali Hai's Mike Gibbons cautioned, "I'd learn a bit about quality before buying."

To his list of take-home souvenirs, we added a few more. On a value-for-money scale of one to ten, we awarded native shell and mother-of-pearl jewelry, some now *tres chic,* an eight.

The pictorial books by Erwin Christian won a five, not because they are priced right but because they are so beautiful. There are many beautifully illustrated books on Polynesia in the bookshops.

Local art and crafts, a matter of personal taste, can rank a noble ten, or a lowly one-half. Value is in the eye of the beholder.

Perhaps the very best value for money are the fruits of Polynesia easily found in the Papeete Market: the translucent sweet meat of the lychee in the Spring or its soft prickly cousin, the rambutan, that debuts in February and stays half the year. When neither of these round succulents with the large seeds are available, you'll still find the similar Dragon Eye. Just peel back the skin and avoid the large seed inside.

Autumn brings the golden red mango, truly the nectar of the gods. Slice it over a sink—it's juicier than a Georgia peach—and attack it watermelon-patch style. Of course, you can scoop its sweetmeat with a spoon which is more genteel, but not as satisfying. Among the other Fall exotics are a tart little seed pod called the tamarind that children love and, everybody's favorite, the custard apple, a clustered cell fruit of outstanding flavor.

Year round you'll find sugar cane, pineapple—wee little things that

215

are so sweet that the locals sprinkle lightly with salt—papaya, banana and watermelon in your choice of red or yellow.

Did you know that pistachios and cashews also grow in French Polynesia?

But it is not these delectables for which Tahiti's marketplace is famous. Vanilla has carried Tahiti's agricultural banner abroad.

A thriving export industry until the mid-1960s when the artificial stuff dropped prices dramatically, vanilla is, in fact, a member of the orchid family. The only member of the clan with a dominate fragrance. It doesn't look like an orchid; it doesn't produce gorgeous blossoms. It does produce gorgeous perfumery from its black, withered, prune wrinkled, skinny pod.

Grown mainly in the Society Islands—Tahaa, Raiatea, Huahine—and in the Austral Islands, vanilla grows *in* trees. But it is a vine whose long fleshy stem attaches itself by aerial rootlets to trees.

And, my, what an esoteric sex life it has. The birds and bees have absolutely nothing to do with the propagation of the species. This orchid, a native of Central America, blooms in such a way that only certain insects or humming birds could pollinate it. Until *man* conceived a method to help. He rushes to the vine the moment the virgin vanilla pod blossoms—between sunrise and noon, one authority says—to hand pollinate each bud. Seven to eleven weeks later he rushes back to harvest the pod at its precise moment of maturity.

This hurry-hurry routine happens twice a year.

Exhausting.

Once, you could buy vanilla in elegant bamboo tubes sealed with red wax and bound in sennit at both ends. The *perfect* take-home gift packaged by Winkler Galerie. Now, we understand, Monsieur Winkler has turned his talents to vanilla production instead of packaging since the government launched a plan that envisions an annual export yield of 100 tons. Wonder if he plans to import a flock of humming birds?

Even in plastic packets, the beans are a packable, fragrant and the cheapest souvenir you'll buy in French Polynesia. We bought a 100-pod bundle for under $20 at the Chinese store in Fare.

If the customs regulations of your country frowns on the importation of agricultural products, stash the pods in a bottle of rum for international transport. It sterilizes the vanilla and adds the most heavenly punch to the rum drinks you'll make.

•

The Pareu And Other Draperies

Getting hooked on the pareu is easy. You watch your guy watching the *vahines* dance-walk in that rhythmic, undulating way that makes the flowers on her pareu flutter about as fast as his eyes. Then you see the *mama ruau,* the matrons, looking nearly as graceful, regardless of their shapes and you ask yourself "why not?" First shyly just on the beach, then bravely around the hotel until, almost unconsciously, you are wearing some version of it everywhere.

The pareu, the national dress of French Polynesia, is a length of fabric measuring 1.90 meters (slightly over two yards). It is worn wrapped or draped as a halter, strapless or one-shoulder dress, as a long or short skirt, or swimsuit or sleeping garment. It is used as a beach mat, towel, tablecloth, turban or, in a crisis, a sail for a boat.

Polynesian men wear them also, either wrapped around the waist or draped diaper fashion and anchored securely at the waist.

It is as colorful as it is versatile.

Where to buy it?

Anywhere. Everywhere. There are pre-cut, hemmed pareus in every hotel gift or apparel shop, in most of the general merchandise stores pivoting around the Papeete Market, or in neighbor island Chinese stores, curio shops, boutiques . . . even supermarkets.

In Papeete, there are stores that sell only pareus, *pret a porter* pareus (one-size-fits all wrap-arounds sewn for secure body concealment), and accessories to wear with them. Two stores recommended by residents are Hawaii and Venus.

Tahitian vahines seldom buy them ready made. They go to a fabric store, order 1.9 meters cut off, and, *voila,* a pareu. Much cheaper.

The fabrics at these stores are likely to be imitation pareu motifs printed in Japan, Hong Kong, France or Italy. The purists, Emile Charles among them, will tell you "There is no such thing as a real pareu that isn't printed in Tahiti."

"What's the Difference?"

As textile printer Charles tells you: "Imported impostors lose their luster rapidly. Some are not even colorfast." He invites shoppers to tour his factory, Charles STIA, where "Quality Tahiti" labeled fabrics and garments made from them may be purchased for the entire family at discounts up to forty percent.

The other granddaddy of the Tahitian textile industry, Daniel Adam, guards his printing technique so tightly that nobody even knows where his factory is located . . . not even his closest business associates.

"It is to protect the process he has perfected," explained a manager of one of two retail TAPA stores, the only place you can buy Daniel Adam fabrics.

She swore she had no idea where his studio is located . . . and she had worked for him for twelve years.

"Everyone copies his motifs, you see, but no one can duplicate his technique."

Local devotees concur.

"Their color never moves." (Translation: the color doesn't fade.) The shopper volunteered: "Use cold water for the first washing, to leach out excess surface dye. Then . . . well, my six- or seven-year-old dresses made of TAPA fabrics are as bright as the day I made them."

I didn't ask her if she starred in Rinso Blue commercials.

TAPA stores are located on rue Jean Gilbert and across from Vaima Centre on rue du General de Gaulle.

STIA prints primarily on cotton and cotton blended with polyesters. Daniel Adam uses a wide assortment of fabrics in addition to cotton: jersey, polyester, French cotton voile as sheer as chiffon, polyester voile, sateen, and heavy duty jute. His motifs are both traditional Tahitian and contemporary, in subtle or bold hues. You pay by the number of colors used in addition to by the yard.

Tie-dyeing, the ancient art rediscovered by the T-shirt set a spate of years back, took on the sophistication of fine art in the hands of a few pioneer Tahitian craftsmen a decade ago. Mireille Ravello and Jacqueline Gilbert designed a variety of leisurewear, but it was their stitched-to-the-knee pull-on pareus in voile that concealed no curve of the body—and few of its wrinkles—that won them fame and prime prices.

Today, there are dozens of designers doing innovative—and imitative—lounge fashions. We have our favorites on each island, as you will have yours, among the endless ebbing/flowing of designer talent. French Polynesia's fashion industry is not exempt from fickleness.

Madame Ravello, now living in Paris and still tie-dying, threatens to quit. *If* there is a Ravello wearable art creation in Tahiti, it will be at Galerie Api on Moorea.

Another Moorea local fashion pacesetter is the Shark's Tooth boutique at Opunohu.

Matairea Rima, an unmissable boutique in Fare, Huahine, had a quality selection of art for the body. (It will be a shame if—more likely *when*—the building the shop occupies is razed. The oldest building in Fare is colorfully decorated in five shades of blue, its "floor" is sand.) Shop owner Ghislaine Owen plans to operate a stall in the new thatched roof municipal open marketplace on boat days.

On Bora Bora, the "don't miss" shop is Martine Creations, on the road just beyond the Bora Bora Hotel.

The Bali Hai resort boutiques in Moorea, Huahine and Raiatea also offer interesting original tie-dyed apparel and jewelry.

Papeete, The Paris Of The Pacific

Papeete being a crossbreed—part Polynesian, part Parisian—it is a mixed-bag shopping venue. Some merchants cater to the Polynesians, others to the French, and a few bridge the cultural gap and cater to all.

Those who serve the Polynesians, the *le Truck* commuters, have shops near the Papeete Market, the *le Truck* depot.

Those who serve the French nationals snuggle up to the business and governmental offices sited between Vaima Centre on the waterfront and Avenue Braut along rue du General De Gaulle, about four blocks away.

The transient visitor population saunters easily between these anchors and along Boulevard Pomare whose shops and gaily draped stalls cater primarily to tourist tastes. Here's where you'll find most of the "duty free" shops. (Caution: do not be deluded that all things stocked in a shop self-signed "DUTY FREE" are, in fact, duty free. It is prudent—and more economical—to ask.)

Besides pods and pareus, Papeete has other shopping fascinations. There are things French: couturier labels such as Dior, Louis Feraud, Pierre Cardin, Guy Laroche, Lanvin; French perfumes and cosmetics; housewares, gourmet foods, wines, and wonderful cheeses. The made-in-France merchandise is, generally speaking, accompanied by a made-in-France sales attitude—indifference. *Fiu* (bored).

The prices, give or take an occasional exception, are as if pumped up with helium.

French perfumes are touted to be cheaper in duty free shops than in Paris or New York. Maybe New York. I doubt the Paris claim. My vote for the best prices in Tahiti goes to the *Liberte* shop, one of the Alders of London shipboard concessions.

With floating shops aboard dozens of luxury cruise ships throughout the world, among them the *QE2,* they can afford to sell eligible duty free items at less than most shorebound shops. (Secret: wait until Friday, the day before returning to the Papeete dock, to do your heavy duty shopping. An Alders' tradition is to offer substantial discounts atop some tax-free items. Note: *some* items. Not all. But the sale is worth waiting to peruse.)

If cruising is not on your itinerary, try the Parfumerie & Cadeaux, tucked away in an upstairs corner of Vaima Centre. There, I found the best duty free prices, and, importantly, volunteered information when the item under review was not duty free.

The Souvenir Search

Papeete affords pleasure to the collector of Pacifica souvenirs. Not just French Polynesian treasures, mind you, but cloisonne from China ("the French buy it to take back home") and tribal art from other Pacific island nations, especially New Guinea.

Before we shop for the crafts of a country, we scout the local museum for an overview of what is traditionally made, and of what standard of quality. The Museum de Tahiti et des Iles is a most remarkable heritage barometer.

A dozen years ago, we made one further stop before buying our first handcrafted item in Papeete. Pu Maohi Centre d'Artisanat, a cooperative of Polynesian artists organized in 1977 with the encouragement of the French government, is located on rue Regent Paraita, a cluster of frame buildings under broad-limbed shade trees. One of its primary functions is as a crafts classroom to perpetuate the culture of Polynesia.

Since our first visit to Pu Maohi, the crafts cooperative movement has proliferated. Handcraft centers have been built on the dock in central Papeete, across from the Royal Papeete Hotel just out of the city, at Pahia (P.K. 22), and smaller ones are operated near the village of Faaone and west of the city at Pointe Venus. Additionally, at least once weekly, every major resort hotel hosts a crafts show on its lawn or in its lobby.

Here, you will see the progeny of artists from throughout the island nation.

First focus may fall on the dramatic hand- or machine-sewn *tifaifai,* appliqued cotton coverlets in bold patterns and Gauguinesque colors, that serve the Polynesians as ceremonial and traditional bridal gifts.

"On presentation, it is customary to wrap the recipient in the *tifaifai* to denote the warmth and affection of its giver," our Marquesan landlady had told us.

We witnessed this solemn proceeding on a warm evening at the High Commissioner's residence. The Tongan honorees never once tried to remove the bedspread-sized mantle. (Our informant didn't say how long the bridal couple remain cocooned in their *tifaifai.* But you do see a lot of infants.

Once you found these heirloom pieces only at Pu Maohi, priced—as we wrote in 1977—between $65 to $575. The range might still be valid, but most of the gems you are likely to see will be in the upper scale of that range.

Also, there to entrap your attention may be "cloth" made from the bark of mulberry or breadfruit trees, its floral or geometric patterns stenciled on with vegetable dyes. (Hawaii familiarized the world with a similar item, calling it *tapa.* No such word existed in other parts of Polynesia, however. It was called *ahu.*

You'll see an abundance of woven straw goods—mats, baskets, placemats, glass holders, matchbooks, hats.

The average Tahitian can look at a hat and tell you where it was made. It is no more mysterious than the average American school boy being able to recognize a car's manufacturer.

Cherished are the pure white hats woven from the inner leaf of young coconut palms on the island Tubuai. Because they are rare, of course they are expensive.

To help you recognize the 'state' of the hat, know that the stiff brimmed hats decorated with bark cloth come from the Marquesan Islands. If they are white, they are made from the breadfruit tree; brown is of banyan tree bark. Hats with an open lacy weave are woven on the island of Tahiti. The fragile white versions are made of bamboo; the natural, sturdier ones of pandanus.

Shells and shell novelties adorn each artisan's table or mat: *leis* and *heis* for neck and head, earrings and hatbands, ashtrays and lamps, figurines of animals, real and *imitation* shark's teeth. Goodness. A very interesting pendant is a shark's tooth carved from the lustrous mother-of-pearl shell.

If you see a rope-round hatband of tiny honey-gold shells, stop and marvel. It is made of *pupu ma a moa* shells, smaller than the smallest *petit pois*. These shells are actually mined, not scooped up, from coral, we're told.

Years ago when the ocean waters were higher, millions of these mini mollusks thrived on the reefs. As the water level receded, the pupu died, creating its own layer in the coral. Today, Islanders chip off hunks of coral, painstakingly separate each minute shell from the bedrock, soak it in a brine to detach the encrustations and to restore its natural golden hue. Hues—plural—since the patina varies from a soft buttery yellow to a flaming sunset orange.

For the very best in indigenous artifacts, head for Manuia Curios in central Papeete across from the Cathedral. Frank Silloux, a Chinese whose real name is Shiu ("The French made us change our names so we wouldn't be so 'foreign'.") may have some of the outstanding intricately carved wooden objects or the white bark cloth wall hangings made by Marquesan artisans. Supply of Marquesan objects is sporadic at best; the artisans simply cannot be bothered with "filling orders."

Frank is optimistic about the future of traditional woodcarving, nonetheless. There is now a government-subsidized Centre des Metiers d'Art to teach the interested the traditional techniques for carving wood, shells and, God forbid, the turtle shell.

There is still another reason for an optimistic projection. French Polynesia participates in the Pacific Arts' Festival, one of twenty-seven countries committed to guarding their culture as they guard their lives—with drive, determination and enthusiasm. As inspiration they quote French novelist and art critic Andre Malraux: "A culture can only wither from within."

Shopping hours in Papeete are advertised as 7:30 a.m. until 5:30 p.m. (11 a.m. on Saturdays). However, there is always a long lunch hour, with the extreme limits from 11 a.m. to 2 p.m. Consult the hotel staff for opening hours (and days) for the handcrafts markets.

The Exotic Palette

Until the voyages of Captain James Cook in the mid-1700s, the islands of the Pacific relied on oral history, apart from a few remnants of engraved animals on stone.

It was the illustrators of the Royal Academy and official recording artists outposted from Paris who capitulated these islands of vibrant colors, graceful people and scenic magnificence into the consciousness of the world. And that represents just a bit more than two hundred years.

British artists John Webber, William Hodges, Sir Joshua Reynolds were followed by lithographers for the French atlas and painters for the French Protectorates who were often good or even brilliant artists, but not geniuses.

That was changed by Paul Gauguin, who at age forty-two, shucked his financial career, left his family in Europe and sailed into the South Pacific.

Gauguin had a profound effect on the art world of his day, but no more than he continues to have on the residents of French Polynesia today.

"The rich people of Tahiti suffer the Gauguin syndrome," Patrice Bredel, owner of Galerie Api on Moorea, will tell you.

"Afraid they will 'miss out' on another Gauguin, as their parents did, they'll buy any bold, pure color primitive painting that surfaces . . . whether it is good or not. They simply don't want to take the chance of not recognizing 'genius' again."

Patrice will also tell you that "of the eighty-five artists in residence throughout French Polynesia, seventy-five of them are very bad."

His gallery was very good.

It once was the studio *fare* of a popular contemporary Impressionist, Francois Ravello. With the gallery came the exclusive right to sell Ravello paintings worldwide. Also Madame Ravello's batik pareus, although she is painting more and printing less these days.

We examined a Gauguin woodblock, "Maruru," priced at about $7,000, sketches by Sebastien Charles Giraud, whose life-sized oil portrait of Queen Pomare (circa 1851) hangs in the Museum de Tahiti, and the bold works of contemporary artist Michael Dallet whose works have been exhibited at the Gauguin Museum, an honor bestowed on few living artists.

Additionally, Monsieur Bredel has assembled a fascinating collection of primitive art . . . not all of it for sale.

He also steered us to Galerie Aad van der Heyde, also on Moorea. A good steer.

Compiling a list of the "best" of anything is, at best, subjective. I relied on the opinions of museum curators and independent gallery authorities for this compilation.

Yves Durand de Saint Front made everybody's list. A talent in several mediums now working in stained glass, Saint Front's primitives are highly regarded, as are his murals on view at the Musee de Tahiti, the Cathedral and at the Gauguin Museum.

A painting by the now deceased Piter Heyman, vintage 1966, hangs in the office of the curator of the state museum, a signal honor.

Frank Fay, a sometimes resident, is an abstract painter, sculptor, potter and textile printer. The government commissioned him to paint the Faaa Airport lobby mural which, for some inexplicable reason, reminds me of carnival lights from atop a Ferris wheel.

Jean Charles Bouloc, portraitist and psychological surrealist, recently married a Chinese lawyer. Now, maybe we'll see a portrait of a Chinese in addition to the strictly Polynesian faces that adorn canvases.

Jean Francois Favre is loved by the locals for his delicate watercolors of Tahitian flowers but remembered by tourists primarily for his relatively inexpensive woodcuts depicting Tahitian legends. Very popular.

Jean Shelsher's bold oil naives, gentle watercolors and dramatic charcoals go on exhibit at least once a year at Winkler Gallery, the pioneer among art galleries in Tahiti.

Francoise Seli had a great thing going commercially with her portraits of young people. But she tired of that, wanted to grow in new directions and began dabbling in abstractism. Her work is hard to find. Now, we think she may be teaching.

Rui Juventin, a self-taught impressionist native of Tahiti, is one of a number of young artists who receives tons of publicity for, mainly, his primitives and who the locals are buying "just in case he's this generation's Gauguin." He opened Oviri Gallery in 1985 as a showcase for members of the Artists Association of French Polynesia.

In addition to the galleries already noted, works of art are sold at Galerie J. J. Laurent at Vaima Centre and Galerie Matamua, the upstairs of Tahiti Art in Fare Tony.

The National Gem

Nero's scepter and Constantine's helmet were covered with them.

Mogul emperors ground them into drinks to improve their virility; Charles VI of France to fight insanity.

Richard Burton paid $37,000 for one flawless speciman as a Valentine's Day gift to Elizabeth Taylor, which her dog promptly chewed into an historical footnote.

A necklace of them was found in a dig of a Persian king's winter palace (in western Iran) that dates to 350 B.C.

Krishna, the Hindus believe, discovered the first one at the bottom of the sea and gave it to his daughter as a wedding gift. It is a practice still honored.

The pearl, Queen of the Seabed, was the most valuable of all gems until the latter part of the nineteenth century, when diamonds became a girl's best friend.

Tahiti has a special breed of pearl. They call it a black pearl although its tone ranges from a silver gray to bluish black, or in comparable shades of greens.

Black pearls have been cultivated in French Polynesia since the early 1970s. The protected lagoons of the Tuamotu and Gambier Islands are ideal "nurseries" for the black-lipped oyster that is found only in French Polynesia. It is their dark mantle that colors the pearl.

"Technically, the black pearl is a 'cultured' pearl, but in 1976, the G.I.A. recognized it as a 'natural' pearl," she said. "That's when the sales started booming."

Our informant was Marion Milan, a London transplant who is the public relations manager for Tahiti Pearl Center & Museum.

The importance of the Gemological Institute of America's judgment is tied to the fact that the USA is the world's largest consumer of pearls. Between 1977 and 1985, US pearl sales jumped from about $54 million to over $600 million.

"A necklace of forty baroque black pearls recently sold for $28,000. Mikimoto, the pioneer of cultured pearls, got $80,000 for a double strand of baroques set with diamonds.

"Or you can buy this irregular, pitted, somewhat dull pearl for $35." She held up what I might have thought a pretty pearl a few moments earlier.

"This one, of a good middle-of-the-standard quality, is $800." It was smaller than the $35 stub, but perfectly round and more luminous.

"Like everything, you get what you pay for. If you seek a souvenir, the cheaper pearls are good enough. If you want a real jewel, you must pay.''

She walked us through the museum: a section of panels tracing the history of all pearls, a group of scientific displays on pearl cultivation and the composition of a pearl, a film presentation, and, best of all, a scale model of a typical pearl farm in French Polynesia.

You learn.

An authentically natural pearl occurs when an irritant—a grain of sand, a parasite or a small fish—gets inside the oyster's shell accidentally. The oyster then goes about licking its wound, covering the irritant with layers of the substance its shell is made of. That substance is called nacre.

A cultured pearl forms when the irritant—a bead of shell from another mollusk—is artificially implanted in an oyster's mantle through micro-surgery. (Pearl farmers in Tahiti use mussel shells from the Mississippi River as seed irritants.)

The oyster is returned to the sea for from three to five years, suspended on a grid and checked periodically to see how well it is doing its job. In a way, you can compare the oyster's craft with that of Japanese lacquerware. Unless the layers are thin and smooth, the product will be of inferior quality.

"Like most farming, there are risks. On average, only five percent of the implanted oysters produce commercially perfect pearls in any given year," Ms. Milan informed us.

Even worse, fifty percent will die from the operation. Twenty percent will reject the seed. The remaining twenty-five percent will produce irregular pearls that are usable but are not considered gems.

"Although our waters in the protected lagoons are ideal for pearl farming, there are, also, risks due to the variables of the weather. In 1983, four cyclones destroyed many of the crops throughout French Polynesia. That meant starting all over."

She cautioned: "Buy from a reputable dealer because, in the feverish rush to get black pearls to market, some farmers do not give the oysters enough time to do the proper job of layering shimmering lustrous nacre over the seed. Some producers are harvesting too soon. The pearl looks pretty but thin nacre will wear through."

You are reminded that even in the best quality, the nuclei accounts for up to seventy-five percent of the pearl.

Industry standards for judging the quality of a pearl are good guidelines for individual shopping. Look for high gloss or brilliance (luster), for an iridescent sheen created by the multiple layering of nacre (orient), an unblemished surface (skin) and, if a gem instead of souvenir is sought, a round or pear shape (shape) measuring a minimum of 12.1 millimeters (size).

If more than two pearls are incorporated into a piece of jewelry, they should be of the same quality and color, and matched or graduated in size.

Marion took us to meet Guy Wan, director of Tahiti Perles, whose father, Robert, started the company and now oversees the farms, having recently bought out his largest competition, Jean-Claude Brouillet.

He also sent his son, Guy, a third generation Tahitian Chinese, to Jesuit Schools in America to learn the business and marketing ways of North America.

"Where will the industry be in five years," my companion asked Guy Wan.

"That depends upon three factors: the quality of technicians, governmental regulation, and our marketing ability. Japanese technicians who have performed the surgery from the very beginning are now conducting classes for new technicians, the government seems to be enthusiastic—the Bank of Development conducts an invitational auction every October."

"The Japanese are driving the price up annually."

(The message: "Buy Now—before the price rises more.")

Guy opened the commercial museum and salesroom in 1985, turning an out-of-the-main traffic location into an asset and leaving little doubt how aggressive his merchandising will be. Tour buses pull up to its doors all day long, disgorging sightseers and potential customers.

His ads in Tahitian publications are big and beautiful. But his main focus is the American market which gets most of the quality pearls.

Where will the industry be in ten years?

Pressed for an answer in consumer terms, Guy Wan, the marketer, said, "I wouldn't be surprised if the cost of a single perfect black pearl reached $800,000 in another decade.

A postscript. While prowling around a Kauai shopping center after our return from Tahiti, I saw a jewelry store that advertised itself as the only exclusive black pearl store in America. I would have had to have an appraisal and the appraiser would have to x-ray the pearls for a fair comparison against the pearls found in Tahiti. But, a strand of thirty-five perfectly matched beauties measuring ten millimeters each dazzled the eye.

"How much?"

"It is privately owned but anything over $80,000 would open a dialogue," the manager reported.

Eighty thou sounded reasonable, I told my Pilot, especially by comparison to that single perfect black pearl that is going to cost him $800,000 ten years from now.

He wasn't convinced.

I set about finding a jewelry designer, Alain Kerebel, whom I met a few years back and who did incredible things with chunky gold black pearls.

The one-of-a-kind jeweler is now into creating one-of-a-kind paintings that he sells to people who seek him out at his studio-home on Moorea, or at private shows in New York, Paris and his former home, Leopardville, South Africa. (At a recent exhibition in Leopardville, he sold 150 paintings for a total $200,000.)

Drop in any day from 9 a.m. until 6 p.m. His address? His card says "Take the lane facing the post office half mile you are welcome."

Island Hopping Shopping

As the fruits of the sea, the orchard, the barnyard and the land find their way to Papeete, so too do the fruits of the hand. Papeete is *the* market. Every type of craft made anywhere in French Polynesia can be bought in Papeete, somewhere. Often at similar prices; sometimes even cheaper.

Made-in-Papeete goods, however, if found on neighboring islands at all, will be more expensive.

This is not to discourage shopping on the less populated islands. Note that I specified every "type" of handicraft, not "every" crafted item, being available in Papeete. As tourism grows—and because the government continues to encourage the making of crafts—more and more emphasis will be placed on producing items special to French Polynesia. Both factors will inspire better quality crafts. We have seen a vast improvement in workmanship in the past decade.

Adopt my cardinal rule: "If you like it, buy it when you find it." You can never be sure you'll find it elsewhere.

If you are outer-island bound, shop the boutiques in the hotels and villages. You just may find the treasure of the trip.

13. Local Living

The Banana Patch At "Pee-Kay Twenty"...
Polynesian Kindness ... Food, Booze ...
Transportation ... Love, Hate ... Sex And
Tahitian Time ...

From the beginning of our 1977 Tahiti exercise, the year of the
initial research, we sought a base camp removed from the noise and
bustle of the city, a retreat for note gathering and writing.

At first we were told it would be no problem. At the end it was
a real problem.

In olden days many visitors would go to Tahiti and rent a *fare* on
the beach and hire a housekeeper for two or three months. Those days
are gone.

All of the housing is taken by the French military officers and
nuclear technicians and support personnel.

At one time we had the entire tourist office looking for a house for
us, a real estate agent and a host of new-found friends.

After two months of touring we were ready to settle down for base
camp work but we were still homeless . . . and desperate.

We were so desperate that we were on our way out to see a house
fifty-five kilometers out in the country for $1,800 a month – including
a car – when we saw a sign *"maison à louer"* (house to rent) at P.K.
20, beside the road. We turned around and had a look.

Two small bedrooms. Tile bath. Kitchen. Linoleumed living room.
Neat and new. $330 a month plus utilities. Two houses removed from
a fairly nice beach.

Earlier we had looked at a shack on top of a mountain for $500 a
month.

The winding road out to P.K. 55 where the $1,800 house was
located took over an hour to drive.

It was no contest. Back to P.K. 20 . . . our new home.

The biggest disadvantage of P.K. 20 was its location ten yards from
the road.

All traffic goes on the narrow road to and from Papeete. The produce to market traffic started *early.*

Les trucks started at 4:30. Our neighbor across the road owned a truck but he didn't start until 5 ayem which we knew because he had a cassette machine on his truck which would loudly play rock-and-roll with the first turn-over of the truck engine.

Also our stretch of road happened to be on a straight-away — one of the few — and all drivers including heavily loaded dump trucks considered it a point of honor to make up time at our doorstep.

The first few dawn mornings we clung to each other in terror.

As a matter of fact the first few nights were almost sleepless. My clock indicated a routine that went: 10:30 cat fight...1:30 dog fight...3:30 cocks crow...4:00 second dog fight...4:30 traffic starts to roll...5:00 "The Supremes" from across the street...6:00 red-eyed coffee.

The best part of P.K. 20 was the *propriétaire*...the land owner who was a retired American photographer-plantation owner who married a dumpling of a Marquesan lady.

Her name was "Tei" and she giggled. She cooked and she laughed and she giggled.

She spoke French in a bell-toned Marquesan accent and during our two month stay at P.K. 20 there was seldom a day when she didn't appear at our door with a dish of one sort or another.

Because I would kneel at her feet she came to know that I adored her *poe,* the fruit compote made into a tapioca pudding and covered with fresh coconut cream.

She would bring over a platter still warm and we would say to ourselves, "We'll be good and just eat the corners." And we'd finish the entire, million-calorie platter.

Tei also made a *poisson cru* out of fresh bonito that was the best we tasted. Incredibly good.

Other days it would be breadfruit prepared Marquesan fashion...first allowed to get soft and then baked, pounded into a paste and again covered with coconut cream.

The taste of breadfruit at first is bland, but as your palate becomes appreciative of its nuances, it becomes a vice. The smell of cooking breadfruit from Tei's kitchen next door would leave me biting the typewriter.

She also introduced us to many new Tahitian fruits...delivered to the door of course. Soursop. Rambutan. Wild oranges.

Often we would find a plate of fresh bananas...or a pineapple a grapefruit on our outside table...or a new shell she had found in the lagoon.

When she would be faced with her generosity, she would duck her head and squeeze her eyes shut with pleasure and she would giggle. Near the end of our stay she also introduced us to her magic of making "punch."

Split two or three inches of fresh vanilla beans and soak them in a bottle of dark rum for a few days to give a rich perfume to the rum. Pour a healthy jigger into a glass, add half a lime, half a teaspoon of sugar, fill with ice and top with water. "P.K. 20 Punch."

Have two before lunch and you are sure of having an afternoon nap.

Fred, her hard-working yardman-husband, said he married her because she was the easiest woman in the world to get along with. What a roly-poly delight.

Our tucked-away house by the side of the road was hidden by a grove of banana trees. We started by calling it "The Banana Farm" but that has a connotation of "The Nut House" and we settled on its geographic name of "Pah-eae-ah, Pee-Kay Vin."

Paea, our district, was just beyond Punaauia, where the wealthy — foreigners mostly — lived. Famous writers, airline executives, the international globetrotters.

At P.K. 18 the High Commissioner had his country house. Tarahoi Iti. A cluster of thatched-roofed *fares* dotting a perfect beach.

Our bank manager lived in Punaauia.

Marlon Brando had a house in Punaauia.

We were just over the tracks so to speak.

However the economies were pleasant. Our water was heated with propane gas and our hot water came from a French *chauffe-eau*, an ingenious French device that automatically turns up the gas under a hot water heater when you turn on the hot water tap. Our oven and range also used propane gas which cost about $10 a tank at the Chinese store. In two months we used three tanks.

Our electricity bill for two months came to less than $40 although we didn't have a telephone or television and only one good reading lamp. We carried our own portable radio and evenings we picked up the Breakfast Show from the Voice of America in Washington (insipid) and an occasional B.B.C broadcast from Australia (excellent).

Food

Our favorite supermarket was the downtown air-conditioned market in Vaima Center.

Three times a week they brought in beef and lamb by air from New Zealand. The cost was about $3 to $5 a pound. Local pork was more expensive and a Sunday roasting chicken cost $10. Not a turkey. A chicken.

At Vaima's you could also buy cheese air flown in special temperature-controlled containers from France. Also pâtes and terrines.

A slice of ripe Brie, a tranch of pork pâte and a salad was our favorite at-home lunch. Vaima's also sold crusty French luncheon rolls. (French bread, 19¢ a loaf, fresh twice a day was available in all markets.)

In larger markets you could buy Skippy peanut butter from the United States and marmalade from England.

There was fresh milk, ice cream ($5 a half-gallon) and New Zealand butter.

Fresh eggs, brown or white, $2 a dozen.

Fresh strawberries at $2.50 a basket, fresh artichokes, $2 each. We learned to shut our eyes to the prices. Remember, the year was 1977, and prices have continued to ascend.

One day at Market Tamanu, I backed off from paying $2.50 for a single roll of Zee paper towels in a reflex reaction, and then turned around and bought dripless candles for twice the amount.

What you find in Tahiti is a wide variety of products which reflects the ability of the people to pay any price for any product they desire.

The Chinese run the stores, the wholesale markets and the importing. If you find a young Chinese from Tahiti enrolled in Harvard and he says that his father is in lettuce, don't laugh.

Beer, wine and hard liquor are available in almost all food stores. Vodka, Scotch, gin, bourbon. Name it. Local beer and imported beer.

And, all are expensive.

Wine runs the gamut from Dom Perignon—lots of it—stacked up like cordwood at jolting prices, to Algerian red wine, guaranteed to flush you out. Nothing is cheap.

Surprisingly, Tahiti's close relationship with France doesn't seem to carry any mother-country advantage in the price of French wines. They are cheaper in New Zealand or California. Liqueurs are also astronomical.

At one time absinthe was a favorite drink in Tahiti and you still see large quantities of Pernod and other absinthe brands.

Today, the favorite drink is rum based, but the price of a good rum that won't take your head off will blow your mind.

Oh, yes, and you can buy Schweppes tonic and Perrier water and Evian water. The local bottled water is "L'eau Royale." (The tap water is perfectly safe.)

About Cars

For a month-to-month automobile we shopped all over Tahiti for a car with enough power to get us up hills and around other cars and enough body-weight to save us from being crushed if we were hit by a scooter.

The best we could find was a beaten up Daihatsu. Two doors. No radio. Scroungy looking but very smooth running and, best of all, problem free.

Our rental dealer, who had the warmth of a pawnshop owner with bowel troubles, let us have the car with minimum insurance, no mileage charge, for $425 a month.

Petrol was about $1.60 for an American gallon.

One day we received a message that a Tahitian family — friends of Honolulu friends — were looking for us.

At a rendezvous we met the family of Leopold Dauphin, a member of the Gendarmerie. Three gorgeous daughters.

In succession they had us to tea, had us to dinner, gave us a two-hour boat cruise across the north shore of Tahiti from Point du Pêcheurs to Point Venus and offered us a car.

If you have a chance, cruise the waterfront. It is much prettier than the road.

You get to see many otherwise hidden waterfront houses...and beautiful ladies taking sunbaths...you see the waterfront of Papeete and the hotels...if the weather is clear you get a view of the Diadème peaks, and it is truly beautiful...and also the tomb of Pomare V from the sea.

The Dauphins who were off to Paris the next day offered a choice of cars starting with a two-cylinder Citroen. We opted for a rugged Land Rover...a white, completely-equipped-for-safari, four-wheel-drive, diesel-driven hunk of machinery.

We called it the "Lion Hunter" and turned back the red pile of junk to our smiling car dealer.

Diesel fuel, incidentally, cost half the price of gasoline.

The Dauphins' trip to Paris was sort of a standard voyage for Tahitians. The Tahitians love to travel. On their itineraries they go to Honolulu for fun and shopping. They used to go to Honolulu for medical care but that became too expensive and they now go to New Zealand.

They go to Los Angeles for Disneyland.

Mrs. Dauphin's mother also left for a trip to take in Honolulu, Los Angeles, London, Paris, Switzerland and Germany. You couldn't say she would be lonely. She was going with two hundred and sixty other Tahitians! It was their second trip together in less than six months. They take their own floor show.

What a party.

Love And Hate Attitudes

Delicate ground.

Still, a visitor to French Polynesia will soon become aware that there are strong nationalistic feelings in the air.

Probably no professional pollster could accurately capture the true relationship between the French and the Tahitian.

The responses would be too discreetly guarded.

We found a strong anti-French attitude among Tahitians of the lower economic echelon.

The more educated the Tahitian, the more he appreciated the hard currency of the French, the vast economic contribution and also the French organizational ability and technical and scientific assistance.

But the more educated the Tahitian the more sensitive he was to the fact that French Polynesia is becoming the last major nation in the Pacific without full independence.

What the Tahitians would like to have is full independence and still retain the full economic support of France.

France, if it is to continue its nuclear experiments, feels it must retain the remote islands of Mururoa and Hao under any circumstances. An airfield capable of flying experiments directly to France and a deep-water port making the nuclear islands independent of Papeete are interesting developments.

The attitude of the French nationals is divided between those who can't wait to get back to France and never see French Polynesia again...and those who would never leave.

The first are French snobs who would never speak to a visitor anyway.

The second are those who remember too well the Paris winters, the Paris prices and the Paris taxes. These Frenchmen look at the complaisant *vahines,* the balmy weather and they especially appreciate their non-existent income tax. They'll speak to you.

We found the strongest group of French admirers to be the local Americans who understood the "no-thanks" position of foreign dominance, no matter how benevolent.

"Without the French," we were repeatedly told, "the Tahitians would be lost."

The independence movement in French Polynesia has many people worried. Without the French funding, Tahiti would collapse.

As our little Tei put it, "If they throw out the French, I have fear."

"Why, Tei?"

Silence. Big sigh. Then: "Who would rent my house?"

The attitude towards tourists is interesting.

Among the young it is not a problem. Quite the contrary. The boys love the girls and the girls love the boys.

Some of the older, sensitive Tahitians, particularly those strong in the church, regard tourism as a negative influence.

"You came with your Bible and your Mother Hubbards and we accepted them.

"Now you come with your *Playboy* and your bikinis and, by example, tell us to change. No. We prefer the moral codes of your fathers and our fathers."

Another delicate area.

The attitude of the Polynesian in the hotel or the restaurant is frequently one of indifference. They are not antagonistic towards the visitor. They are just *fiu*...bored...bored with their jobs.

But watch the joyous smile of the Tahitians at dance. Now, that is work that they enjoy.

With Polynesians the magic touch is to get to know individuals' names. Show an interest in them, their work, their island, whatever.

The Tahitians will respond to kindness with the same response they would give you in their homes. Lovely smiles. Soft voices. Gentleness.

Be patient. They have their own time style. Go along with it.

Don't be like the visitor we saw in a restaurant who grabbed a passing waitress by the arm and said, "Hey, Cutie, how 'bout getting us some wine!"

He's probably still sitting there. Thirsty.

Tahitian Time

Clocks are bright objects to work for, admire, then give to the baby to break.

Appointments are casual.

Future dates are vague.

Promises often forgotten.

I had five tennis dates with Tahitian opponents and two of them were kept.

A true story told to me over coffee by the person involved concerned a visit to a nearby island, Tetiaroa, not long after the war.

An expensive yacht had gone on the reef and it held as ballast several tons of valuable lead in its keel.

My story-teller, Homer Morgan, and a pal set out to salvage the lead and were taken to the island by a friend who had a ship.

The two adventurers were successful in their salvage operation and waited to be picked up by their friend and they waited and ate fresh fish and lobster and waited and ate fresh fish and lobster...and waited.

Three months later in Quinn's a bunch of local imbibers were sitting around and one of them asked, "Hey, whatever happened to Homer? I haven't seen him around lately."

"Oh, my God!" said Homer's friend and got up and ran to his boat. He left in the middle of the night to pull them off.

Homer said he picked up a very good tan.

Love And Marriage, Tahitian Style

The Tahitian attitude about marriage is loose.

It was rumored that our truck owner across the street had several wives. None of them his.

The liaison of a "Tahitian marriage" is a common practice. Children of such arrangements are never a problem because every Polynesian loves children and there is always a bed and family love and food.

A visitor who is romantically inclined should be handsome and have money, preferably lots of money.

The willing *vahine* of yesterday who was happy with a present of a new "robe" as a sign of appreciation of her favors would now like to have a Vespa but would prefer a convertible Fiat. You can buy it locally. About $12,000. Inflation is everywhere.

Also it has been reported that a romp in the evening doesn't guarantee you a stimulating conversation at breakfast because a large number of the girls are limited to monosyllabic repartee in English. This is one country where you will not laugh a woman into bed. Brilliant dialogue will get you a lonely cup of coffee.

However, an attractive, pocket-jingling European has a huntress appeal to many *vahines* and the unsuspecting European male may find himself bagged, bedded *and advertised* before he suspects any rules of the game.

He takes it for granted that any love-making remains a discreet bit of knowledge between the two of them. Not at all. She has gone back to her girl friends and given a blow-by-blow account of the evening including the most intimate details and if the gentleman gets a good report he becomes marked for the hunt by the girl friends! It doesn't happen if your hair has gone to grey. Promise.

The attitude of sex in Tahiti is not immoral. It is not that casual. In fact in many groups it is puritanical.

Still the heritage of the natives of French Polynesia is different.

In the Marquesas, for example, a husband even at the time of Stevenson and Gauguin would have no thought but of honor in sharing his wife with a friend. Not an enemy. Only a friend.

The difference in attitude spills over into homosexuality.

There are boys in families who are raised as women (*Mahus*). They aren't necessarily homosexual. They are just feminine.

And the practicising homosexuals are taken in stride (*Raeraes*).

I remember pointing out one of the most attractive dancers in all of Papeete and was deflated to learn she was a lesbian. It only bothered me.

And one of our favorite waiters in Papeete was absolutely darling. He was cute. Walked with a swish. Charming smile. Sometimes when kidded he would hit me on the shoulder with his towel.

His name was Dorothy.

He'd always been called Dorothy.

In Tahiti it is just another part of life.

Before leaving Papeete and winding up our adventure, we got Muk on the phone on Moorea to say goodbye. Couldn't resist asking if a story we had picked up on our island-hopping were true.

It was conveyed to us that Muk, the Bali Hai bachelor who had told us that you had to learn to hit a woman to gain her respect, had been beaten up so badly in Lahaina, Maui by his Tahitian girl friend that they had to call the police.

"Muk, was this true?"

"True?" he exploded over the phone. "Holy Moly, she nearly killed me. We had closed Harry's Windsock Bar at the little airport and were having a few at the Lahaina Yacht Club when I decided it was time to go and get cleaned up. She said she wasn't going anywhere now or later. I grabbed her and said I didn't ask her if or when but was telling her we were leaving *now* and dragged her out and down the main street.

"And then I let go. That was a mistake.

"She is an excellent soccer player and she jumped up and grabbed me by the hair and let me have it with her feet from my ankles up to my eyebrows.

"Someone called the police and it took three of them to get her off me, handcuffed and into a police car. They took her down to the station and fed her more booze to calm her down.

"A police sergeant came to the hotel almost whimpering, 'We've handled Samoans, pro football players and drunken yacht crews but this hundred-and-ten-pound Tahitian is too much for us. We're bringing her back.'

"I cried before the policeman, 'Please, officer, don't do that. She'll murder me.'

"But they brought her back. Fortunately, there was an oak door between the living room and the bedroom and as soon as they let her in one room I locked myself in the other.

"In the morning she was a kittycat and I looked like I had stepped in front of a threshing machine.

"You have to learn to bat a Tahitian woman but you have to learn an alternative move too."

"What's that, Muk?"

"Run for your life," he said.

● ● ●

14. Once Around Lightly— By Cruise Ship

The Sea View . . . Beautiful Lagoons . . .
Shore Excursions . . . The Movie Star Captain

It was not that long ago when the only way to see the islands of French Polynesia was by ship.

The experience could be fairly wretched, or romantic, depending upon your ability to handle storms at sea.

With the advent of the airplane the need for passenger ship transportation all but disappeared but now the idea of ocean travel by luxury ship—adventuring without unpacking—has been gaining great favor among vacationers.

Although luxurious might be too rich a word, interisland cargo ships still carry migrate passengers at most reasonable fares.

In 1986, the Raromatai Ferry joined the interisland trade. This giant-sized ship operated by the Compagnie Maritime des Iles Sous-le-Vent, a company owned by the Cowan family—Cowans are everywhere—carries 350 passengers and has a separate deck for take-along cars.

It features airline-type seating, a limited number of one- and four-berth cabins, a restaurant, and a snack bar.

The ferry runs from Tahiti to Huahine to Raiatea, Tahaa and Bora Bora. A typical schedule will leave Papeete Friday night, call on the other islands Saturday morning, and arrive in Bora Bora by lunchtime.

The ferry is not the only way to go. There are several boat services that ply the waters between islands. Other private and government ships with passenger accommodations for from twelve to forty serve some forty islands within French Polynesia. Have you always cherished the romantic notion of cruising the South Pacific on a long voyage, off the track, in *non* luxury liner conditions? Take your

239

seasick pills, good books to read, and get aboard.

For example, the *Areanui* does a seventeen-day trip to the Tuamotus and the Marquesas.

A class "A" cabin with shower, toilet and air-conditioning costs about $2,500 for the entire trip. A class "B" cabin—share toilet, no shower—is about $1,800.

All cabins are exterior and are on the aft end of the ship. Lots of motion. The fare includes three meals a day. That assumes you feel well enough to eat.

Government-owned boats go only to the Gambier and Austral Islands. For more information on small ships contact the Tahiti Tourist Promotion Board:

In the U.S.A., Suite 200, 2330 Westwood Blvd., Los Angeles, CA, 90064.

In Australia, BNP Building, 12 Castelreagh Street, Sydney, N.S.W. 2000.

The Tahiti address is, OPATTI, P.O. Box 65, Papeete, Tahiti, French Polynesia.

More comfortable ways of exploring French Polynesia are available.

Exploration Cruises has conducted seasonal interisland tours for several years, and, in 1986, went on a year-round sailing schedule.

During our last visit, their ship in place was the *Majestic Explorer,* a 152-foot ship large enough to accommodate eighty-eight passengers. In summers the ship had been in North American service for Alaska cruising.

Its shallow draft, about ten feet, allows it to poke its bow up to a beach and discharge passengers on a bow gangplank directly onto land. The promotional slogan of the line is "cruise the Tahiti the big ships can't."

(The shallow draft also results, we were told in Papeete, in a rolling ship in rough seas.)

The standard cruise schedule is a week-long voyage from Papeete to Opunohu Bay on Moorea, to Raiatea, to Bora Bora—two nights—to Tahaa, to Huahine, back to Moorea, this time anchoring in Cook's Bay, and return to Papeete.

Four-day excursions are marketed by permitting passengers to join the ship in Bora Bora for one night for its normal return to Papeete.

However, the biggest cruising news for Tahiti was the introduction of American Hawaii Cruises to Tahitian waters.

The American Hawaii Cruise is a fine way to see the islands, especially for the first time. You learn which islands you want to come back to and where you want to spend your time. One thing is for sure. You'll never see a string of more spectacular anchorages anywhere in the world.

The impact of American Hawaii Cruises advertising in the North America market is having a major positive effect on Tahiti tourism. The manager of the Beachcomber Hotel said, "Oh, we feel it every day."

Tahiti has had a steady tourism count of just over 100,000 visitors a year for the last ten years. The *Liberte* alone will bring at least 30,000 new visitors to Tahiti each year, visitors who probably would never have seen the islands without the marketing experience of the San Francisco-based shipping line.

Prior to the startup of the Tahiti cruises, the company had enjoyed great success with two large cruise ships that circle the Hawaiian Islands on seven-day tours, starting and ending in Honolulu.

Expanding on the same format, AHC bought an American-built carrier, the former *Brazil* and later the Holland American Line's *Vanderam,* spent a fortune gutting and refurbishing the ship, christened it the *SS Liberte,* and put it into a similar weekly cruise pattern through the Society Islands.

We had the good fortune to be on the first shakedown cruise, December 21, 1985.

Every berth on the ship was taken. When the company first advertised the shakedown cruises—offering attractive fare discounts, to be sure—the marketing people expected 1,200 responses. Over 18,000 requests poured in.

The cruise package tempted passengers with:

(1) A total fare, including an airfare charter, that was less than half the normal fare.

(2) A chance to experience seven different islands with magical Polynesian names—Tahiti, Rangiroa, Huahine, Raiatea, Tahaa, Bora Bora and Moorea—in air-conditioned comfort.

(3) Six meals a day in addition to several bars, a casino, a disco, organized games, free movies, lively musical entertainment every evening, and dancing to live orchestras.

We left the dock at Papeete on a Saturday night and slipped into the Sea of the Moon heading two hundred nautical miles northeast.

Sunday was a day at sea—a day of needed rest for passengers who had arrived Saturday on overnight flights from the West Coast. A day to breathe salt air, lounge in deck chairs, and sleep.

Our destination was Rangiroa, the only island in the Tuamotu group where we would make a landing.

We could not believe that the massive 23,000-ton ship with an 85-foot beam was actually going into the lagoon through the narrow Tiputa Pass. We had drift-snorkeled in the pass on a previous trip and knew from a face-mask perspective how skinny it was.

"How in the world are you going to do this?" we asked the captain. "The mouth of the pass is only three hundred yards wide."

"Oh, we've vasolined both sides of the ship," said Captain Cal Bourke, with just a slight smile.

It all depended on perfect timing. The tide had to be at maximum high tide. There could not be any lateral wind. The course had to be absolutely true.

Monday at 4:30, in the first pearl cast of dawn, we stood forward near the bridge nervously watching the dot on the horizon slowly form into a low-lying atoll as we approached it. The pass finally became visible as we moved ponderously toward it.

It was so small.

Closer and closer the *Liberte* inched into the passage until, finally, we were in the middle of an aisle of green water being washed by offshore waves. People were standing on the beach—waiting for us to grind our hull on the rocks?—and then we were through the gap and into the deep blue water of the lagoon.

The life boats from the ship went over the side to serve as ship-to-shore lighters. The people on tours went first and then the independent wanderers.

On shore at the tiny village of Tiputa, under the shade of a huge tree, this first ever cruise landing party was met by the mayor who greeted us in French.

"We don't have much to offer you here but we give you our hearts. You can use the post office to write your postcards and use the town hall if you want to change your clothes."

What kind of cultural shock does the off-loading of seven hundred passengers have on a remote Polynesian village of five hundred residents?

Surprisingly, very little. The passengers formed little groups and wandered off, most to the beach, or made short walks through the village and then returned to the coolness of the ship.

The greatest economic effect was on the proprietor of the little Chinese store. He sold more soft drinks, beer, postcards and T-shirts that morning than he has ever sold in a two-hour period before.

We bought shells from a young lady who had set a small table up in her yard and then found a snack shack where a few locals were sharing beers and gossip under a canopy of trees. We took a beer and sat down to watch the sea and cool off from the humid December day, to be immediately surrounded by a crowd of small urchins who watched with great joy as I wrote each of their names in my notebook.

"Angelina? How old are you? Seven?"

It was recorded.

"Clara? *Quel age avez-vous?* Ten?"

It was recorded.

And so it went. Rachel, 11. Ernie, 7. Taiata, 7.

Sweet, unaffected children with the giggles and *joie de vivre* that characterize children everywhere.

We weighed anchor and departed on the outgoing tide.

Note: the treacherous tides and the shifting winds posed too great a threat to the ship and, within the first six months, Rangiroa was removed from the schedule. The latest schedule limited the cruise to just the Society Islands. The proprietor in the Chinese store must have been heartbroken.

The next morning, the ship anchored in a deepwater lagoon of Huahine. We were disappointed, hoping that we would dock at the pretty little town of Fare.

The shore tours were typical of paid-for options available on every island: a glassbottom boat cruise or outrigger cruise, a beach picnic, an archaeological tour, a snorkel and swim cruise, a horseback ride or a tour ending with a Tahitian *tamaaraa* (feast) at the Bali Hai Hotel.

We by-passed the elective activities and took *le truck* into the village, shopped, walked to the Bali Hai Hotel where we peeked in at the *tamaaraa*. The cruise passengers were bedecked in *heis* and *leis*, dressed in just purchased pareus, and dancing with the Tahitian dancers, taking pictures as the pig came out of the *himaa*. It was a well done party. Good job. We thought the passengers had more fun at this party than any of the other elective activities we saw.

We sailed at four in the afternoon for Raiatea.

As the sun began to set, a far-off canoe carrying two *vahines* paddling slowly and rhythmically in the fading afternoon light were silhouetted against a dark green bushed shoreline. They passed along the lagoon, their paddles barely disturbing the water . . . the only sound, an occasional tinkle of laughter. Finally, the canoe turned a corner of the shore and disappeared. Where had it come from, where was it going? Who knows? Was it staged for our benefit? Believe me, no. It was a typical, peaceful South Sea vignette you won't find except in the Pacific.

That night we dined with Captain Bourke, a handsome, gray-haired officer, who would have made a totally believable and more handsome replacement for the captain of "Love Boat."

"I used to be a captain of oil tankers. Big, monstrous, dirty things. One day in port we had had a terrible time . . . hourly emergencies . . . repairs . . . work almost around the clock. I remember I was on deck, covered with muck and oil, dead tired, when a cruise ship went by. Standing on deck was this immaculate figure of a man, the captain. Trim. Pressed. Neat whites and gold braid. I realized then I was in the wrong job and resolved to change.

"Funny stories? Oh, every cruise captain could write volumes of funny stories about on-board experiences. One of my favorites concerns an eighty-two-year-old passenger on a cruise to Bermuda who was found wandering around the ship's lobby at two in the morning . . . absolutely naked.

"Well, they wrapped a blanket around the old gentleman and took him to the purser's office, and after a great deal of questioning and scrutinizing their files, they finally figured out his cabin number.

"The purser called his wife and told her that her husband had been found wandering around the ship without his clothes on.

" 'Oh, are the dogs with him?' she asked."

Having dinner with the captain is always a treat personally and, predictably, good source material professionally.

The next morning's port was Raiatea.

We elected a half-day shore excursion to Tahaa, the small island that shares the lagoon with Raiatea. We off-loaded the ship in the middle of the lagoon once we were inside the reef and took a small boat—which got lost—to a relatively remote marina hotel, Marina Iti, on the southwest coast of the island. (It was, after all, the first time the ship's personnel had made the run.)

Started in 1985, the isolated Garden of Eden has ten beds, a large thatched-roof hut that served as lounge, dining room, bar, library and self-entertainment center. The proprietors were Philippe Robin of Lyon, thirty-six, and his vibrant, petite wife, Marie Adeline.

"We seem to be a stopping place for passing yachtsmen whose women are *bored,*" he told us. "They want to get off a ship and *play.*"

Several large yachts were anchored off the inn's pier as if to prove his point.

"We also have charter yachts available here."

Part of our expedition was to tour the island which we did in Tahaa's public transport, *le truck,* in a driving rain. The driver of the truck spoke no English. The hostess from the ship spoke no French.

We had a little map and knew that the truck was taking us to Vaitoare and then to Haamene which was the usual route for the vehicle. ("Price per passenger: 150 francs. *Paiements interdit cote chauffeur,*" said the sign. "Don't pay the driver on his side of the truck," it said. Or you might get hit by another vehicle, is what it didn't say.)

A hurricane the preceding year had destroyed many trees and houses on the island, but new houses were already in place. A sparkling new school had been built in Haamene, population one thousand.

"Is there any place to shop," asked one passenger. No, Lady.

Coconuts were the island's industry and drying sheds stood in front of almost every beachfront house. The white road was of ground coral. The lime in the coral makes the road concrete hard.

Back at the "hotel," we had a drink and a Polynesian lunch with food cooked in a thatched-roofed *himaa.* Very good. Following the meal, most of us put on diving masks and snorkeled in front of the hotel until it was time to board our small craft and return to the ship.

While we were on the shore excursion, the ship had been continued on to Raiatea and tied up at Uturoa, the principal village. It was the only dock we saw besides Papeete, and was the first time that many of the crew had had a chance to go ashore. They celebrated.

Because it was the first cruise, the *Liberte* snaked out of the reef-rimmed harbor before darkness fell.

The next morning, when we awoke, the ship was already anchored in the lagoon of Bora Bora before we were on deck. A shame. Approaching Bora Bora from the sea is one of the dramatic sights of French Polynesia with its clean lagoon and peaks shooting up to the heavens. We elected to go on a snorkeling tour which took us out to a far reef. Snorkeling inside the lagoon where the warm water is only shoulder high in spots is great fun. You are on your on to swim through the coral heads and play peek-a-boo with a thousand colorful fish. It is an underwater theater of pleasure.

One of the guides spotted an octopus under a rock. He took a shell fish, broke it in half with his knife handle and put the pieces in front of the octopus's hideout. Small fish nibbled at the shell until the octopus darted out, scared them away, grabbed some food, and darted back in again. Once he came out too far and the guide grabbed him.

The octopus was about the size of two dinner plates when he spread his tentacles. He writhed in the guide's hand who would let him go to watch the creature spurt forward in the water. Then the guide would grab him again; once, standing on the sandy bottom, the guide put the octopus on his head and let the tentacles curl through his hair and over his face. The women squealed as best they could with snorkeling tubes in their mouths.

He invited the participation in the fun; there were no takers.

Young octopus being an island delicacy, the guide would eventually kill it to be enjoyed as part of the family dinner.

Anchorage the next day at Captain Cook Bay on Moorea is the prettiest anchorage in Tahiti—or anywhere else, for that matter.

Tours took passengers off for sightseeing drives, to *tamaaraas,* and to snorkeling parties. The favorite seemed to be the *Liki Tiki* snorkel runs, operated by the Bali Hai Hotel successfully for years. The *Liki Tiki* is a canopied platform built across two canoes and is loaded down with booze, beer, edibles and is made for snorkeling parties . . . or just parties. With Tahitian music twanging away, pretty girls with little on—and caring less—trying to throw their hips out of joint, and people singing and drinking, it becomes more than festive.

People return to the ship with heads wreathed in flowers, a rum punch in each hand, mumbling about moving to Tahiti. They don't remember it the next morning.

Moorea is a beautiful island and another place where you can rent a car for a half day and go tootling around.

Don't take a motor scooter. One bump in the road and you could be a basket case for the rest of your life. It has happened too many times to chance.

The next morning we would pass through the Sea of the Moon and be back in the hustle and bustle of Papeete but we had a honeymoon last night on board.

Because of the tides and current, the captain elected to move our anchorage from Captain Cook over to the next bay, Opunohu, which is almost as pretty as Captain Cook. There we spent the night. The move was made just at dusk and we took a bottle of champagne to a private corner on deck where we were alone with the splendor of the sky and the spires of the mountains, Mouaputa and Rotui. We sipped the bubbly and toasted the pewter colored waters, the last of the sun setting behind clouds, the first stars just appearing in the sky, and told ourselves how lucky we were to have all this—and each other.

Ahhhh—the magic of Tahiti.

INDEX

.